Making Chó Bò
Làm *Trouble*

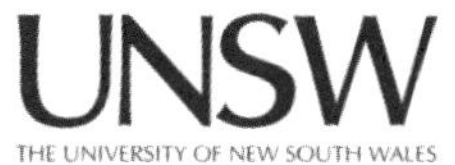

Making Chó bò*: Troubling Việtspeak

Collaborating, translating, and archiving with family in

Australian contemporary art.

Hong An James Nguyen

A thesis fulfilling the requirements for the degree of Doctor of Philosophy

UNSW Art & Design

2020

Making Chó Bò Làm *Trouble*

James Nguyen

Published by Discipline

Contents

Introduction

Chapter 1
Troubling Translations

Chapter 2
Troubling Archives

Chapter 3
Troubling Tongues

Conclusion

DECLARATION RELATION TO DISPOSITION OF PROJECT THESIS/DISSERTATION

I hereby grant to the University of New South Wales or its agents a non-exclusive licence to archive and to make available (including to members of the public) my thesis or dissertation in whole or in part in the University libraries in all forms of media, now or here after known. I acknowledge that I retain all intellectual property rights which subsist in my thesis or dissertation, such as copyright and patent rights, subject to applicable law. I also retain the right to use all or part of my thesis or dissertation in future works (such as articles or books).

.... Signature

.... Date

ORIGINALITY STATEMENT:

'I hereby declare that this submission is my own work and to the best of my knowledge it contains no materials previously published or written by another person, or substantial proportions of material which have been accepted for the award of any other degree or diploma at UNSW or any other educational institution, except where due acknowledgement is made in the thesis. Any contribution made to the research by others, with whom I have worked at UNSW or elsewhere, is explicitly acknowledged in the thesis. I also declare that the intellectual content of this thesis is the product of my own work, except to the extent that assistance from others in the project's design and conception or in style, presentation and linguistic expression is acknowledged.'

.... Signature

.... Date

COPYRIGHT STATEMENT

'I hereby grant the University of New South Wales or its agents a non-exclusive liscence to archive and to make available (including to members of the public) my thesis or dissertation in whole or part in the University libraries in all forms of media, now or here after known. I acknowledge that I retain all intellectual property rights which subsist in my thesis or dissertation, such as copyright and patent rights, subject to applicable law. I also retain the right to use all or part of my thesis or dissertation in future works (such as articles or books).'

'For any substantial portions of copyright material used in this thesis, written permission for use has been obtained, or the copyright material is removed from the final public version of the thesis.'

.... Signature

.... Date

Abstract

* Chó bò is the approximate Vietnamese homonym for ~ *trouble*. Bluntly translated, chó bò is a *dog~cow* or *dog~crawl.* This linguistic joke for many Vietnamese people learning English represents a capacity to make trouble.

This PhD thesis comprises original research and artistic work made with my family. As people from the Vietnamese diaspora, our experiences are formed by dispersals and estrangements as settler-colonisers on this continent. Our daily encounters in the realms on which this thesis is focused—contemporary art, academia, and family enterprise—are folded into distinct systems of colonial power and violence.

I often make work with my family in video-performance and the documentary form. Our inter-generational, political, and language differences add to the conceptual complexity of what it means to collaborate, make art, produce archives, and confront our position as displaced people. This thesis aims to address how our artistic collaborations utilise linguistic and archival approaches to articulate the systemic racism we encounter as people from a refugee background, but who are also embroiled in the colonial infrastructures of our new home.

Aligning with thinkers such as Gloria Anzaldúa and her critique of coloniality, to Gayatri Chakravorty Spivak and Hito Steyerl on minoritarian forms of translation, and Sara Ahmed on racism in the

university, this thesis describes how collaborations with my family can trouble the contradictions of colonial violence within our relationships. Reconnecting with individual members of my family through art, I have gained a better understanding of my language and culture; I have also found important artistic and political connections with peers. Collaborating with my family has forced me to rub against the researcher-research subject binary, the archival visibility of being invisible, the rhetoric of institutional inclusion, and the weight of being displaced and displacing colonial subjects. The work we have produced together methodologically uncovers and critiques the opaque confrontations of institutional power, racism, and colonial violence in the everyday. As a family, we continue to make uncomfortable pronunciations like chó bò, producing the epistemic trouble necessary to face the colonial realities of our resettlement.

Artwork Website

https://chobotrouble.com/

Chúng tôn trọng và cảm ơn

người Wurundjeri và ~~Boon~~

Boon Wurrung của

đất của giới ta

từ ~~đất~~ đất nước của tổ tiên

từ đất nước Kulin

trên mảnh đất ~~đã~~ thế

từng bị người khác lấy đi

mà không phải nhường.

Nhưng có chúng tôi đang

sống, làm việc, ~~hát tả~~

thăm viếng, cũng như
ngày hôm nay chúng tôi đi từ ~~một~~ nơi khác để
~~đang~~ thăm viếng và
trình diễn ~~các câu chuyện~~
~~và~~ chia sẻ những câu
chuyện.

pp. 14–15
James Nguyen, Acknowledgement of Country in Vietnamese, 2017. Pencil on paper. Courtesy of the artist.

Acknowledgements

Cho tôi trân thành cảm ơn người Wurundjeri và người Boon Wurrung của đất nước Kulin, và người Gadigal của đất nước Eora. Tôi thêm cảm ơn những dân tộc đã sống đầu tiên ở Úc Châu và Việt Nam, và các tổ tiên của những người ấy. Tôi đã sáng tạo ra các tác phẩm này trên nơi bị người khách lấy đi, mà chưa bao dờ nhường. Trên những đất nước này, tôi đã tới từ nơi khác, đến sống bình an, và may mắn được chia sẻ những công việc này. Và sau, tôi gửi lời cảm ơn đến Ba Mẹ, Dì Cậu, Anh Em trong gia đình của tôi, và hai thày giáo viên Dr. Jennifer Biddle, và Dr. Verónica Tello, tới các bạn nghệ sĩ, các người yêu mến trên quãng đường nhỏ này.

I acknowledge the Wurundjeri and Boon Wurrung of the Kulin Nation, and the Gadigal of the Eora Nation. I pay respects to the Peoples, Lands, Traditional Custodians, Elders, and Creator Ancestors of these Great Nations, as well as other First Nations people throughout Australia and Vietnam where I conduct my work. I live on stolen lands that were never ceded. I am thankful for the many privileges and the safety afforded to me and my family as uninvited guests on these lands.

Thank you to Ba ~ my Dad Nguyễn Ngọc Cu, Mẹ ~ Mum Nguyễn Thị Kim Dung, Dì ~ Aunty Nguyễn Thị Kim Nhung, Cậu ~ Uncle Nguyễn Công Ái, Em ~ my Brother Joey Nguyen, our Cousins, Elders, and other extended family who

gave up so much time and kindness to create this work with me. I am especially grateful for the profound care from my PhD supervisors, Dr Jennifer Biddle and Dr Verónica Tello, throughout the research. I thank all my friends, artists peers, partners, and loved ones who have persisted on this journey with me.

Additionally, special thanks to Sophia Cai, Lucreccia Quintanilla, Ciaran Begley, Phương Ngô, Nikki Lam, Bhenji Ra, Rainbow Chan, Kay Abude, Andy Butler, Soo-Min Shim, Abigail Moncrieff, Georgia Banks, John Di Stefano, Eben Kirksey, Brian Martin, Xi Liu, Sheila Pham, Lap Xuan, Hung Le, Nguyễn Thị Thanh Mai, Hoàng Trần Nguyễn, Victoria Pham, Joel Sherwood Spring, Bron Belcher, Shivanjani Lal, Alana O'Neill, Cyrus Tang, Vipoo Srivilasa, Sheila Pham, Siying Zhou, Jess Chen, Yin-Lan Soon, and Damian Gibney, my long-suffering partner. I am also thankful for the University of New South Wales Art & Design for their community of students, researchers, and staff, the technical facilities, studios, and research scholarship that kept me afloat. In shaping this manuscript, I would also like to thank my assessors Michelle Antoinette and Nikos Papastergiadis, and the team that published this book Helen Hughes, Amy May Stuart, and Zenobia Ahmed.

Foreword

It is a privilege and honour to write this foreword to a very important book Làm Chó Bò ~ *Making Trouble* by James Nguyen. I have been following James' work and practice for many years, a practice that calls to question the problematics of representation and the real issues that face "us" in so-called "Australia."

Growing out of PhD research, James steps out a sequencing and interconnectedness through family, linguistics, and creative practice, generously allowing us insight into his locality and Place. In doing so we witness how creative practice in this instance offers reconnection to a complex past, a convoluted present, and a questionable future. The power of subversion through relational practice foregrounds Làm Chó Bò ~ *Making Trouble* through creativity, family, and community—disrupting the tropes of coloniality, linearity, settler narratives, and the mentality of migration. It starts from the position of Vietnamese diaspora and takes us into multiple narratives and identities predicated on institutional racism and colonial violence.

A significant contribution to disrupting the tropes of coloniality is calling out the imaginary of coloniality whilst identifying its real "affects" in the world and on people. Disrupting the linear time and trajectory of western culture is vital to this book as it builds on the amnesiac condition in Australia.

In this we are reminded that amnesia is not just a matter of simply forgetting; if there is nothing to remember, then there is nothing to forget. James' book, and in particular his practice through connection and relationality, interrogates and builds on this amnesiac trajectory, making the comfortable uncomfortable. Through modes of "resettlement," this book propositions important interventions in order to create a revival of identities and resistance to amnesia. Belonging and reconnection allows us to shift the disconnection and separation that the western discourse creates, and James does so through non-linear means. This re-setting is vital for now and future generations. The tropes of coloniality in Australia have continuing affect and impact on these unceded lands and territories, where Country and Place have been overshadowed by the colonial agenda. This important and timely book by James offers us some insight into modes of disputing these linear discourses created by colonial mentalities and linearities. James presents an acumen into traversing the colonial terrain from a diasporic positioning, and in doing so strategises ways of diversifying approaches through family, relationality, and practice. The synergies between practice and research provide alternate ways of looking at the world, and in particular the complex matrix of coloniality and diaspora on the unceded lands in so-called "Australia."

Through creative actions and interventions, Làm Chó Bò ~ *Making Trouble* furnishes us with a platform where we can look towards beautiful, substantial, and real solutions.

Professor Brian Martin
(Bundjalung/Kamilaroi/MuruWarri)
August 2023

Introduction

A Troubling Anecdote

Sitting on the couch, I was reading *Thinking, Judging, Freedom*—a collection of writings on Hannah Arendt. Calling from his desk, my partner at the time asked if I was collaborating with another academic, whose major research funding grant he was in the process of reviewing.

Distracted, I asked him to repeat his question and the name of the academic. Scrolling through my inbox, I located an email from a few months earlier. In this exchange I was invited to join the academic as an "Artist-Activator." My contribution would be to catalyse discourse, sharing my personal experience as a Vietnamese refugee and research on Union Carbide's manufacturing of Agent Orange, and how these chemicals still continue to leach into the waterways of Sydney's immigrant suburbs[1]—long after industrial production stopped decades ago.[2]

1
To read further about this chemical history, see Boi Huyen Ngo, "The Haunting of Agent Orange within the Waters of Rivers and Bodies for Vietnamese Australians," *Australasian Journal of Ecocriticism and Cultural Exchange* 6 (Summer 2016/2017): 5-6; and Eben Kirksey, "Chemosociality in Multispecies Worlds," *Environmental Humanities* 12, no. 1 (2020): 27-29.

2
My role in this collaborative workshop was to share with audiences my experience, as a local growing up, living, and working in the suburban surrounds of Homebush Bay. Famously, this area was the site of the Sydney 2000 Olympics. Prior to this, the area had been reserved for intensive industries, including the manufacturing of pesticides and herbicides by Union Carbide.

The overarching "feminist methodologies" outlined in the email aimed to interrogate the hidden human and environmental disasters bubbling underneath Sydney. In my reply email, I had politely declined, citing a high workload and clashing exhibition schedules. Despite my upfront (but friendly) refusal to participate, this academic continued to include my name as a collaborator in their grant.

Looking up the academic and their affiliates online, it appeared that I may have been the only person of colour from Australia to be included on the project. Feeling a pang of tokenism, unwittingly included in a grant application I was not taking part in, I wondered if I was included to bolster this academic's career ambitions? Sara Ahmed points to the commodification of diversity in academic research.[3] To Ahmed, "diversity" is now circulated

The most contentious industrial herbicide Dioxin-the chemical constituents of Agent Orange, a chemical defoliant used in the jungles and farmlands of Southern Vietnam between 1962 and 1971-were manufactured then buried, and are still leaching into Sydney's local waterways. There is both clinical and anecdotal evidence for in-vivo birth defects and cancer in Vietnamese civilians, Australian army personnel, and communities living near Gregory Falls in far North Queensland associated with Dioxin exposure and testing. I had previously made work, collaborating with my Aunty Kim Nhung to unpack the irony of how Vietnamese refugee communities had ended up resettling in parts of Sydney that had not only once manufactured, but continue to be contaminated by the same chemical weapons from a war we had fled, but could never escape.

3 Sara Ahmed, *What's the Use?: On the Uses of Use* (Durham: Duke University Press Books, 2019), 147.

like a currency amongst researchers and national funding bodies. Syndicated and traded, diversity is used to underwrite an established culture of individualism and neoliberal careerism. These institutions continue to avoid investing in the resourcing and duty of care needed to guarantee cultural and academic justice—that is, beyond the rhetoric of corporate inclusion and tokenistic anti-racism.

Coincidentally, my primary research was engaged with exactly this type of opaque institutional rhetoric, as I had been seeking UNSW HREC (University of New South Wales Human Research Ethics Committee) approval to formally gain permission to undertake research with my family. The collisions of inclusion (especially those involving my family and our subject-position as Vietnamese-Australians with a refugee background) expose how representational politics inevitably protects not the people *being* included (me, my family, and collaborators), but the institutions *doing* the including (further outlined in Chapter 2). Discussing this scenario with a few close friends, I heard how this encounter with such academic mischief was not unique. My anecdote was instantly recognisable as yet another example of opaque racism and tokenism within academia and its economic modalities. For this PhD, I myself had regularly colluded in various cynical exercises of academic box-ticking. Via the cycle of performance reviews, HREC ethics online training courses,

competency workshops, and other administrative performance benchmarks just to certify that my conduct was unquestioningly ethical, and my research was stuffed full of academic excellence. I open this thesis with an anecdote that exposes the false contingencies of higher research, and parts of the artworld linked to academia. Here, my encounter with institutional care and oversight was ultimately due to my intimate partner relationships. Was it right for me to learn about a violation of academic consent through an intimate disclosure? My lover, and not the academy, verified with me confidential academic information to ensure I could give or refuse consent. This was a salient lesson on academic access and fairness.

Focusing my attention back to family, and my intimate and peer relationships, I was reminded of the many subtle forms of institutional exclusions historically deployed on the people around me and other diasporic artists working in Australia. My family's involvement in my arts practice was a way for us to reconnect. To start rebuilding bonds that were broken due to the many language and cultural barriers that shape migrant and refugee narratives. I had at one point recruited my family to help me make art, not just because they were around, but because I knew I could rely on them. They would regularly check in to offer help, generously giving me their time and plenty of unsolicited feedback. Different family members would drop in from time to time—learning to set up the camera, stopping by

the hardware store, and troubleshooting last-minute projects and exhibitions.

Benefiting from their playful derision as well as their concern, and readiness to engage in what they often saw as my ridiculous pursuits, I soon realised that I started to have productive conversations with my family. The complex conceptual concerns of my practice, often beyond the limits of two broken languages (Vietnamese and English), were beginning to find a dialogue in the hows and whys of what we were making and doing together. I even began to absorb and trust their aesthetic and critical judgement.

Increasingly drawn into my work, my family started to make more active and assertive input into the conceptual concerns of what we produced. As a family making art together, we would slip between an amateur film-crew one moment, then spontaneously switch to a brains trust, an art collective, and occasionally a performance troupe—navigating various artistic or conceptual obstacles in our way. The works and projects we developed as a family eventually found reception in places like academic symposiums at universities, performance festivals, and art galleries. As we gained exposure and further opportunities in these spaces, so too did we start to recognise the subtle and pervasive ways in which our work and our bodies were being co-opted and reshaped by these institutions and their audiences. The conditional and contradictory barriers to gaining entry into the artworld, much like the university (and its carnivorous funding pool) was not so far removed from how my

family had encountered those all too familiar forms of institutional mishandling and negligence when entering this country as asylum seekers.

Drawing from historic and current experiences, I saw how the PhD was an opportunity to think about the ways in which my family and I should go about navigating the various epistemic obstructions and obfuscation of the various artistic encounters with the artworld, the university, and, eventually, the Vietnamese community in Australia. Our covalent exchange of broken and brokered languages, our informal ways of communication, and our unconventional means of navigating the power structures surrounding our practice as a family became increasingly important to me. My family's experiences with the artworld and university ultimately shaped my own artistic approach. By encountering different forms of institutional violence and opaque exclusion firsthand with my family, I started to see how these linguistic and dialogical strategies were in themselves a valuable form of knowledge production. As we continued to make work and accrue more conversations and ideas between each other, we recognised a particular archival urgency. Motivated to capture our expanding and increasingly complicated ideas and arguments, I started to focus my attention on improving my own linguistic fluency and cultural competency to better understand my family whilst making art. In a way, these relationships—and the constant push and pull of contradictory expectations

and awkward forms of care—became a refreshing respite from the academic careerism, anti-racist hypocrisy, and colonising rhetoric that lurked at the edges and spread from the centre of the university and the Australian art scene.

First, I will ask: how does working with my family to make art expose the troublesome nature of self-representation? To address this question, I have to take into consideration how my family have used the creative means of translation, language-brokering, and minoritarian exchange to bring to the fore the banality of systemic racism inside the university, the artworld, and the broader economies that as a family, we are exposed to.

By articulating the racism and colonial infrastructures that dictate how my family can make art in Australia as immigrants, this thesis urgently addresses the situational bind and specificity of being historically colonised and displaced refugees, who now find ourselves problematically resettled into the colonial matrix of the settler-colony. How, then, do we make art about the racism and coloniality of the institutional infrastructures around us, when we ourselves form part of the matrix of racism and prejudices of our own diasporic doing?

As we encounter multiple forms of epistemic violence, such as institutional marginalisation, paternalism, tokenism, and the de-legitimisation of "non-academic" knowledge, how do the artworks that we make, and the discourses we are engaged in, avoid repetitively reperforming our traumas, personal testimonies, and subject-position as people from a refugee background?[4] In answering this question, it becomes especially important to clearly outline the terms and conditions for how our practice operates. The following clarifications (although themselves incomplete and variously problematic) are useful to provide some context for our work and research. This gives the reader a better understanding of where my family and I might be coming from.

I start with my use of the term Nhà ~ *family.* When I refer to my family in this thesis, it refers to family members who are biological relations and those linked by marriage: there is Ba ~ *Dad,* Mẹ ~ *Mum,* Thàng Em ~ *Younger Brother*, Các Dì Cô ~ *Aunties*, Các Cậu ~ *Uncles*, Các Anh Em ~ *Cousins*, and their spouse/partners/children, etc. These relationships are either organised as my "immediate family" or my "extended family."

In my immediate family, there is Nguyễn Ngọc Cu (Ba ~ *Dad* and husband of Nguyễn Thị

4
Patrick Williams and Laura Chrisman, *Colonial Discourse and Post-Colonial Theory: A Reader* (London: Routledge, 1994), 95.

Kim Dung), Nguyễn Thị Kim Dung (Mẹ ~ *Mum* and wife of Nguyễn Ngọc Cu), Thàng Em ~ *Younger Brother* Joey Nguyễn, and Tôi ~ *Myself*.

My extended family are in Australia and Vietnam. In Australia, there is Nguyễn Thị Kim Nhung (Dì Nhung ~ *Aunty Nhung*, younger Sister of Nguyễn Thị Kim Dung), Nguyễn Công Ái (Cậu Ái ~ *Uncle Ái*, younger Brother of my Mum and Aunty), and numerous other relatives not involved in this research. Members of my extended family based in Vietnam include Các Anh Em ~ *Cousins* from my Dad's side of the family. They have explicitly asked not to be named due to business sensitivity, and like the majority of my kin who remain in Vietnam, are not Việt Kiều ~ *Overseas Vietnamese* like me, that is, Vietnamese people from the exogenous diaspora who have now resettled outside of Vietnam. My Brother and my Uncle's Partner have largely opted to be observers rather than participants throughout this research.

As I relate my practice with my immediate and extended family to the important work being done by my peers, non-filial collaborators, partners, lovers, etc., my definition of family will be extended to a queering of the artistic and political "chosen family." The relationships that make up this expanded family, although non-biological nor necessarily culturally affiliated, have been maintained long-term, and are profoundly relevant to my work, and the work made with my immediate and extended family.

As an individual, I might lack various resources that would otherwise cushion and protect me from the prejudices of the colonial-settler state. That is why I rely on, through my collaborations, multilayered and shifting family relations—those drawn from immediate, extended, and expanded family, forming thick relationships, providing critical dialogues, and transformations to situate me in the world.

Nikos Papastergiadis points out that since the 1990s, "a distinctive turn towards collaborative and social forms of artistic practice"[5] has become associated with globalisation, distributive labour, diverse output, and disruption of global media in an "increasingly polarised world."[6] Delving into the close collaborations I share with my immediate family, our dialogues and forms of mediation are complex and do not guarantee smooth forms of productivity or even togetherness.

In more extreme circumstances Michael D. Shin has pointed out that in the context of the Cold War and the Korean-American War, collaborations were not always a benign thing.[7] Collaborations might emerge not out of free-will, but also from desperation, coercion, and necessity.

5
Nikos Papastergiadis, *Cosmopolitanism and Culture* (Cambridge; Malden: Polity Press, 2012), 11.

6
Ibid., 156.

7
Michael D. Shin, "Yi Kwang-su: The Collaborator as Modernist Against Modernity," *The Journal of Asian Studies* 71, no. 1 (2012): 115.

Collaborators are not always trustworthy. As an artist doing the primary language and cultural brokering between my family and the academic and artworld establishment, apparent power differentials have led another of my artistic collaborators, Ciaran Begley, to point out that I may not only be collaborating with my immediate family in art, but rather, I might be actually collaborating with the power structures of the artworld in order to recruit my family into these fraught spaces. As a linguistic, cultural, and art-world intermediary, I sit between these collaborative allegiances. Might I be, in fact, in cahoots with the artworld? Collaboration therefore can go hand in hand with the betrayals of ambition and careerism. At times, I might be instrumentalising my language-brokering skills to selectively communicate, bend translations, and instrumentalise power to my benefit at the expense of the people, infrastructures, and systems I am apparently collaborating with.

Considering the dynamics of shifting power in how collaborations happen in the family, I occasionally use other terms that better articulate the variable nature of these fraught relationships. The terms "complicity," "conspiracy," and "collusion" are at times more accurate at describing the tactical and subversive intent of working with my family under the structural remit of the university, the artworld, and even the Vietnamese friends and communities around us.

Working with my family throughout this thesis, the term "self-representation" describes how

we articulate ideas amongst ourselves and how we might become visible to the artworld and its audiences, along with other institutions and infrastructures. Initially relying on the term self-representation, I will gradually adopt Hito Steyerl's use of presencing to "leave behind the endless debate about representation."[8] Instead, the term "self-presencing" is used to navigate how my family engages with each other. This is how we situate ourselves through the particular strategies of translation, collaboration, and archival production. This thesis provides an opportunity for me to unpack how my family creates the space to produce and share knowledge, even when we are deep inside institutions of profound exclusion and asymmetrical power. Of particular concern are: the immigration department; the university; the capital economy; and the artworld. And because these institutions are themselves never straightforward, the reader cannot expect our experiences as a family in these spaces to be straightforward either.

The legitimacy of my family is often called into question at border crossings, in academic research, and when participating in the artworld. The ability to make ourselves known in these worlds is outside of our control. According to Ien Ang, the conditional criteria to simply be present is regularly accompanied by the expectation that immigrants stay silent and

8 Hito Steyerl, "The Language of Things," *Under Translation*, June 2006, https://transversal.at/transversal/0606/steyerl/en.

compliant.[9] Gayatri Chakravorty Spivak also notes the conditional auspices that allow the subaltern to speak.[10] Having to perpetually seek legitimacy and permissions, to continually perform standards not expected from other citizens, presencing becomes relentless work. For my family, the ability to freely self-represent and articulate our thoughts, such as blending our accents to demonstrate good English, become unknowing re-enactors of the arbitrary Dictation Tests of the Australian Immigration Act throughout 1901–58.[11]

Beyond the neoliberal conceit of individualism as a valid form of self-representation, my family and I often find our presence and representation to each other to be essential to how we make work for each other. Art in these private moments is not burdened with having to seek permissions and approval from external publics and institutions around us.

Throughout this thesis, the term "self-determination" is used to supplement the concept of self-presencing. Self-determination suggests our awareness that, although we can have all the determination and intention to be present and say what we need to say, the capacity for others to actually stop and listen, or to accept us as equal and legitimate participants in their world, is not something that can be assumed. The determination of my family to presence ourselves into discourse becomes as important as our representation and reception by others. Centring our intentionality through self-determination and presencing,

we avoid wasting the greater part of our energies on doing self-representation and presenting ourselves to others. Again, it is almost impossible to completely disengage or ignore powerful infrastructures like the immigration department, the UNSW HREC approval process, the artworld, and even the Vietnamese community.

9

Ien Ang, *On Not Speaking Chinese: Living Between Asia and the West* (London; New York: Routledge, 2001), 11.

10

Gayatri Chakravorty Spivak and Rosalind C. Morris, *Can the Subaltern Speak?: Reflections on the History of an Idea* (New York: Columbia University Press, 2010), 45–48.

11

The National Archives of Australia describes The Immigration Restriction Act of 1901 as a foundational piece of legislation that was the first piece of legislation enacted by the new Federated Parliament of Australia in 1901. Also known as the White Australia Policy, the exclusion of non-Anglo Europeans into Australia was enshrined through a series of legislative restrictions placed on Asian and non-white aliens. Under the Immigration Act, migrants who entered Australia between 1901 and 1958 could be asked to take a dictation test. To pass the test, they needed to write fifty words in any European language as dictated by an immigration officer. After 1905, the officer could choose any language at all. A Chinese immigrant, for example, could be asked to write out fifty words in French, Italian, or another language. Few migrants could pass the test under such circumstances. This meant that it was easy to fail an applicant if they were from an "undesirable" country or culture.

The Immigration Restriction Act 1901, accessed July 6, 2023, https://www.naa.gov.au/explore-collection/immigration-and-citizenship/immigration-restriction-act-1901.

These institutions continue to exert both tangible and extraordinary power on our lives.

An important way for my family to gain artistic and academic presence is by producing artistic documents and archives. The archive, according to Michel Foucault, extends beyond the material content and documents that make up said archive.[12] For Foucault, what is equally, if not more important are the conditions that manifest and made possible these archives in the first place. These include the structural apparatus, political institutions, and the constructed cultural rules and resources that facilitate how material archives come into existence. To Foucault, the archive is neither complete nor coherent. Recognising how archives do not just appear in and of themselves, archives should be closely scrutinised and never "accepted without question."[13] Echoing Foucault, these archival contingencies allow for what Tina Campt describes as a way of synthesising "a collective and relational practice of enunciation."[14] The archive, as critiqued by Achille Mbembe, is dangerous for people undergoing major disruptions such as migration.

12
David Bate, "The Archaeology of Photography: Rereading Michel Foucault and *The Archaeology of Knowledge*," *Afterimage* 35, no. 3 (2007): 3.

13
Michel Foucault, *The Archaeology of Knowledge* (London: Routledge, 2002), 28.

14
Tina M. Campt, *Image Matters: Archive, Photography, and the African Diaspora in Europe* (Durham: Duke University Press, 2012), 241.

Forced archival presence in the form of documents, notes, photographs, and recordings are ways for migrant bodies to become legible, accounted for, surveilled, scrutinised, and ultimately violated by the state. In Australia, Aboriginal woman born and living on D'harawal Country Bronwyn Carlson[15] and Torres Strait Islander man Martin Nakata describe how the forced movement of Aboriginal and Torres Strait Islanders along with their legal and cultural identities continue to be enforced by "very narrowly prescribed, government-instated modes of political representation."[16] Consigned to frontier denial and neglect, Wiradjuri Celtic artist and curator Brook Andrew points out in *Nirin* for the *22nd Biennale of Sydney* how Indigenous presence and memory is pushed off the "edge and often out of sight" in ways that deliberately erase massacres and genocide.[17] With the settler-colonial archive conspiring to deliberately remove Indigenous archives, Bundjalung, Muruwari, and Kamilaroi man Brian Martin describes how Australia cultivates "the act of forgetting, but also ... a condition that perpetuates

15
Bronwyn Carlson, *The Politics of Identity: Who Counts as Aboriginal Today?* (Canberra: Aboriginal Studies Press, 2016).

16
Martin Nakata, "Indigenous Memory, Forgetting, and the Archives," *Archives and Manuscripts* 40, no. 2 (July 2012): 102.

17
Jennifer Lavers, Hannah Catherine Jones, Paschal Daantos Berry, and Brook Andrew, "Diaspora Footprint Cycle Puzzle Oceans," in *Nirin: 22nd Biennale of Sydney*, ed. Jessica Neath, Sarah Gory, and Susan Acret (Sydney: The Biennale of Sydney), 53.

the consequential apathy that prevents memory from being put into practice."[18] The archive, therefore, when used for documenting and erasing minoritarian subjects is an instrument of state-sanctioned violence that does not offer protection or archival assurance for many bodies still being recorded and archived.

Beyond the accumulation and organisation of human lives though state documents and documentation (which includes documentary forms), many refugees and their families still desire to gain legitimacy with these same "lawful" archives. The line between coercion and visibility offered by archival presence is complicated. The archival impulse sometimes cited in contemporary art easily slips into a form of archival impost. The motivation to create documentation and archives for my family as a personal record, and the need to produce documents and archives exclusively for legitimisation in the eyes of the state, is troublesome. For my family, archival evidence and proof (as demanded by the immigration department) is carried into other institutional encounters in Australia; as we cross one border, we encounter subsequent and familiar archival demands embedded within the artworld and academia.

Reflecting on these troublesome forms of exclusion, I was inspired by the Vietnamese homonym chó bò ~ *trouble.* Utilising trouble as

18 Brian Martin, "Immaterial Land and Indigenous Ideology: Refiguring Australian Art and Culture" (PhD diss., School of Communication and Creative Arts, Deakin University, 2013), 3.

the titular thematic across this thesis, I refer to the difficulty of speaking English with a Vietnamese accent. As a linguistic and conceptual device, chó bò or *trouble* slips between being in trouble, causing trouble, and asking for trouble. Chó bò or *trouble* itself is inevitably perceived as troubled, troubling, and troublesome.

These terms complicate the slippery subject-position of Vietnamese and Asian immigrants as outsiders charged with importing trouble, as people who are haunted by trouble, or those who refuse to leave their troubles behind. Catriona Ross describes how Australian literary culture specifically represents Asian foreigners as a troubling threat to its Anglo-colonial sovereignty. She describes how persistent racist representations of Asian Australians gives an "insight into the historical and cultural unconscious of an anxious settler nation."[19] Seen by more established settler-colonisers as an existential threat, people like my family, who not only look but also sound different, are a troubling reminder of the historic precarity of Australia as an isolated penal colony. These historic perceptions of trouble continue into the present, painting Asian immigrants not only as perpetual outsiders, but perpetually troubling to the Australian way of life.

19 Catriona Ross, "Prolonged Symptoms of Cultural Anxiety: The Persistence of Narratives of Asian Invasion Within Multicultural Australia," *Journal of the Association for the Study of Australian Literature* 86, no. 5 (2006): 86.

These experiences challenge popular definitions of trouble by mainstream feminists, such as Donna Haraway, who conceptualise trouble as an emergent condition of the present. Calling on her collaborators to "sit with the trouble," Haraway appeals for people to become accustomed to the emergence of these troubling times, as if it were a choice—or not—to "sit with" the trouble.[20] Being actually perceived *as the trouble*, my family has no choice in the matter; our tolerance and experience of trouble is quite distinct from Haraway's.

As this thesis unfolds, the troubles my family face are recognised as not merely external phenomena that encircle us, but as profoundly linked to our troubling condition as displaced people, who have been resettled in and recruited into the prevailing settler-colonial nation. Trouble for us must be conceptualised and enacted in a more internalised and reflexive way. As a tool of epistemic and decolonial disruption, trouble becomes a weapon. Trouble can defend us from the racism and ignorance directed at our families, but trouble can also be a way to keep each other from enacting the same persistent forms of colonial violence again and again. Trouble is—an inevitable reality of—our history, future, and ever present.

As people displaced from elsewhere, my family—like many others exiled from Vietnam

20 Donna Haraway, *Staying with the Trouble: Making Kin in the Chthulucene* (Durham: Duke University Press, 2016), 2.

throughout the many historic waves of Han, French, Japanese, and American-led occupations—have been largely resettled into coloniser or colonial-settler countries especially since the Vietnam-American war. Our significant cultural and colonial traumas become psychologically, emotionally, and politically laminated over the colonial traumas of our host countries. The contradictions that members of my family and I encounter as people now living in Australia, and our recruitment and gradual assimilation into the settler-colonial frameworks of Australia, must be confronted. This subject-position, as both colonised and colonising people, as displaced and displacing, has to date not been well articulated by the Vietnamese diaspora in Australia. This thesis approaches diasporic decolonialisation through the intimate conversations, translations, and artworks made with my family. As a family, we attempt to grapple with the contradictory subject-position of being people who were historically colonised, but yet continue to be profoundly colonising in our deepest hopes, aspirations, and desires.

The capacity for self-determination, and to represent ourselves within these troubling realities, is profoundly important to how my family and I have navigated these spaces together. Decolonisation for my family demands the decolonising of the self, for each other. Decolonisation entails challenging the Vietnamese community as much as dealing with the racist and colonial infrastructures around us. As we continue to work together as a family, the willingness

to engage in these conversations and to reassess the Vietnamese preoccupation with being profoundly colonised will hopefully lessen our own tendency to blindly enact enduring forms of violence wrought through our continuous resettlements.

Reducing the scope of my research to only the art-works that I have made with family during the period of my candidature, and under the auspices of the UNSW HREC approval system, seems at first limiting and counter-intuitive when pushing the limitations of self-representation. However, the decision to narrow the content of my output to artworks with my family is necessary to contain the length, scheduling, and administrative limits of my research. I will mention some independent parts of my practice as well as cross-collaborations with friends and colleagues outside my family only where relevant.

Critical to the contextualisation of my family relationships and our practice as makers is an acknowledgement of our subject-position as people from the Vietnamese diaspora. My family and I are part of the tens of thousands of Vietnamese people who fled and subsequently resettled in Australia following the Vietnam-American War. The traumas of war, recurrent refugee testimony-making, and restaging of intergenerational loss, described by Michael Rothberg[21] and elaborated by Marianne Hirsch as "traumatic realism,"[22]

21 Michael Rothberg, "Between the Extreme and the Everyday: Ruth Klüger's Traumatic Realism," *A/b: Auto/Biography Studies: EXTREMITIES: MEMOIRS AT THE FIN DE SIÈCLE* 14, no. 1 (January 1999): 93-107. https://doi:10.1080/08989575.1999.10846758.

is true for my family. However, this will not be the primary artistic concern for the type of work we have produced or are interested in addressing. Similarly, the autobiographic nature of the materials discussed in the thesis and the various culturally specific inflections that contribute to the dynamics of my family might appear quite ethnographic to some readers. Fred Wilson[23] and Coco Fusco's[24] critique of westernised forms of ethnocentric viewership debunks this assumption as primarily that of a colonial gaze focused on difference that decentres the normalcy of non-western people. Seeing our work as cultural oddities and curiosities, rather than recognising our inherent and deliberate artistic methods and contributions beyond our perceived "Otherness," is not *our* bias. It is incumbent on readers to acknowledge and recognise these biases within themselves.

On engaging and producing contemporary artworks for exhibition and research, my family and I are fully aware of the spectacle and rhetoric

22 Marianne Hirsch, "Surviving Images: Holocaust Photographs and the Work of Postmemory," *The Yale Journal of Criticism* 14, no. 1 (Spring 2001): 5-37.

23 Fred Wilson, in conversation with Ivan Karp in "Constructing the Spectacle of Culture in Museums," in *Thinking About Exhibitions*, ed. Reesa Greenberg, Bruce W. Ferguson, and Sandy Nairne (Hoboken: Routledge, 1996), 180-191.

24 Coco Fusco, *The Bodies That Were Not Ours: And Other Writings* (London: Taylor & Francis Group, 2001).

of inclusion and diversity in these spaces. This thesis will address the institutional biases inherited from the paternalistic and colonial treatment of people according to an inflexible researcher-researched model of knowledge production. As an artist actively seeking the awarding of this research degree, and who is involved in the life, recording, and production of art with other members of my family, I have both an insider and outsider perspective. I am both an observer and an "artist-activator" between these worlds. Research principles organised around perceived notions of unbiased positionality, impartial objectivity, and the indisputable separation of labour between the researcher and those being researched are inevitably complicated by the type of research I am doing with my family. I will not be writing this thesis to justify the validity of my approach, nor legitimise my practice according to the conceit of objectivity. More useful is the recognition of complexity inherent in doing this type of research with my family. More important are the potential artistic questions that extend beyond pure research towards something compromised and troubling, yet perfectly capable of epistemic rigour, artistic innovation, and self-criticality.

My family, as part of the Vietnamese community in Australia and the Vietnamese diaspora displaced throughout the world, can never be one neat or coherent entity. Neither can we ever be representative of, nor interested in speaking for, multitudes. From past experience, there is a

tendency for many artworld and academic audiences to misinterpret the work my family has made to be somehow representative and indicative of the experiences of other people with a similar background. My family and I resist this completely as we will not be burdened, nor are we conferred with any right to represent, or be representative of, the wider Vietnamese community in Australia and beyond.

I am also very aware that there are profound and deep divisions within the Vietnamese community. Particularly relevant is Kieu-Linh Caroline Valverde's analysis on the divisions of the global Vietnamese diaspora.[25] The emotionally charged and at times dangerous political divide of transnationalised Vietnamese communities in Australia and those abroad remain important considerations as to how this research is framed.

I will make it clear from the outset that all participants from my family, any people named, either directly, or only having loose association with producing this research, are afforded the right of refusal and simply cannot be compelled to make any public statements that may be taken beyond the context of this thesis. Especially information that could compromise private freedoms and their right to exist as part of the Vietnamese community

25 Kieu-Linh Caroline Valverde, *Transnationalizing Viet Nam: Community, Culture, and Politics in the Diaspora* (Philadelphia: Temple University Press, 2013), 4.

and diaspora without political intervention or punishment. This research will not be used for the purpose of minimising or contracting the expansive lives of so many people sharing a similar Vietnamese background. Further, as individuals, each member of my family has our own ambitions and desires. Even the term "family" is itself problematic and will be discussed later in Chapter 1. To us, family, community, diaspora, and our collaborative relationalities are inevitably nebulous and dynamic.

Although my family plays such a significant role in my arts practice and research, it does not mean that all of the materials and content that we have produced as a family during the period of this PhD is totally open for public and academic scrutiny. As a family engaged in this research, we have the right to refuse, as well as the right to express our need for distance and for the purposes of exhibition and publication. Similarly, we have determined what is excluded from research, and what cannot be recorded or retained. We have discussed and executed ethical conduct and the academic expectations of this PhD to the best of our abilities.[26] We have benefited from the support and help of my supervisors Dr Jennifer Biddle, Dr Verónica Tello, and many others from UNSW Art & Design.

26 The PhD research was conducted in full compliance with the UNSW HREC (UNSW Human Research Ethics Committee): project no. HC180430, including all terms and conditions associated with this approval.

Choosing to base my research around artworks made with my family is a complex and challenging enterprise. The process has been one that is dynamic and elastic in its conceptual reach and breadth as well as its humour—at times contracting to the intimacies of one-on-one exchanges, into rapidly exponential outbursts of joy, failure, and humiliation. What remains central, however, is how the methodology of working with family offers the capacity to recognise and navigate the systemic barriers, contradictions, and compromises we encounter as people in the present.

Chapter Outline

This thesis is organised under three main chapters.

In Chapter 1, I start reconnecting with estranged members of my family. I focus on building and forming a new relationship with Cậu Ái ~ *my Uncle* Nguyễn Công Ái and Các Anh Em ~ *my Vietnam-based Cousins* focussing on how our connections were dependent on the language-brokering and translations embedded in various family enterprises. The artistic and relational outcomes of these translations and interactions were performative (with Cậu Ái ~ *my Uncle*) and entrepreneurial (with Các Anh Em ~ *my Cousins*). By helping my Uncle to set up and connect to the National Broadband Network (NBN) on his zucchini farm in Adelaide, we produced a performance piece and video work accounting for the speechless presence of migrant labourers and workers in regional Australia. Similarly, translations with my Cousins in Vietnam dealt with the racism of international capital. Working in their business, I edited their emails and press-releases, mediating the communications of their start-up with the language-brokering skills I learnt in Australia. By adapting my language in these two family-run enterprises (a zucchini market garden in Adelaide, and a biotech start up in Vietnam), I gained new insights into the economic colonisation and ubiquitous privilege of the English language. Responding to the dumb racism and linguistic

supremacy of English in these family enterprises, my Uncle, Cousins, and I found ways to orchestrate minor linguistic deceptions and artistic manoeuvres to expose and even exploit linguistic prejudice.

In Chapter 2, I recount how Ba ~ *my Dad*, Nguyễn Ngọc Cư had helped me to gain UNSW HREC approval to do research with my family. Again, engaging in another subversive collusion, my Dad worked to translate the "HREC Participant Information Statement and Consent Form" for me. Essential in fulfilling the HREC demands of the university, his auto-translations blurred the impossible segregation between the "researcher" (me) doing approved research on my "research-subjects" (my family—including my Dad). The institutional expectation to distinguish those with the capacity to *do* research and those who can only participate by *being* researched is profoundly problematic for researchers like myself who are from the same communities we are researching. I was surprised to find these divisions were the case, and further dismayed that my insight and entanglement in the lived experiences of my own family were treated as a procedural nuisance by the university. The persistence of colonial, paternalistic, and medicalised frameworks in higher-degree research were clearly still apparent. Translating the "HREC Research Participant Consent Form" from English into Vietnamese, and signing the forms he had just translated, my Dad crossed this researcher-researched divide. Using his

language skills to help me subvert the university's own means of epistemic segregation, his translations met the compliance and documentational needs of the UNSW HREC approval process, yet was conceptually troublesome in subverting the procedural violence of academic research. Similar to the world of business enterprise seen in Chapter 1, minoritarian voices in the university are rarely equal partners in research and knowledge production. These opaque prejudices regularly establish subtle conditions for cultural exclusion. In an effort to protect my family through a series of inflexible ethical procedurals, the university ironically sanctioned a contradictory system of burden and patronising care on the family.

In Chapter 3, I spent time with Mẹ Dung ~ *my Mum*, Nguyễn Thị Kim Dung, and Dì Nhung ~ *my Aunty*, Nguyễn Thị Kim Nhung. Working with my Mum to translate her poetry from Vietnamese to English, and with my Aunty to translate what has become protocol in Australia: a formal Acknowledgement of Country in institutional spaces and public events from English to Vietnamese.[27] Our collaborations suddenly became more located in the literary work of translation. These acts of informal translations with Mẹ Dung ~ *my Mum*, and Dì Nhung ~ *my Aunty*, gave me a little insight into their lives. They are regularly excluded from social and economic opportunities afforded to the men in my family. My Dad and I, compared to my Mum and Aunty,

speak *good* English. Language in our family is drawn across a distinctly gendered line. Central to their own form of linguistic troublemaking, the work of my Mum and Aunty stirred up the latent misogyny of the family and of their Vietnamese neighbours. Rather than supporting their work as marginalised members of this community, a number of Vietnamese men, including my Dad, sought to minimise the legitimacy of my Mum and Aunty as women who didn't speak good English, and who continued to work low-skilled piecework.

Helping to translate my Mum's poem, which described the resettlement of our family onto the stolen lands of the D'harawal/Tharawal, the work of language-brokering that as a child I had grown to resent, was consequently an invaluable tool for reconnection. With these translations came the painful realisation of my own linguistic deficiencies. Before embarking on this PhD, I was utterly unaware of my Mum's poetry. I too was completely indifferent and ignorant of her artistic ambition and

27 An Acknowledgement of Country, according to Reconciliation Australia, is an opportunity for anyone to show respect for Traditional Owners and the continuing connection of Aboriginal and Torres Strait Islander peoples to Country. It has become common protocol at public events and can be given by both non-Indigenous people and Aboriginal and Torres Strait Islander people. "Acknowledgement of Country and Welcome to Country," Reconciliation Australia, September 26, 2022, https://www.reconciliation.org.au/wp-content/uploads/2020/09/acknowledgement-of-country_welcome-to-country.pdf.

inner life. Helping me to appreciate the linguistic inheritance and the context of my Mum's poem, my Aunty directed me to the canon of Vietnamese feminist poets who were, again, completely unknown to me. Through the orthographic separation of the Vietnamese language from the Han-Chinese script, and prior to its Romanisation under French occupation, I came to learn that Vietnam's revered national literary renaissance was built on an ancient feminist legacy. These revelations highlighted my own linguistic disconnect. Described by Gloria Anzaldúa[28] and later by Walter Mignolo[29] as a willingness to trade-up the wealth of my linguistic inheritance by exclusively speaking good English, my daily compliance in someone else's tongue made me what Rey Chow[30] calls a willing traditore ~ *a traitor* to my own language.

The intimate process of language-brokering and translation with my Mum and Aunty was a powerful and political awakening. By translating an Acknowledgement of Country into Vietnamese with

28 Gloria Anzaldúa, *Borderlands = La Frontera*, 2nd ed. (San Francisco: Aunt Lute Books, 1999).

29 Walter D. Mignolo, "Geopolitics of Sensing and Knowing: On (de)coloniality, Border Thinking and Epistemic Disobedience," *Postcolonial Studies* 14, no. 3 (September 2011): 276. https://doi:10.1080/13688790.2011.613105.

30 Rey Chow, "Translator, Traitor; Translator, Mourner (or, Dreaming of Intercultural Equivalence)," *New Literary History* 39, no. 3 (2008): 570, https://doi:10.1353/nlh.0.0048.

my Aunty Nguyễn Thị Kim Nhung, we engaged in complex and often unspoken dialogues linking colonisation and the displaced refugee. Taking for granted the Acknowledgement of Country as a cosmetic exercise in previous work, I learnt, through Dì Nhung of our family's active role in Vietnam's dispossessions of tribal lands between the wars. Making art and sharing language as deployed in the life of my family has helped my relatives and I to uproot these complex and uncomfortable histories. Doing informal translations, we start the long process of reclaiming culture, reconnecting with family, and speaking up about the most troublesome aspects of misogyny, racism, and colonial violence embedded within ourselves and our multiple communities.

CHAPTER 1

Troubling Translations

Having outlined the chapters and established the terms and premise for the thesis above, I will keep the introduction to this first chapter brief. I will discuss the various forms of linguistic mediations and collaborations with my family, both in Australia and Vietnam. Through my encounter with estranged members of my family, I use language as a cultural and practical medium to navigate the distance between the artworld I occupy, and the family enterprises of my Uncle and Cousins. I look at how our work—as family, as artists, and as collaborators in business—is ultimately dependent on how we deploy our broken languages to reconnect, make art, and engage with the global economy.

Whilst western art history continues to be concerned with prioritising the achievements of individuals, the work that my family and I create together specifically deals with our individual concerns, yet is only realised together and collaboratively discussed, produced, and shared. Working with my family, these types of endeavours seek to develop viable ways to communicate and connect the individual to the shared concerns of our family. By reconnecting with estranged family members, this chapter explores multiple forms of language-brokering, mediation, and linguistic collusions. For example, it explores what it means to conceptualise the practice of art beyond the individual, to rediscover and reconnect family networks and solidarities, and through this, express ourselves artistically and economically. By providing

an alternative to the individualistic pursuit of art, perhaps the family as a source of dialogic and linguistic engagement can generate unexpected forms of epistemic resistance and refusals through our reconnections.

At the Border of a National Broadband Network

Getting back in contact with my estranged Uncle Nguyễn Công Ái, I had not expected to be waiting on hold with Telstra (Australia's largest telecommunications corporation). Trying to ignore their repetitive and annoying on-hold music, I was waiting for information about local Telstra-approved contractors who could dig a cable-trench from the roadside to my Uncle's property. This trench meant that he could connect his small market garden to the NBN (Australia's National Broadband Network) and have regular contact with distant relatives.

Cậu Ái ~ *Uncle Ái* was a few years younger than my Mum and Dì Nhung ~ *Aunty Nhung*. Unlike the other siblings who came to Australia in the 1990s, Cậu Ái didn't stay in the city. As soon as he arrived, he left and headed out bush. My Mum and Aunty would occasionally get reports from family friends about their Brother's vague movements, doing seasonal fruit picking throughout parts of regional Australia.

In 2016, I decided to reach out and contact Cậu Ái myself. Following two years of patchy phone calls and multiple road trips (occasionally with my Aunty coming along), we visited my Uncle in his off season. Cậu Ái at that time also decided to use all his savings to start a small-scale zucchini market garden in the Smithfield Plains, on the outskirts of Adelaide. Setting up this small enterprise, Cậu Ái needed an internet connection, and not confident with English

(despite working in regional Australia for over two decades), he asked me to help him set up his NBN. Like many other Australians (even those who speak fluent English), retrofitting their existing copper cable to the NBN fibre-optic network was inevitably an expensive and confusing exercise. I found it fitting that reconnecting with my estranged Uncle, also meant a rather banal and all too familiar tele-communications odyssey with Telstra.[1] Put on-hold, I realised this was the first time I had used my English-brokering skills to help my Uncle. Like many other immigrant children, I had grown quite used to the endless requests of parents, elders, and neighbours to help translate and broker this English language for them. Mediating on their behalf, I made countless calls to resolve issues with Telcos, local councils, schools, and other public/private institutions and organisations for my family and their neighbours.[2] These regular requests were a nuisance. But sitting here, putting up with Telstra's on-hold music for my Uncle suddenly felt meaningful.

1 Gary McLaren, "What Now for Australia's NBN?: How Australia's Politics, Insular Policies, and Preference for Monopolies Have Made Australia a Broadband Backwater," *Australian Journal of Telecommunications and the Digital Economy* 6, no. 4 (2018): 34.

2 Shu-Sha A. Guan, Patricia M. Greenfield, and Marjorie F. Orellana, "Translating into Understanding: Language Brokering and Prosocial Development in Emerging Adults From Immigrant Families," *Journal of Adolescent Research* 29, no. 3 (May 2014): 331-55. https://doi:10.1177/0743558413520223.

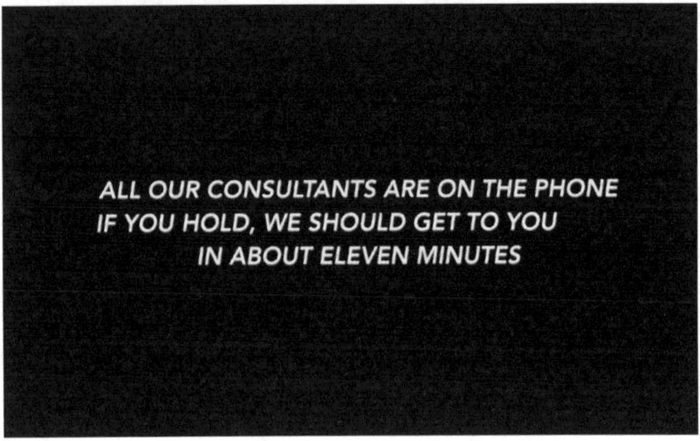

ALL OUR CONSULTANTS ARE ON THE PHONE
IF YOU HOLD, WE SHOULD GET TO YOU
IN ABOUT ELEVEN MINUTES

Figs 1, 3–6 (pp. 70–71)
Phone recording of automated Telstra messaging service, screenshot taken from screen text for *On The Border Of Things (Part II)*, duration 16:15 min, courtesy the artists Nguyễn Công Aí, Nguyễn Thị Kim Nhung, Hayley Forward (composer), and James Nguyen, produced by Bron Belcher for Next Wave Festival, 2018.

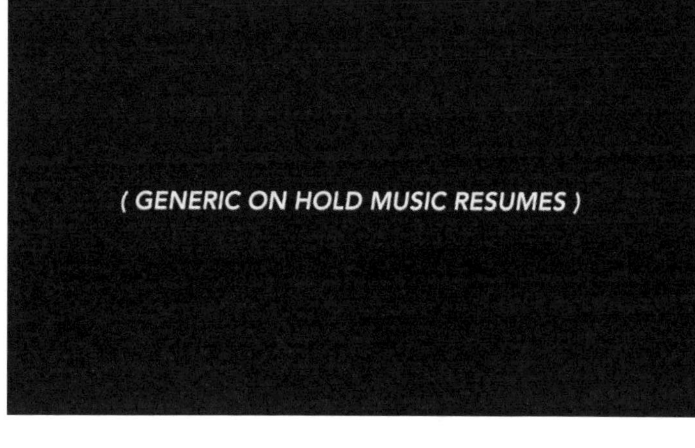

Fig. 2
Audio description of automated Telstra National Broadband Connection, screenshot taken from screen text for *On The Border Of Things (Part II)*, duration 16:15 min, courtesy the artists Nguyễn Công Ái, Nguyễn Thị Kim Nhung, Hayley Forward (composer), and James Nguyen, produced by Bron Belcher for Next Wave Festival, 2018.

Organising a "conduit and socket" and a three-foot deep trench for the network cable, I fielded calls as my Uncle tried to keep on top of his bumper harvest of zucchinis. Between the labour and necessity of connecting to this piece of national infrastructure, I realised that I was the actual conduit for my Uncle, for Telstra, and their over-booked local contractors. I knew Cậu Ái's poor English would be a profound barrier. Not confident in English, my Uncle's previous attempts at connecting to this piece of publicly owned national telecommunications infrastructure was regularly scuttled; pushed to the back of Telstra's customer service priorities. By deploying the assertive tone and language of complaint as a fluent English speaker, my requests on behalf of my uncle suddenly became actionable to Telstra and their contractors.

The realisation of how easy it would have been for my Uncle to be deprioritised and deferred by Telstra sharpened my own sense of frustration each time I was transferred from one service operator to another communications manager. In my boredom, I decided to start recording Telstra's on-hold music. I was most likely being recorded on the other end for Telstra's "training purposes" anyway.

Listening to the on-hold soundtrack of corporate indifference, I reflected on the many broken lines of communication, ongoing separations, and daily deferrals that my family had encountered. Our lives had, to a degree, been put on-hold, exiled from the places and people we had left behind.

I WAS WONDERING IF YOU HAD ANY ELECTRICIAN WHO COULD DO A CONDUIT AND SOCKET?

IT DEPENDS ON HOW LONG THEY HAVE TO RUN THE CONDUIT, BUT BASIC ELECTRICAL RATES IS $110 FOR THE FIRST THIRTY MINUTES AND THEN $66 EVERY THIRTY THERE AFTER PLUS MATERIALS

THEY SAID IF IT'S DUG IN THE RIGHT PLACE, THEN THERE'S NO PROBLEM, BUT IF IT'S IN THE WRONG POSITION, THEN THE COST OF THE TRENCH WOULD BE AN EXTRA $1800

THANK YOU FOR YOUR TIME
WAS YOUR QUERY RESOLVED TODAY?

We now were caught waiting in limbo, because of our broken and mixed-up language, waiting for a ditch to be dug, waiting for decisions from the immigration department, waiting for lost friends, lovers, and family members who had simply disappeared in the middle of the night. Migrant families, like my own, might experience the loneliness and alienation of these diasporic dispersals in what Sara Ahmed refers to as our "uncommon estrangements."[3] These estrangements allow immigrant lives to drift away from one another, to be reformed anew as we establish new lives elsewhere. My small task to broker the customer service language of Telstra, connecting to the NBN, had helped me to actually reconnect with my Uncle. Streamlining the multiple quotes from contractors and simplifying the procedures to connect his market garden and home to the internet became my own performance of filial duty; something I could not fulfil all those years he was away, doing fruit picking in some distant place.

Telling my family about how I was recording these endless phone calls with Telstra, my Aunty and Uncle laughed at the absurdity of having reconnected, only now to be put on-hold by Telstra.

3 Sara Ahmed, "Home and Away: Narratives of Migration and Estrangement," *International Journal of Cultural Studies* 2, no.3 (December 1999): 329-47. https://doi: 10.1177/136787799900200303.

Sharing stories about people and friends from their youth, Dì Nhung started to sing in mock cải lương ~ *a traditional Vietnamese opera*, playfully recalling stories of home as she wailed and waited for the NBN. Recording this spontaneous and hilarious moment, I asked Dì Nhung and Cậu Ái if we could work on what was just sung. We quickly composed and wrote a series of songs that were completed well before the NBN was actually installed. The absurd failures of Australia's telecommunications network ironically brought us together. Over time, we developed a performance titled *On the Border of Things (Part II)*, which was latter presented at Next Wave Festival. Taking place on the back of my ute (a utility truck), roving across multiple locations in Melbourne throughout the festival, our mock-Vietnamese opera was backed by a pre-mixed track of the Telstra on-hold music. The instrumental accompaniment was a soundtrack produced and composed by artist friend Hayley Forward.

Not keen on performing, my Uncle helped write these Vietnamese songs but chose to be present only as a voice-over on the soundtrack. Instead of deferring to English, the performance involved my Aunty and I singing Vietnamese lyrics in front of a screen playing English subtitles. Having translated these lyrics into English, I in turn, became the conduit for English-speaking audiences to decode our opera. In these performances, my Aunty and I would dance, get dressed for the next song, play air-guitar, and simply wait around whilst the Telstra

track played. The on-hold music became a formal device or musical interlude that structurally disrupted the flow of the live performance. As we were being perpetually placed on-hold and kept in limbo, we would sing and wait for the NBN to connect us to our relatives.

According to Charles Green's *The Third Hand* (2001), family collaborations offer artists the opportunity to make work beyond the concerns and limitations of the individual; to be part of an expanded identity or "composite subjectivity."[4] Green assumes that a shift away from individualistic practice towards something more democratic and less bound to established modes of concentrated authorship could bring a new perspective to artmaking. Contemporary collaborations are also described by Nikos Papastergiadis as a departure from art history, offering a way for artists to mediate and construct new forms of "discourse that enables a cosmopolitan dialogue," beyond a merely Euro-centric one.[5] These collectivist registers, so natural to how my family share our absurd anecdotes and make art together, extends the experience of the sole individual, the authorial, and the linear "evolution of progress" of western art history.[6]

Since the Renaissance, the west had privileged the sole author. Sven Lütticken describes how this was established through a series of preoccupations whereby "the *persona* became the primary artistic

4 Charles Green, *The Third Hand: Collaboration in Art from Conceptualism to Postmodernism* (Sydney: UNSW Press, 2001), x.

5 Papastergiadis, *Cosmopolitanism and Culture*, 11.

6 Ibid.

material and focus of artistic practice."[7] But perhaps the overt European preoccupation with personality and persona was instigated by Giorgio Vasari when he published *Le Vite de'più eccellenti pittori, scultori, e architettori ~ The Lives of the Most Excellent Painters, Sculptors, and Architects* (1550).[8] Vasari created a biographic convention where authorial attribution and fame became intrinsic to how an artwork would be appreciated and admired by the artworld. The so-called "Lives" that Vasari did write about were neither comprehensive nor objective. Rather, they reflected what Vasari personally decided was "excellence." This preoccupation with persona and biographic immortality still continues today.

Reviewing a recent survey of Australian artists from a number of years ago, curator Sophia Cai writes about the implicit bias of exclusion for "comprehensive" surveys of individual artistic practice. Citing Melissa Loughnan's book *Australiana to Zeitgeist: An A–Z of Contemporary Australian Art* (2017), Cai notes the contradictions of a comprehensive A to Z overview of only a small selection of contemporary Australian artists.[9]

7
Sven Lütticken, "Personafication," *New Left Review* 96 (December 2015): 103.

8
Giorgio Vasari and Betty Burroughs, *Vasari's Lives of the Artists: Biographies of the Most Eminent Architects, Painters, and Sculptors of Italy* (London: Allen & Unwin, 1960).

9
Melissa Loughnan, *Australiana to Zeitgeist: An A-Z of Contemporary Australian Art* (Port Melbourne: Thames & Hudson, 2017).

Prioritising the artistic achievements of a select few, these surveys invariably fall into obsolescence when these artists fall out of fashion. Cai notes the difficult task for a singular author, who might not have the cultural networks to relate with a "broader narrative than her own. A perspective beyond the white Melbourne art world."[10] The selection bias that accompanies the myth of the individual genius in western art history is nothing new. The Vasarian tradition of prioritising particular individuals whilst overlooking more inconvenient forms of artistic achievement, like Renaissance women painters, as opposed to painters of Renaissance women, reveals how this literary tradition can shape and perpetuate the idiosyncratic tastes and biases of the art historian. As Gayatri Chakravorty Spivak points out, the racial double standards of individual privilege are also apparent in Feminist discourse. Where "feminist literary criticism celebrates the heroines of the First World in a singular and individualist [way], and the collective presence of women elsewhere in a pluralized and inchoate fashion."[11] The irony here, is that even when embedded and working from the so-called "first world," non-white practitioners in Australia could still be written out of surveys

10
Sophia Cai, "A White Utopia," *Sophia Cai*, June 2017, https://www.sophiacai.info/a-white-utopia-1.

11
Gayatri Chakravorty Spivak, "Imperialism and Sexual Difference," *Oxford Literary Review* 8, no. 1 (1986): 237. https://doi:10.3366/olr.1986.028.

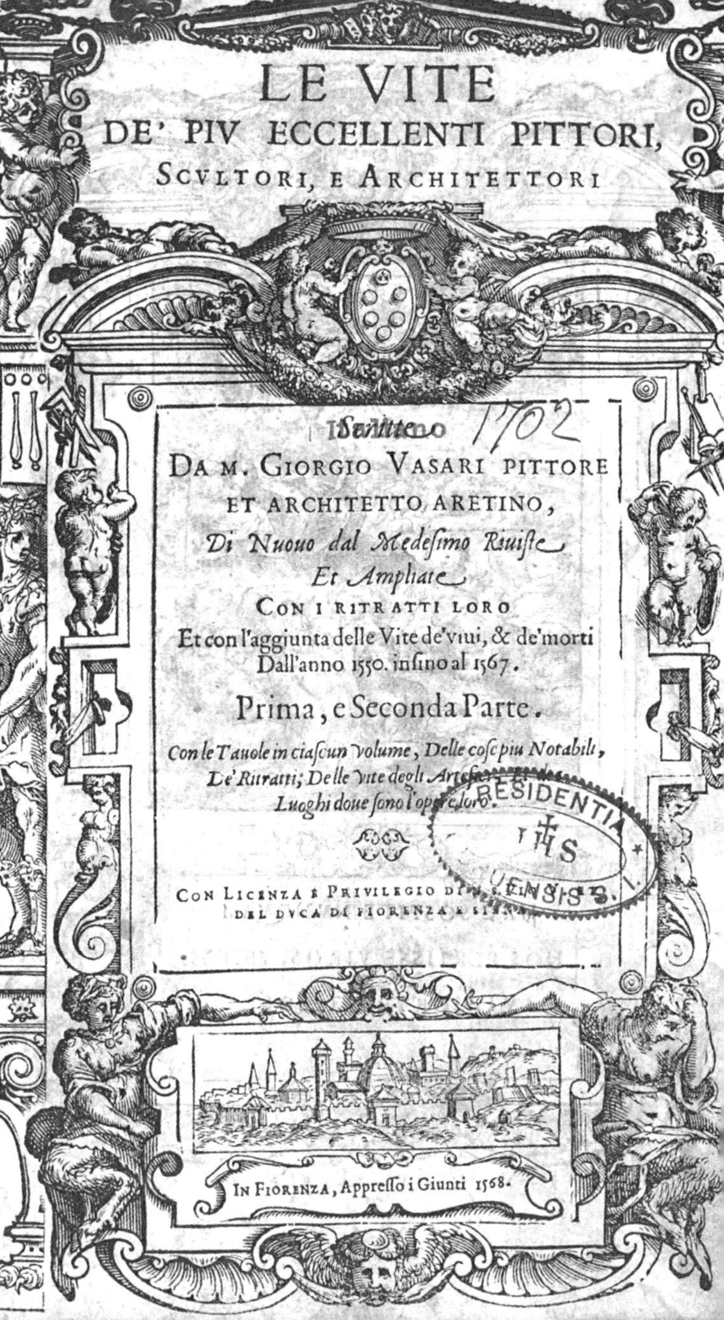

LE VITE
DE' PIV ECCELLENTI PITTORI, SCVLTORI, E ARCHITETTORI

Scritte

DA M. GIORGIO VASARI PITTORE
ET ARCHITETTO ARETINO,

*Di Nuouo dal Medesimo Riuiste
Et Ampliate*

CON I RITRATTI LORO
Et con l'aggiunta delle Vite de' viui, & de' morti
Dall'anno 1550. insino al 1567.

Prima, e Seconda Parte.

*Con le Tauole in ciascun Volume, Delle cose piu Notabili,
De' Ritratti; Delle Vite degli Artef[illegible]
Luoghi doue sono l'opere loro.*

CON LICENZA E PRIVILEGIO DI [illegible]
DEL DVCA DI FIORENZA E SIENA.

IN FIORENZA, Appresso i Giunti 1568.

that benchmark individual excellence. By basing her selection criteria on a few notable individuals, it becomes quite easy for Loughnan to avoid the complexity and diversity of artistic practice that consitutes the messy Australian contemporary zeitgeist.[12] It therefore remains particularly important to challenge the banal but established modes of art historical privilege that perennially site the achievements of a handful of white artists under the guise of individual excellence. Individual achievement in these circumstances is anything but individual. These individuals are regularly supported by an enduring art historical framework, and the contributions of many cultural power brokers who may not knowingly promote and protect these systemic biases. Authorship and authorial control must therefore always be scrutinised to ascertain why particular individuals are deemed worthy of inclusion to the persistent exclusion of others.

12
Ibid., 235.

Fig. 7 (p. 78)
Title page from Giorgio Vasari, *Le vie de' piu eccellenti pittori, scultori, e architetettori*, 2nd ed. (Florence: Giunta, 1568).

What Is the Author and Why Are they Dead?

Michel Foucault's *What Is an Author* (1969) reflects on the hierarchical privilege of individual eminence in fields of science and academic research. Foucault describes how the individualisation of authorship and the importance placed on attributing ground-breaking discovery to the individual are primary organising principles in the western academic tradition. Establishing a "system of valorisation" to reiterate and reward the author, academic institutions benefit by underwriting and monopolising the power to "describe and designate" both what is considered knowledge, and who is determined to have excellence. By strictly regulating the legitimacy of these individuals, academic institutions can protect their ownership over systems of knowledge production to maintain their control over who and what knowledge forms are ultimately privileged, endorsed, and financially supported.

The absurd comparisons of Foucault and Vasari—the latter, the lauded father of western art history—with Melissa Loughnan, a former Melbourne gallerist (and now a colleague and friend in the Melbourne art scene) reveals the eventual complicity of all forms of authorship, and the selection bias of artists and researchers like myself (in this thesis), and other gallery workers, writers, theorists, curators, academics, and small-time art critics within our many circles of authorial privilege.

Foucault notes that "in our culture, the name of an author is a variable that accompanies only certain texts to the exclusion of others."[13] "Others" not only refers to the exclusion of drafts or unofficial texts, but often also the marginalisation of so many forms of knowledge perceived to be not excellent or non-intelligible to the academy. For Foucault, it is *outside* of the author and authorial constraint where knowledge has the space to engage and become valuable to society.

In *The Death of the Author* (1967), Roland Barthes proposes a decentralisation of power to challenge the primacy of what he calls a capitalist society focused on authorial ownership. For Barthes, the interpretation, exchange, and contestation of text becomes essential to the dialogue and experience of art beyond the limitations of authorial control. He writes:

> a text consists of multiple writings, issuing from several cultures and entering into dialogue with each other, into parody, into contestation; but there is one place where this multiplicity is collected, united, and this place is not the author, as we have hitherto said it was, but the reader: the reader is the very space in which [meaning is] inscribed, without any being lost, all the citations a writing consists of; the unity of a text is not in its origin, it is in its destination; but this destination can no longer be personal.[14]

Barthes' argument for the decentralisation of meaning away from the author (and even the individual reader) toward dialogue within a culture of others is an argument for dialogical agency and exchange.

In relation to working with my family—practicing art as non-native English speakers, and brokering multiple languages just to decode the conventions of the artworld and the organisations around us—reading never is a singular or linear process. What Barthes terms as a "reader" of texts, for my family, becomes a "translator," "mediator," "interpreter," and "negotiator" of spoken and written language. That is, the reader must also broker the language and texts not only for themselves, but for the other family members around them. Artworld encounters with my family are ultimately shaped by how we *share* these readings and interpretations. For us, translation is the pragmatic and paradigmatic centre of an artwork, its production, and its interpretation. The locus of the original text or artwork makes no sense without the collaborative and collective effort to unpack and decode text through multiple processes of translation, validation, and contestation with other family members.

13
Michel Foucault, *Language, Counter-Memory, Practice: Selected Essays and Interviews* (Ithaca: Cornell University Press, 1977), 124.

14
Roland Barthes, "The Death of the Author," in *Image, Music, Text*, trans. Stephen Heath (London: Fontana Press, 1977), 148.

Unlike Barthes who saw reading and interpretation of text as interconnected (but ultimately an individual enterprise), reading and translating produces what Papastergiadis calls a "cosmopolitan imaginary," that is, a dispersed and dynamic process of collaborative and translational exchanges and relationships.[15] To me, reading is done *for*, and *with*, the family and with other people around us, as much as it is done *for* and *by* the individual.

15 Papastergiadis, *Cosmopolitanism and Culture*, 159.

The Third Hand and the Language of Things

Charles Green in *The Third Hand* unpacks the collaborations of artists specifically working together with their families to produce artistic knowledge. Green cites the Boyle Family, Anne and Patrick Poirier, and The Harrison Studio as producing "architectural, archaeological, and ethnographic descriptions of the loss of what could be loosely termed as shared cultural memory, which was clearly taken by thc artists as the condition for the maintenance, re-creation, and renovation of social organisation."[16] The foundations for practice in these families contest the unilateral concepts of authorship that was prevalent under Modernism. To Green, family collaborations introduce a new way of working beyond the individual. The family becomes a site for producing new narratives, memories, and perspectives for decentralised artistic production. Families operate beyond a singular authoritative author. Green's collaborative art family shifts western historiography from the individualistic preoccupations of modernism towards a postmodern authorial breakdown of the west.

One thing that Green does not account for, however, are the linguistic dispersals and cultural disruptions that emerge when immigrant families collaborate. Even though he was writing about

16 Green, *Third Hand*, 60.

non-Anglophone and bilingual European migrant artists like Christo and Jean-Claude, Marina and Ulay, and Gilbert and George, Green focused on how these artists primarily use language as an aesthetic gesture. He describes how text and language are conceptual strategies to stand in for the dematerialised art object:

> Their works, in theory at least, preserved or, more importantly, re-created and represented information and were intended, therefore, not to be beheld but instead to be read, like archives of books. The reverse was just as true in practice. The appearance of a proliferation of useful-looking, impressively assembled information was probably more important than actual veracity or utility, for few people ever bothered to read all the information on display in works like the Harrisons or in Art & Language's endless file-card systems.[17]

Besides seeing text and written language as representative of the archive or an aesthetic choice, Green does not mention how some of these multilingual art families may have used language and translation beyond the aesthetics of their document-heavy and highly text-based practices. By not considering the full impact of linguistic exchange, speech, and mediation in the practice of these family collaborations, Green's analysis on the artistic

17 Ibid., 63.

family limits discussion on how the contestations of text, translation, and interpretation in multi-lingual art families could shape these collaborations.

Whilst Foucault, Barthes, and Green have introduced important ideas of distributive authorship, language, and knowledge production into contemporary collaborative dialogues, their institutional critique of power and authorial control has become institutionalising itself. The fact that their positions are reiterated again and again (into discourse including in this thesis) demonstrates the circular nature of academic power and authority. As I delve more into my own argument, I will begin to integrate other texts, linguistic devices, alternate voices, and perspectives of close peers and family members who are not necessarily supported by the academic or artworld establishment.

By engaging with western art history, from Vasari through to Loughnan's *Australiana to Zeitgeist*, my family's encounter with the artworld as non-native-English speakers is just as architecturally, archaeologically, and ethnographically complex as those families discussed by Green. However, in a contemporary setting more accustomed to migrant and diasporic presence, there is an increasing awareness of how the multilingual family can collaboratively use language beyond just as an aesthetic device. Hito Steyerl and Papastergiadis' writings on translation, interpretation, and mediation are particularly useful for understanding how my family might apply language to our artistic and

collaborative practice. In "The Language of Things" (2006), which responds to the writing of Walter Benjamin, Steyerl explores how translations between the language of human beings and the language of materials in the world can facilitate a productive transfer and exchange of knowledge and power. This conceptual view of connectivity and communication between people and the worlds that they inhabit views knowledge as ultimately produced beyond "a politics of the original content," or by one singular authorial source (per Foucault and Barthes).[18] More importantly, Steyerl views knowledge as enacted through multiple processes of reading, translation, and interpretation. Moving beyond text, Steyerl describes how the documentary form is an important site of translation. She writes that the "documentary image … translates the language of things into the language of humans … it is half visual, half vocal, it is at once receptive and productive, inquisitive and explanatory, it participates in the exchange of things but also freezes the relations between them."[19] This reflects my own experience of language-brokering between my family and the host country where we now live; everything had to be constantly albeit partially decoded, pictured, and interpreted to function.

18
Hito Steyerl, "The Language of Things," *Under Translation*, June, 2006, 20. https://transversal.at/transversal/0606/steyerl/en.

19
Ibid., 21.

Here, to navigate the alienation of connecting to the NBN, language-brokering and mediation are deployed by myself and my family to negotiate our surrounds. According to Steyerl, engaging in the documentary process affords an opportunity to translate, review, process, and vocalise such experiences. As the documentary medium and our family translations merge into the process of art making, our documentary interventions (where we record, produce, and engage in conversation and exchange) are part of the tools that help us to mediate the everyday as conduits for one another.

These cultural translations, as described by Papastergiadis in *Cosmopolitanism and Culture*, mediates the differences, and perhaps alienations, that arise from the hybrid encounters of colonialism and multiculturalism in Australia. At the interface of immigrant resettlement, the cultural differentials between old and new settlers establish what Papastergiadis calls a "transformative dynamic" between majoritarian and minoritarian identities that rupture and challenge the delusions of a cultural singularity, authority, of absolute autonomy, of purity. These forms of cultural translations include interactions between difference (but can also transcend difference); he calls this the process of "mobility." Papastergiadis describes how translation and mediation opens up movement across borders, and across the "insufficiencies of existing cultural structures, and necessitate the invention of new points of cross-cultural connection."[20]

Translation and cultural mediations, therefore, are sites for new knowledge and creative exchanges beyond our differences.

20 Papastergiadis, *Cosmopolitanism and Culture*, 137.

The House of the Artist

Whilst developing *On the Border of Things* and reconnecting with Cậu Ái, I also made a series of return trips back to Vietnam, reconnecting with my family over there. Catching up with my older Cousins, one of the first things I tried to do was describe my art practice to them in Vietnamese. Often the person doing the language-brokering in Australia, in Vietnam I was the one who needed help to simply describe myself as an artist. Drawing from half-remembered Vietnamese words, I used the term Hoạt họa ~ *cartoons*, describing myself as a họa sĩ ~ *illustrator or cartoonist*. It was not until my Cousins saw my website and artworks that they informed me of a more appropriate term; Nghệ sĩ ~ *artist.* Beyond correcting this most basic translation for the term artist, I also learnt that the Vietnamese classifier to introduce the article of an artist was: nhà Nghệ sĩ ~ *house of the artist*, preferentially used over người Nghệ sĩ ~ *person of the artist*. My family would introduce me as:

> "Đây là nhà Nghệ sĩ James Nguyen"
> ~ *This is the (~ house of the artist) James Nguyen.*

Rather than the awkward:

> "Đây là to người Nghệ sĩ James Nguyen"
> ~ *This is the (~ person of the artist) James Nguyen.*

These linguistic nuances reminded me of how dependent I was on my family (my house) to mediate, translate, and broker the most basic of terms in my Mother tongue. Language-brokering with my family, when used to articulate our place in the world, flows both ways. Through this process, I slowly began to recognise the subtle rationale embedded in the Vietnamese language itself. Significantly for me, it was the conceptualisation that art is a process bound to a "house," or a canon of on-going traditions, rather than the individual invention of an artist that really resonated.

I know many contemporary artists in Australia currently working with, or closely engaging with family in their practice. These include Jason Phu, Lara Chamas, Phương Ngô, Truc Truong, Lộc Nguyễn, Shoufay Derz, Leyla Stevens, Sione Monu, Claudia Nicholson, Angela Tiatia, Salote Tawale, and Shivanjani Lal among others. Many of these artists are also my friends and, like me, have regularly received support from the communities established by organisations like 4A Centre for Contemporary Asian Arts in Sydney,[21] and more recently Hyphenated Projects in Melbourne.[22]

21 An established CAOA in Sydney, 4A Gallery was started by a group of Asian artists in 1996. The organisation opened with an exhibition of Asian-Australian artists Emil Goh, Lindy Lee, and Hou Leong who were curated by Melissa Chiu, 4A's first curator and director. It is during writing, currently led by Thea-Mai Baumann. This organisation set the precedent for Hyphenated Projects in Melbourne. Both organisations draw from diaspora-initiated projects and exhibitions to give minoritarian voices space to connect throughout Australia and the Indo-Asia-Pacific. "About Contemporary Art Organisations Australia," CAOA, accessed June 23, 2023, http://caoa.com.au/about/.

22 Hyphenated Projects is an artist-run organisation started in 2018 by Phương Ngô, Tammy Wong Hubert, and Nikki Lam. They have presented a large-scale biennial exhibition titled *Diaspora Biennial*, and are currently developing ongoing projects. "About Hyphenated Projects," Hyphenated Projects, accessed May 28, 2020, https://www.hyphenatedprojects.com/.

These artists and organisations have over time become my other family, my family of peers whose work in one way or another is in contact with my own. Undeniably, but not exclusively from POC and overseas First Nations backgrounds, this community of diverse artists is my other nhà, my expanded artistic family and *home*.

A Sydney-based artist whose work I often think about, having first met as exhibiting artists at Underbelly Arts Festival in 2014, is Bhenji Ra. A performance and interdisciplinary artist, as well as Ballroom Mother and Sister, Ra is a prominent figure in both the Sydney Ballroom and contemporary art scene.[23] Ra, like me, has had an established collaborative practice with her immediate family. At Underbelly, she worked with her Filipino-Australian Mother, Friends, and Aunties as part of the *Bay Angels* (a Filipino diaspora women's line-dance troupe). Utilising the tropes of country music, Ra, her Mum, and the *Bay Angels* performed something that was simultaneously Country Western and Filipina, integrating line-dancing and popular Filipino dance. The costuming, choreography, and camp art direction had the energy and inclusive atmosphere of Ra's club aesthetic, celebrating the intersections of her trans,

23 Contemporary Ballroom culture in Sydney, Australia follows social, political, and organisational parallels with the New York Ballroom scene. The House of Slé was the first Ballroom house in Australia. Like New York City, each House is led and headed by "Mothers," or "Fathers," who are generally more experienced, senior members.

queer, and immigrant life. On the phone with Ra, I learnt that doing performance with her multiple families was a way to celebrate these relationships, dispelling the fear and alienation in her communities. Manifesting a cycle of connection and caregiving as a form of feedback and tribute to her own Mother, her Aunties, her queer family, her Ancestors, Ra's collaborations are a synthesis of all these relationships. It feels arbitrary to divide Ra's practice between her multiple families, between her immediate family and her chosen queer family.

Gaining attention in thc international Ballroom scene, Ra has played the role of Ballroom Mother in the House of Slé among her Sisters—the other founding members being Koco Carey, Taimania F'oai, Jamaica Moana, Fetu Taku, and Eliam Royalness. This Ballroom family catalysed Sydney's current queer and trans POC Ballroom culture. Inheriting the conventions of the New York Ballroom Scene, Slé formed itself across queer solidarities, community building, and fundraising that evolved from regular parties, competitions, and dance classes. Ra's expanded family goes beyond the limits of kinship and seeps into the rest of her life. Embedded in the practice and conventions of the cultural traditions of the scene, and the cultural inheritance of Filipina and Oceania, these fluid formations of family straddle histories of Trans and Queer movements with diasporic migrations.

A moment that profoundly shaped and consolidated these networks of care and queer

solidarities came in early 2018, when four members of the Slé family were brutally attacked in a parking lot in Western Sydney. One of the victims was the Mum of a member of Slé. This event highlighted the ever-present dangers and violence that threaten the lives and freedoms of queer and trans families throughout Australia. The House of Slé is not just a designation for queer affiliation and Ballroom tradition however, but as a House, the Slé family draws from the ancestral and historic survival of violence and trauma, as well as the corresponding activist organising principles that brought together queer, trans, gay, and diasporic intersectionality in movements like Stonewall. Ra has told me that in doing the work of activism, fundraising, and community building, audiences often expect her to perform a certain identity that fulfils her role as a Ballroom Mother. However, she feels her place in the Slé family is not tethered to these external obsessions with personality and celebrity. Rather, she points to the importance of drawing from the collective energies and charismatic individuality of all the diverse members of Slé. Here, each person is responsible for the work of co-creation to feed into cycles of care that actively resists the extractive desires of individual fame expected by a casual audience.

Reminiscent of the Vietnamese designation for an artist, nhà Nghệ sĩ (~ *house of the artist*), the House of Slé, and the creative and protective communities that bypass the short-lived expectations

and attention span of a mainstream public, should establish long-term approaches to withstand the persistent manifestations and outbursts of prejudice, exploitation, and violence against trans and queer bodies. The House offers protection through what Ra calls "deep archiving," a profound and long-term memory accumulated from political struggle. The House as a tradition of Ballroom is not only a cultural form for Slé. It is a reminder of the social and political structures that need to be kept alive to honour the historic and social achievements of Trans and Queer ancestors. Significantly, the Ballroom scene in Sydney is not unaffected by Australia's ongoing racist colonial-settler histories, nor the forms of terrorisation of Queer and Trans bodies of colour globally. The recurrent eruptions of transphobic and racial violence that target these communities emphasise the importance of seeking connection, dialogue, and community through expanded definitions of the family (including biological, political, and chosen). Family is also a strategy for defence and survival. The House, or nhà, is also the inheritance of struggle and resistance. It is a place of shelter where our estrangements can develop contiguous solidarities, forming new strategies and artforms of care and resistance.

That being said, the family is neither an untroubling nor intrinsically good thing. Haesook Chae describes how in economic theory, Karl Marx and Friedrich Engels saw the monogamous, heterosexual, and marital family as problematic, with gender and economic biases inherent in the normative family.[24] Georg Hegel describes the family union between husband and wife as akin to a "one-sided and unequal" relationship between a master and a servant,[25] while for Marx and Engels, the family unit is built upon paternity and property.[26] Chae points to the double standards of men who seek social emancipation whilst continuing to enslave women as property within the family. In order to "participate in praxis and in association with others, the same principle of equality should be consistently applied to both the family and the nondomestic spheres."[27]

24 Haesook Chae, "Marx on the Family and Class Consciousness," *Rethinking Marxism* 26, no. 2 (2014): 270, https://doi:10.1080/08935696.2014.885216.

25 Georg Wilhelm Fredrich Hegel, Terry W. Pinkard, and Michael Baur, *Georg Wilhelm Friedrich Hegel: The Phenomenology of Spirit* (Cambridge: Cambridge University Press, 2018), 114, https://doi:10.1017/9781139050494.

26 Friedrich Engels, *Origins of the Family, Private Property, and the State*, trans. Ernest Untermann (Salt Lake City: Project Gutenberg, 2010), 76, https://www.gutenberg.org/files/33111/33111-h/33111-h.htm.

Claiming broader egalitarian social access, the normative oppressions within the family must be challenged. Melinda Cooper argues that to this day, the rhetoric of heteronormative monogamy remains a powerful tool for neoliberal and neoconservative politics that limits definitions of the family to a so-called nuclear family. This politic also seeks to divest governments from the responsibilities of social welfare, housing, education, and healthcare by shunting them into the family home.[28] As the American contemporary family is increasingly indebted, taking on the expenses of higher education, housing, healthcare, etc., it mortgages itself to a rhetoric of moral righteousness. Core family values, according to Cooper, are used to regulate sexuality and institutional submission as the family is economically pushed to breaking point. Absorbing the compounding burdens of debt and rising interest rates within heavily privatised economies, the family increasingly relies on wider networks of support. Cooper points out that many vulnerable families in America have turned to the mega-churches and the once easy credit of banks as a neoliberal safety net for economic precarity and social alienation.[29]

27 Chae, "Marx," 262.

28 Melinda Cooper, *Family Values: Between Neoliberalism and the New Social Conservatism* (Cambridge: MIT Press, 2017), https://doi:10.2307/j.ctt1qft0n6.

29 Ibid., 315-16.

Perversely for queer families, there is a simultaneous war contesting bathrooms—and as Sophie Lewis notes, immigrant families are being brutalised "at the US border by one of the armed wings of a state that is all about 'family values.'"[30] These impossible pressure points on the family have compelled academics to propose entirely radical approaches to reimagining the family. In the face of ingrained economic precarity, climate change, mass human displacements, and migration events seen in emergent diseases and ongoing resource uncertainty, the family must somehow move beyond the limits of neoliberal, economic, and moral righteousness to organise new systems of care that can adapt to these uncertain futures.

30
Sophie Lewis, "Full Family Now: Surrogacy against Feminism, Response by Sophie Lewis," January 16, 2020, https://www.societyandspace.org/articles/response-by-sophie-lewis-full-family-now-surrogacy-against-feminism.

Responding to the urgency of such global crises, Donna Haraway has famously called for a radical rethinking of the family, one which exceeds the human species itself. To Haraway, extreme human crisis necessitates extreme forms of kinship and queering:

> Kin is a wild category that all sorts of people do their best to domesticate. Making kin as oddkin rather, or at least in addition to, godkin and genealogical and biogenetic family troubles important matters, like to whom one is actually responsible. Who lives and dies, and how, in this kinship rather than that one? What shape is kinship, where and whom do its lines connect and disconnect, and so what? What must be cut and what must be tied if multispecies flourishing on earth, including human and other-than-human beings in kinship, are to have a chance?[31]

The domestication of the term family, and the clear ideological, genetic, and racial boundaries surrounding it, compels Haraway to challenge the reader to think beyond their "own kin." Perhaps in times of crisis, the family needs to collaborate with unconventional relations, seeking safety in numbers.

31 Haraway, *Staying with the Trouble*, 2.

When urgent decisions are made to determine who lives and who dies, kinship has to transcend the conventional divisions between the individual, the family, and other living species. The urgency for Haraway is to form unexpected alliances and relationships. To make "odd kin" and reconnect with estranged relations previously neglected or seen as unconventional.

Haraway's expansion on the family is aimed at creating solidarities and consolidating relationships to gain resilience in times of crisis—much like my own family and Ra's. Haraway writes: "staying with the trouble requires making oddkin; that is, we require each other in unexpected collaborations and combinations, in hot compost piles. We become-with each other or not at all."[32] Haraway offers the diversity of inter-species kinships as a tactical form of resilience, pressing that

> staying with the trouble requires learning to be truly present, not as a vanishing pivot between awful or Edenic pasts and apocalyptic or salvific futures, but as mortal critters entwined in myriad unfinished configurations of places, times, matters, meanings[33]

Opening up the family to an expanded definition of relations is all well and good, but Haraway seems to

32 Ibid., 4.

33 Ibid.

infer that the awful pressures of war, colonisation, economic catastrophe, and genocide can be tolerated on some level if the reader perseveres to "stay with the trouble." In facing a collective crisis, Haraway conceptualises trouble as a choice, to opt in and out of, to be with, or not at all. As if trouble might be something readers and their oddkin can choose to stay and compost in.

This notion of *choosing* to stay with the trouble, feels problematic, particularly from a migrant point of view. The catastrophic experiences of being exiled from one place, and to have to endure recurrent forms of expulsion and forced resettlement, is profoundly traumatic. Yet immigrants and refugees have fundamentally chosen *not* to stay with trouble. They do whatever is in their capacity to avoid and escape trouble. Even as we are resettled into supposedly safe and liberal nations like Australia, Aotearoa, Canada, and the United States, many Vietnamese migrants remain outsiders and are treated by the mainstream as perhaps a type of "oddkin." I wonder if the oddkin that Haraway surrounds herself with, ultimately, has any say or ability to refuse being absorbed into her various bumptious piles of compost? Despite arguing for an expanded form of kinship, and collaborations in times of crisis, Haraway's organising frameworks still prioritise and reinstate the urgent interests of the individual—the reader, at the centre of her white feminist formations—even whilst facing the overwhelming violence, disruption, and cascading uncertainty of globalisation.

Unlike the trouble that Haraway describes as something to be stayed with, the trouble that my family, peers, and our expanded families encounter on a daily basis is not something that is simply external to us. My family is continually reminded of being the source of trouble, of not fitting in, of speaking with the wrong accent, doing low-paid work no one else wants, failing to assimilate, etc. Seen as perpetual outsiders, we *are* the trouble. For us, the family somehow has to take ownership of these troubling prejudices. Perceived by others as simultaneously invisible and troublesome, the immigrant family has to utilise its networks, intersectional solidarities, and strategic forms of language and communication to make trouble for our own benefit and protection. Trouble, when made with the family has the capacity to disrupt the violence placed on us as troublemakers. We do not just sit with trouble.

Translating Emails, the Traduttore, Traditore

The ability to reconnect and engage with my family has been through language-brokering and mediations. Language exchange and translation is a tactic of collaborative production as described by Steyerl and Papastergiadis. Upon landing in Vietnam, I was quickly recruited by my Cousins for their new start-up. Reminiscent of my Uncle's market garden, my Cousins asked me to help them with their corporate communications, using my English skills to gain an advantage for their company. The rapid economic rise and flow of global capital into Southeast Asia has meant that doing business in fluent English is now essential for many Vietnamese industries. Good English is often a deciding factor on whether contracts, commissions, and investments can be secured. My job was to translate and edit company emails for my Cousins, helping them with media releases, and proof-reading corporate presentations and other communications. They would regularly forward me a variety of texts and digital matter to edit. These exchanges were neither artistic nor aesthetic uses of my language and translation. However, the to-and-fro of language not only gave me a valuable opportunity to participate in the life of my Cousins; through the family enterprise, I gained a deeper insight into the racism of global capital.

Doing regular edits and translations with my Cousins, I began to notice familiar forms of systemic

exclusion and exploitation similar to what my family had encountered in Australia. Reading Yifeng Sun and Paul Bandia, I recognised the transnational violence of language, as much as the opportunity for self-determination found in multilingual and multinational literacy. My Cousins worked with partners based in Singapore, the United States, and Europe to open up new markets and finding new opportunities in Vietnam. The business demanded clear communication skills in both industry language and a version of multinational Globish. Globish was developed by a non-native English speaker Jean-Paul Nerrière who was working as vice president for IBM when he decided to put together a condensed vocabulary of 1500 words to streamline business communications in English.[34] Proposed as the universal language of global capital, Nerrière's Globish was designed to function across the global supply chains.[35] As a communications tool that unified the flow of transnational capital and production, Isaac Chotiner in *Globish For Beginners* (2017) compares the linguistic ambitions of Globish with the imperialism of the British East India Company. Training and recruiting the administrative pedagogy of India's

34
Jean-Paul Nerrière, "Do You Speak English or Globish?" *Gerer & Comprendre* 100 (June 2010): 57, http://search.proquest.com/docview/742323477/.

35
Dmitry N. Tychinin and Alexander A. Kamnev, "Scientific Globish Versus Scientific English," *Trends in Microbiology* 21, no. 10 (2013): 504–5, https://doi:10.1016/j.tim.2013.07.004.

TRANSLATE PLEASE

To: James Nguyen

Hi anh Tep
Can you help me to see it advance
And Could you support me translate to Vietnamse, Please tell me with suitable time for translate it. You are translator and I am writing Vietnamese
Thank you for your time

Thanks & Best Regards

COMPANY PROFIL...v.docx   COMPANY PROFIL...rev.pdf

Fig. 8
Screenshot of an example of email communications (with identifiable details redacted). *Family request to translate and correct the grammar of the "Company Profile,"* James Nguyen, 2019.

merchant classes, colonial English was deployed to siphon resources and capital back to London.[36] Chotiner's observations of linguistic colonialism and economic imperialism is similarly echoed in Steyerl's reflections on IAE (International Art English). According to Steyerl, the universalisation of artworld English reinforces a homogenous and hegemonic form of pompous and verbose artspeak throughout the world:

> no gallery in Salvador to Bahia, no project space in Cairo, no institution in Zagreb can opt out of the English language. And language is and has always been a tool of Empire. For a native speaker, English is a resource, a guarantee of universal access to employment in countless places around the globe. Art institutions, universities, colleges, festivals, biennales, publications, and galleries will usually have American and British native speakers on their staff.[37]

The native English speaker is given the privilege of both access and movement across the global jurisdictions and economies that have acquiesced

36
Isaac Chotiner, "Globish for Beginners," *The New Yorker*, June 19, 2017, https://www.newyorker.com/magazine/2010/05/31/globish-for-beginner.

37
Hito Steyerl, "International Disco Latin," *e-flux Journal* 45 (May 2013), https://www.e-flux.com/journal/45/60100/international-disco-latin/.

to IAE. Contemporary forms of migration and freedom of movement remain biased towards these colonial modalities of language, and as Chin-Tao Wu points out, "the biennial … has, despite its decolonizing and democratic claims, proved still to embody the traditional power structures of the contemporary western art world; the only difference being that 'Western' has quietly been replaced by a new buzzword, 'global.'"[38] The economics of globalisation in art and business betrays the enduring impact of western imperialism on contemporary life. In frustration, Steyerl proposes to:

> communicate in a language that is not policed by formerly imperial, newly global corporations, nor by national statistics—a language that takes on and confronts issues of circulation, labour, and privilege (or at least manages to say something at all), a language that is not a luxury commodity nor a national birthright, but a gift, a theft, an excess or waste, made between Skopje and Saigon by interns and non-resident aliens on Emoji keyboards.[39]

As global communications become increasingly reliant on universal English, both global business and the business of the artworld continue to perpetuate established forms of cultural and linguistic dominance.

38 Chin-Tao Wu, "Biennials Without Borders?" *New Left Review* 57 (May 2009): 115.

39 Ibid.

Found in Sent - jamesnguyen.com.au Mailbox

James Nguyen 24 December 2019 at 2:28 pm

Re: check grammar

To:

Sorry for late reply I've just arrived in Sydney lol.

This one is for holiday period between now and 1st January 2020:

"Please be advised that our company will be closed for holidays between now and the 1st January 2020. We will resume regular business operations on the 2nd January 2020, until then we will have limited presence over the holiday period and will attend to urgent matters only."

Or this for only the one day holiday on the 1st of January 2020:

"Please be advised that our company will be closed for holidays on the 1st January 2020. We will resume regular business operations on the 2nd January 2020. We will have limited presence during the closure and will attend to urgent matters only."

Ta J

shing you a Merry Christmas and a Happy New Year

We inform you that our company will be
closed on 01/01/2020 and resume working on 02/01/2020.
During the Company closure there will be a limited presence in order
to manage urgent matters only.

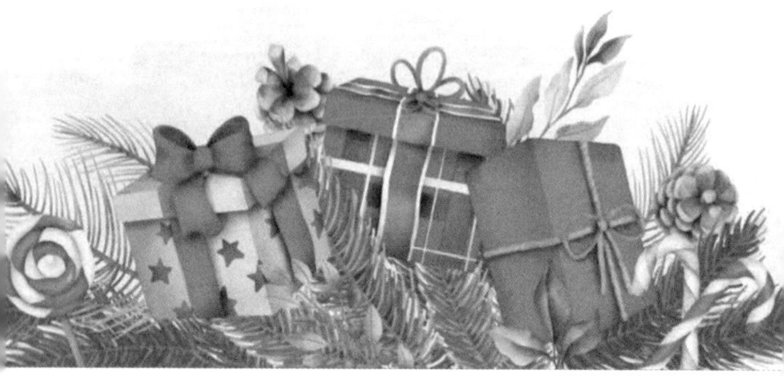

Fig. 9 (p. 112)
Screenshot of an example of company email communication of holiday closures (with identifiable details redacted). *Family request to translate and correct the grammar of email materials,* James Nguyen and Nguyen family, 2019.

Fig. 10
Screenshot of an example of response to company email communication regarding holiday closures. *Family request to translate and correct the grammar of email materials,* James Nguyen and Nguyen family, 2019.

Hi anh Tep
Please see email below and this is my content send to ██████

Hi ██████

We're pleasure to announce you that We won this project that you support price for us
But In the competiton period, After convince to customer to choose ██████ and We choose suitable product and then quotation to customer. But There is a another supplier was quotation to our customer with the same product that the price is lower than we buy from ██████ 10% for ██ and 5% for battery (Eg: ██████████████████████████)
We have some difficut. But with your support as so as the customer's help make us become winner

Although, We won but we're confuse the price. According to me, With the ██████ 3 phase for Industry, We need more support from you for projects, especialy with PO is stock in the future as so as previous PO.
With the last PO , we hope that more discount. If not your additional discount, it is difficult to release the good.
Once again, we're thank you for your support this project. But we hope that you can review the price for us again

Thank you

Hope this is more clear:

Hi ██████,

We are pleased to let you know that we can finalise a new project if you can assist us with some pricing issues.

After convicting to our customer to choose ██████ and assisting them to choose a suitable product with our best quote, we were told by our customer that another supplier quoted a lower price for the same product.

The price quoted to them was even lower than our purchase from ██████ by 10% for ██ and 5% for battery (Eg: ██████████████████████████
We have some difficulty in negotiating these prices and hope that you can assist us to match these prices for our new customer.

If we can match the price, they are happy to go with us. From what I can understand, the ██████████████, we would need more support from you for new projects and customers, especially with PO stock in the future. With the last PO, we hope that there might be more of a discount.

Without these additional discounts, it is difficult for us to release the goods in our stock.

Again, thank you for hearing us out and any help you can provide is much appreciated.

Thank you

Hello

We are pleased to support your project with attached suggested price.

This is equivalent to 25% reduction, to help you secure this deal.

Few important points:

1) Some are not in our official price list, and the prices sent by was the DISTRIBUTOR PRICE, meaning after see some misunderstanding for 2 . I have corrected them in the file.

Overall price is still much lower anyway

2) On the batteries modules, you may have some stock, or at least pending Orders. You purchased them at 10% discount, but I suggest to go more aggressive for this project and provide you 20% discount

3) Next time, please synchronize first with or to ensure the BOM is correct and get support. I am not handling project myself and rely on the team

4) Also, next time, please provide the name of the end user and the location. It will help us to better assign the resources and protect if needed.

I hope this discounted price will help you secure such deal!

Thank you

Hi anh Tep

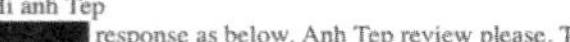 response as below. Anh Tep review please. Thank you

---

Hello

Congratulations!

On the price with others resellers, the point is well taken. While we are checking on the as well, are you able to explore competitions? What prices do they sell.
We would be able to fix this in one shot.

Thank you

James Nguyen

Re: Price support for Manufacturing project

To:

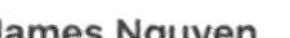

Dear

Thank you for supporting us to aggressively secure the customer. Your help is very Much appreciated.

We will go through next time for our queries, but thank you for taking it on board this time to personally provide us with assistance.

Global forms of linguistic imperialism—be they Globish or IAE—are, however, never completely totalising. Collaborating with my Cousins, I quickly learnt to work within these systems of bias to broker and impersonate good English and benefit their company.

Investing heavily in professional English translators on their staff, my Cousins ended up paying me to be part of their communications strategy. For my Cousins, I would edit and smooth out emails and company communiques with naturalised English (Fig. 9, 10, and 11). We also had regular online meetings to collaboratively translate more complicated materials such as business strategies (Fig. 8), company directives, and sales pitches to potential partners. Although I lacked the technical language, my background as a pharmacist, arts administrator (fluent in pompous art press releases), and my naturalised English gave me a specific skillset for gauging the subtleties of language-brokering within the start-up economy. The way in which I edit the emails and press releases allowed my Cousins to convincingly "pass" as "Native-English-Speaking." This regularly conferred the company with a competitive edge, with perceived status, and prestige among their local and international business

Fig. 11 (pp. 114-116)
Series of screenshots detailing an example of email communications (with identifiable and sensitive details redacted). *Business negotiation of a reduction in the purchase price from an international supplier*, James Nguyen and Nguyen family, 2019.

partners. As a new Vietnamese-owned and -run enterprise, my Cousins adapted the linguistic tool of empire and globalisation for their own benefit. As non-native English speakers, we could collaborate to simulate the language of exploitation, securing advantage and opportunity for ourselves and their staff in Vietnam.

The email drafts above detail a series of excruciating price reduction requests with one of our international suppliers. Accompanying some very minor tweaks—such as "we need more support from you for projects" to "we would need more support from you, for new projects and customers"—these international partners suddenly responded in a more engaged and agreeable way. For example, "we are pleased to support your project with attached suggested price … We would be able to fix this in one shot." Suddenly responsive and cordial, these communications became more prompt, professional, and timely. Respondents were more likely to be open for negotiation, to afford my Cousins more flexible conditions, and good-will. Eliciting such positive responses, I found my language-brokering to be problematic yet also satisfying. My language contributions could manipulate the business bias for "good" English, in collusion with my Cousins, giving an illusion of our English fluency to create chó bò ~ *trouble.* This bluff helped my Cousins to shape the implicit prejudices of their international partners, benefitting their bottom line. Strategically codeswitching between awkward Globish and

"Native-English," my Cousins and I would out-manoeuvre the language biases of these so-called "multinationals."[40]

Described by Rey Chow as traduttore, traditore—the idiomatic Italian accusation that the *translator is a traitor*—this type of collusion with my family used linguistic deceptions to our own benefit.[41] With my Cousins, we worked together to exploit the imperialism of global capital. For us, these small acts of transgression and corporate duplicity have real-world impacts. Language done with my family cannot undo the systematic racism and coloniality built into global systems of capital, but like making art with my family, these minor email edits sharpen the opportunity to trouble and take advantage of the economics of racism and prejudice surrounding us.

40
Marlene Hansen Esplin, "Self-Translation and Accommodation: Strategies of Multilingualism in Gloria Anzaldúa's *Borderlands/La Frontera: The New Mestiza* and Margarita Cota-Cárdenas's *Puppet*," *MELUS: Multi-Ethnic Literature of the United States* 41, no. 2 (2016): 176, https://doi:10.1093/melus/mlw012.

41
Rey Chow, "Translator, Traitor; Translator, Mourner (or, Dreaming of Intercultural Equivalence)," *New Literary History* 39, no. 3 (2008): 570, https://doi:10.1353/nlh.0.0048.

大南國音字彙合解大法國音

DICTIONNAIRE
ANNAMITE-FRANÇAIS

(LANGUE OFFICIELLE ET LANGUE VULGAIRE)

PAR

JEAN BONET

PROFESSEUR À L'ÉCOLE SPÉCIALE DES LANGUES ORIENTALES VIVANTES
ET À L'ÉCOLE COLONIALE

TOME PREMIER

A-M

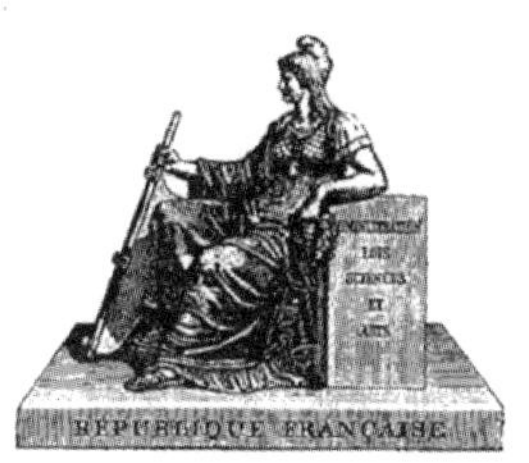

PARIS

IMPRIMERIE NATIONALE

ERNEST LEROUX, ÉDITEUR, RUE BONAPARTE, 28.

M DCCC XCIX

Speaking the Langue Vulgaire: Lap-Xuan and Rainbow Chan

Having to regularly mediate and broker language with my family—i.e., being called on to do translations for my Uncle and Cousins—can become exhausting. It was therefore refreshing to encounter the playful texts of Vietnam- and Australia-based artist Lap-Xuan during a chance studio visit in Sydney. I was struck by how her work elicited in me the pleasure of linguistic recognition and immediacy. Blu-tacked to her studio walls were a series of printed A4 sheets. In Times New Roman font, Lap-Xuan had printed Chinese, English, and Vietnamese word combinations around an inter-linguistic homonym:

I (English),
Ai (Vietnamese—translated into English ~ *who*), and
爱 (Mandarin—translated into English as ~ *Love*).

The various phonetic equivalence of the pronoun "I," when paired with a range of everyday verbs such as "do," "eat," "die," etc., resulted in a playful and evocative admixture of contradictory meanings. For example,

I-Die,
Ai-Die (~ *Who-Die*) and
爱-Die (~ *Love-Die*).

Reading across these word combinations and their absurdities was a satisfying experience for Vietnamese/English speakers like me.

Lap-Xuan's linguistic assemblages are impactful in that they confer power to a small subset of readers who could understand two or more of the languages in her word game. I could engage with her work because of, rather than in spite of being bilingual. The violence of being excluded by a lack of fluency in the majoritarian English language in the social and business life of my family is reversed here. Lap-Xuan's game addressed me and all those bilingual or tri-lingual Vietnamese, Mandarin, and English readers. As natural language brokers, we could appreciate and gain access to the conceit of her work. Lap-Xuan deliberately places exclusive dominant language speakers beyond understanding, demonstrating the inherent violence of the expectation for comprehensive access to knowledge, universal belonging, and legibility via the privilege of dominant and imperial power. Existing between Vietnamese, Mandarin, and English, Lap-Xuan's text works were also an important reminder of the playful slippage of translation and how language can be enjoyed beyond the burden of family duty or business utility.

Fig. 12 (p. 120)
Image of book title page from Jean Bonet, *Dictionnaire annamite-français (langue officielle et langue vulgaire)* (Paris: Imprimerie Nationale, E. Leroux, 1899-1900).

Reflecting on these word games, I immediately thought about how the term translation would itself be translated in Vietnamese. To dịch ~ *translate* bàng tiếng Việt ~ *with Vietnamese*, or to dịch ~ *translate* từ tiếng Anh ~ *from English*, ultimately carries a mental image of bệnh dịch ~ *a transmissible disease*. This coincidental homonym, linking dịch ~ *translation* with dịch ~ *contagion*, linguistically connects the exchange of words as sites of disease, infection, and trouble. Like the traduttore-traditore relationship, translation in Vietnamese is hardly passive conceptually. In pointing to the violence inherent in the inacuracies, potential errors, and manipulation of meaning that comes from linguistic exchange, Yifeng Sun comments on the violence embedded in translation: "translation necessitates or justifies acts of violence in overcoming the untranslatable."[42] Added to this is the violation of personal agency and freedom of expression when your very being is rendered into someone else's tongue. To Spivak, translations are regularly associated with the submission of marginalised subjects to colonising languages. Translations for the colonised are regularly perceived as "subordinate—translation-as-violation."[43]

42 Yifeng Sun, "Violence and Translation Discourse," *Journal of Multicultural Discourses* 6, no. 2 (July 2011): 162, https://doi:10.1080/17447143.2010.547251.

43 Spivak, "Imperialism and Sexual Difference," 234.

Whilst broadly noting the treatment of minoritarian languages as "a language of servants not worth mastering 'correctly.'"[44] Conversely, Spivak notes the care and respect that European translators have for other European languages and their proto-European texts in Greek and Latin. The primacy accorded to dominant language speakers who pretend to have "no geo-political determinations" is not granted to the inchoate "subaltern."[45]

In the context of the French occupation in Vietnam, the most revealing example of colonial insult to dominant translations is clearly printed on the title page of Jean Bonet's *Dictionnaire Annamite-Français* (1899-1900). The now Romanised Chữ Nôm 𡨸喃 (Annamite Vietnamese) characters are designated as the langue vulgaire ~ *the vulgar local language*. Compared to the counterpart langue officielle. Expanding from Gilles Deleuze and Félix Guattari, Ronald Bogue similarly points to the uneven distribution and bias for Euro-foundational languages in philosophy.[46] Bogue, however, notes

44 Ibid.

45 Spivak and Morris, *Can the Subaltern Speak?*, 45.

46 Walter Mignolo describes the dominance of Euro-foundational languages that prioritise translations from Greek and Latin via the imperialist languages of Italian, Spanish, Portuguese, French, German, English, etc., yet continue to deprioritise and dismiss the translation of others as vulgar and conceptually minor. Walter D. Mignolo, *The Darker Side of Western Modernity: Global Futures, Decolonial Options* (Durham: Duke University Press, 2011), 19, 227.

that although minoritarian languages continue to be marginalised and subjugated, they still have the threatening capacity to cause "linguistic deterritorialization" and disruption to western hegemony.[47] It is under these circumstances of profound domination that the vulgaire becomes effective as a troublesome and resistive force.

By interrogating how collaborations and informal family languages can be deployed to resist linguistic subjugation, Hong Kong- and Sydney-based artist and pop-musician Rainbow Chan incorporates the disappearing Minority Weitou language of her matrilineal heritage into her Cantonese and English indie-pop songs. Chan acknowledges the dominance of both English and Cantonese in popular music, and the effort it takes to achieve a sense of expressive equality between these with her Weitou tongue. Speaking with Chan over Zoom, she notes the challenge of mentally relearning the vocabularies of her matriarchs, and the physical exercise and practice needed to retrain the muscle memory of her tongue and mouth. As a singer, Chan is acutely conscious of grasping the diphthongs and ligatures from which she has been culturally displaced and estranged. In her music, like much of her artistic practice, hybridity, intuition, and epistemic disruption form the conceptual approach for her live sets in which she speaks and

47 Ronald Bogue, "Minor Writing and Minor Literature," *Symploke* 5, no. 1 (1997): 106, https://doi:10.1353/sym.2005.0051.

sings in Weitou. Not doing the additional labour of translating everything into English, Chan refuses to broker and make her other languages comprehensively legible to her largely English-speaking audience. For this audience, Chan only provides the general context for the various languages she weaves in and out of her performance. Chan does not spend much time decoding the explicit meaning of each and every word in her lyrics. Untranslated words to Chan retain a resonant intactness and resistance. She prefers to let the emotionality of pop guide the interpretation of her songs, where untranslated lyrics work to trip-up the expectation of an audience accustomed to the digestibility and accessibility of pop. To Chan, music should never be taken for granted. She demands in her audiences a willingness to take the emotional and interpretive leaps necessary to accept these gaps and respectfully absorb the impasse of encountering a multi-language barrier. Rather than appeasing a primarily English-speaking audience, Chan focusses on doing translations that reconnect with her Mum and family. She is actively invested in a personal pursuit to record, retain, and utilise Weitou in her songs as it suits her and her matriarchs. Sticking what Anzaldúa calls her "wild tongue," Chan's multilingual pop music becomes a non-essentialist and non-nationalistic self-assertion of her hybrid voice and repertoire.[48]

48
Anzaldúa, *Borderlands = La Frontera*, 33.

Both Lap-Xuan and Chan (along with her Weitou-speaking family) deploy specific linguistic oscillations to articulate a diverse, heterogenous, and multilingual practices. Both artists refuse the burden of always making every word entirely legible to English-speakers. Their work also points to the growing power of Cantonese and Mandarin as a linguistic and economic counter to global English, whilst continuing to position their minoritarian languages as deserving of equal status amongst the multiple dominant forces in the Asia Pacific. As Lap-Xuan and Chan demonstrate, it is almost impossible to decouple from the power of dominant languages. However, as these artists continue to find new ways to disrupt text, speech, and pop, they show how important the vulgaire is in generating art and expression via the heterolingual.

While the work of Lap-Xuan and Chan recognises the growing importance of Chinese Mandarin and Cantonese in the emerging and established economies of the region, it is important to reconsider Paul Bandia's critique of the position that translations advance the operational dichotomy in the post-colony. That is, they set a colonising west against a colonised east.[49] Such a binary perpetuates the unidirectional flow of information from the colonising *dominant* officielle to the

49 Paul Bandia, "Postcolonial Literary Heteroglossia: A Challenge for Homogenizing Translation," *Perspectives* 20, no. 4 (December 2012): 419-31, https://doi:10.1080/0907676X.2012.726233.

colonised and *servile* vulgaire with little complexity. These distinctions can reductively frame translation as subordination, compliance, and utility, rather than one of equal instability, fluctuating refusals, unexpected hybridity, and creativity. To Bandia, what is often overlooked is that translation is multi-directional and multi-dimensional. The multilingual therefore can develop its own agency and heterolingual momentum separate to historic forms of colonisation and imperialism. Although Yifeng Sun notes the intrinsic violence in all forms of translation, the fraught slippage of translation is described by Sun as indefinitely covering the spectrum of "abusive" and "gentle" forms of violence.[50] That is, the violations of translation and how they are directed varies in intensity and intention. As demonstrated by the artistic endeavours above, translation also generates potential for the flux between languages, and also between languages within languages. To Sun, translations continue to be both injurious and remedial. As seen in my family and the work of my peers, language is also co-opted in minoritarian life as a way to reformulate play, make jokes, talk back, and refuse explanation as opportunities for troublemaking.

50 Sun, "Violence and Translation Discourse," 160.

The burdens I once felt having to translate and broker language with my parents, neighbours, and elders have now given me a deep appreciation for this ability to reconnect and participate in the life of my family. To broker and exchange language, even through broken English and half-forgotten Vietnamese: these imperfections are themselves invaluable for rebuilding relationships with my Uncle in Adelaide, and my Cousins in Vietnam. The ways in which our communications are so faulty, how we rely on each other to correct and unpack even the most basic of terms, such as "artist" and "translation," give fresh relevance to how language operates in our everyday. The artistic inheritance of Nhà Nghệ sĩ *~the house of the artist*, to the transmissibility and risk of translation as dịch ~ *a contagion*, reveals the potential for violence and betrayal even inside the family home. What was important in these collaborations with my Uncle, Aunty, and Cousins was the potential for language and language-brokering to be a strategy to collude with and conspire against the prejudices we face as immigrants and non-fluent speakers of English. My family, my nhà ~ *house*, provides me with the relationships and opportunities to share our resentments and troubles, responding to unfair access and exclusion. The strategies described by Chow as the traduttore, traditore ~ *the translator is a traitor* articulate this capacity to utilise language and translation to undermine the biases around us.

These traitorous collusions of language have let us work within our dynamic families, expanding the range of topics we share concerning representation, authorship, and coloniality as sites of ongoing struggles of power. Having relied on multiple approaches to broker language, to reconnect with estranged members of my family and their various business enterprises, the following chapters will see me return to Australia, where I will seek to reconnect with my immediate family. I focus on the family histories and collaborations with Ba ~ *Dad*, Mẹ ~ *Mum* and, finally, with Dì Nhung ~ *my Aunty Nhung*. Throughout this process, we will encounter the multiple ways in which the family confronts the archival and institutional violence of seeking approval to enter the university, Australian borders, and our ongoing presence in the settler-colony.

CHAPTER 2

Troubling Archives

This chapter explores the burden of archives in academic research and applications for immigration. How did I arrive at the crossroads of postgraduate research and the immigration department? The creeping and protracted process of seeking HREC approval diverted much of my energy away from my actual research and practice, toward addressing the documentational demands of the university. In this chapter, new knowledge was not found by producing new family-made archives and recordings. Instead, knowledge in this chapter came from satisfying the institutional demands of administrative documentation. Reflecting on these encounters with the university, I began to recognise other occurrences of historic interference, of forced documentation and evidence-making for many immigrants. Our academic and civic participation, much like our artistic expression, is contingent on first gaining permission from gatekeepers to let us in. This process gave me a visceral insight into how my parents had disturbingly encountered parallel systems of documentational coercion as refugees seeking to cross Australian borders.

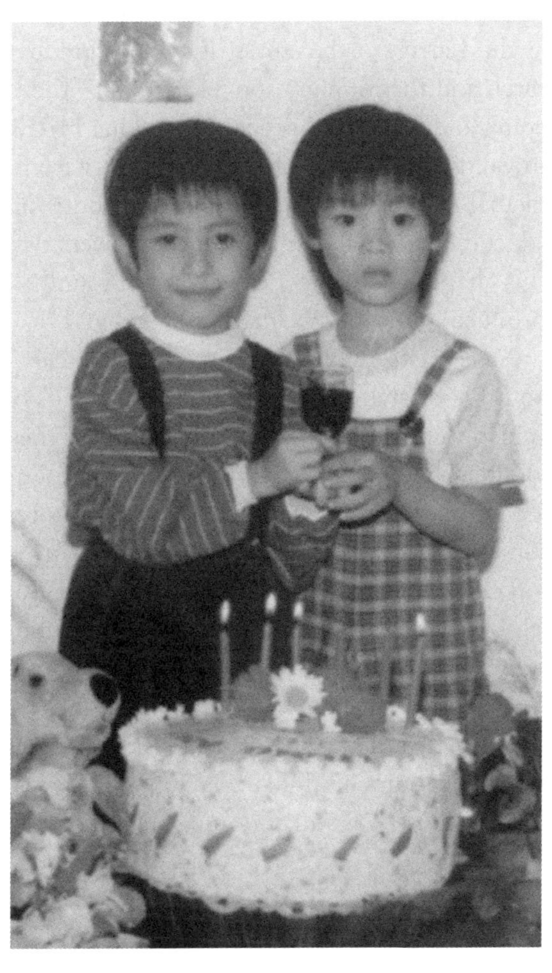

Fig. 13 (p. 136, pp. 140-141)
Series of birthday photographs of James Nguyen. *Nguyễn Family Photo Album,* Nguyễn Thị Kim Dung & Nguyễn Ngọc Cư. Photography by Nguyễn Công Chính 1986-1989.

In the late summer of 2016, I was at my parents' house, reorganising and doing a stocktake of our archive of photographs, letters, and paraphernalia stowed away in the granny flat. Amongst their immigration papers was the family photo album, containing a few awkward photographs of me as a child living in Vietnam. I seemed to be always wearing kitschy t-shirts with koalas emblazoned across the front and posing with new toys that my Dad had sent over from Australia.

The photographs that stood out most were the ones with me and my birthday cake. There was a formula to how the cakes were decorated and displayed. Tilted towards the camera, these cakes stated my name and marked the passing of years with candles and decorative flourishes. Visually this was my annual timestamp. Composed around the props of a birthday party—the cake, new clothes, and toys sent from Australia—my parents steadfastly deployed these formulaic tropes to convince the immigration department of their genuine and ongoing relationship. My birthday photos, as it turns out, were part of the documentation required for the Refugee Family Reunion Visa.

These photos of me, my family, and friends were in themselves a collective performance for immigration. My family archive was not simply a collection of intimate moments or sentimental mementos; rather, our letters, poems, and documents

were produced to maximise the appearance of an ongoing commitment to perform whatever the immigration department's definition of a normative family entailed. These images conveyed a constructed version of family life, bizarrely throughout a post-war period where nothing was normal.

Reflecting on the importance of archive making and the documentary, Okwui Enwezor and Mark Nash survey the limits of documentational truth, representation, and self-representation in contemporary art.[1] Enwezor and Nash describe how the "Documentary Turn" in art needed to challenge documentarian assertions that claimed the inherent truth of images, texts, and testimonies. In "Documentary/Verité," Enwezor notes the inevitable "crisis of the political in current artistic practice,"[2] driving many artists to engage with a new "social and political reality."[3] This trend anticipated how contemporary artists concerned with documentary practices were beginning to think about the truth more critically.

My own documentary turn was accompanied by a return to the recent histories of my family.

1
Mark Nash, "Reality in The Age of Aesthetics," *frieze*, April 1, 2008, https://frieze.com/article/reality-age-aesthetics.

2
Okwui Enwezor, "Documentary/Vérité: Bio-Politics, Human Rights and the Figure of 'Truth' in Contemporary Art," *Australian and New Zealand Journal of Art: Art & Ethics* 5, no. 1 (January 2004): 13, http://doi:10.1080/14434318.2004.11432730.

3
Ibid., 14.

Returning home to my parents, I found how the benign photographs and documents of my childhood revealed a truth beyond a banal birthday photo. First, these images contrasted starkly with global post-war representations of Vietnamese refugees. Photographed and recorded by journalists and documentary filmmakers, their version of the truth was invested in the dramatic imagery of traumatised boat people fleeing war and stuck in refugee camps. My family's mundane-looking documents turned the camera elsewhere, focusing instead on the administrative violence that separated our family over thousands of kilometres. These benign family photographs do not satisfy the truth-seeking desire of photojournalists for frozen moments of suffering that sell newspapers or inspire political outrage. Referring to such images, Enwezor argues that when "the documentary confronts the monstrous," through the grotesque depictions of violence and human rights abuses, the document renders "human suffering to abject status, and spectacle."[4] To Enwezor, these sensationalised representations are a form of death, a memento mori accounting for the inhumane—almost unhuman—and faraway suffering of others. Referencing Susan Sontag, Enwezor questions the ethics of reproducing these types of documents.[5]

4 Ibid., 31.

5 Susan Sontag, "Regarding the Pain of Others," *Diogène* 201, no. 1 (2003): 127-39. https://doi:10.3917/dio.201.0127.

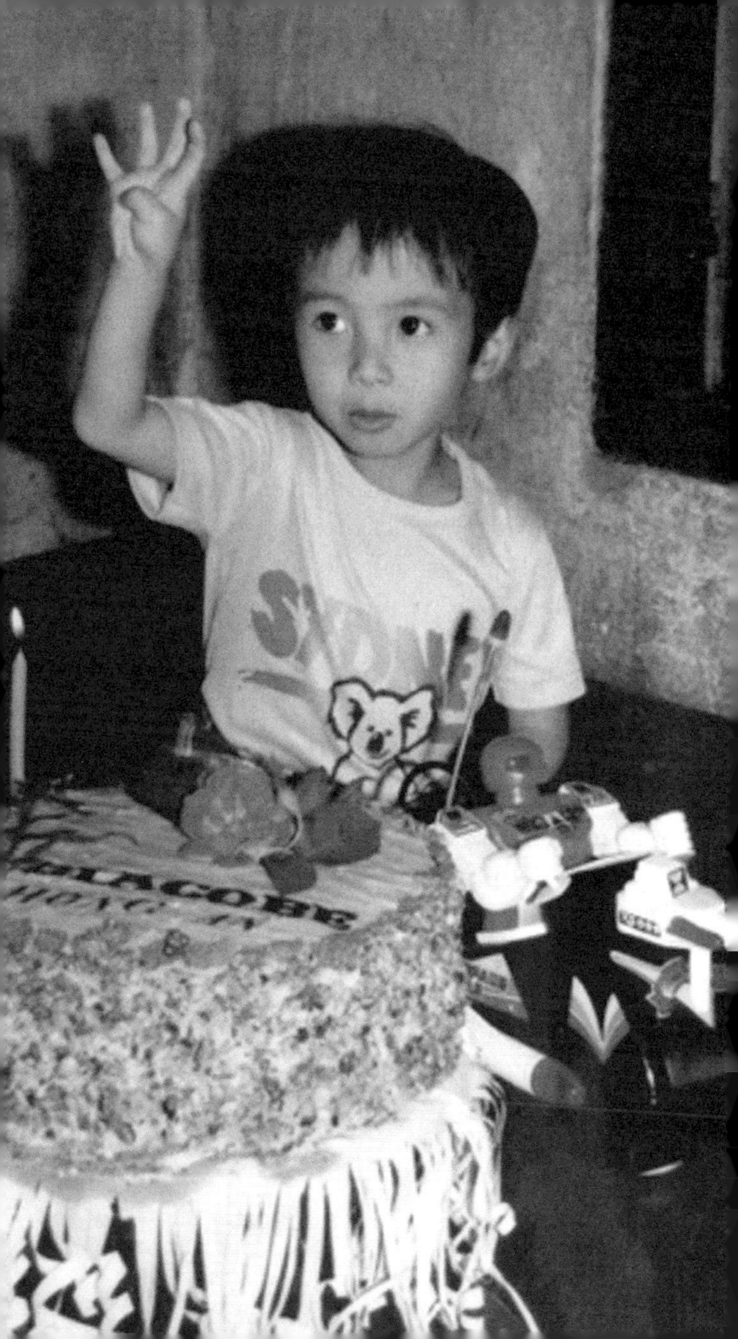

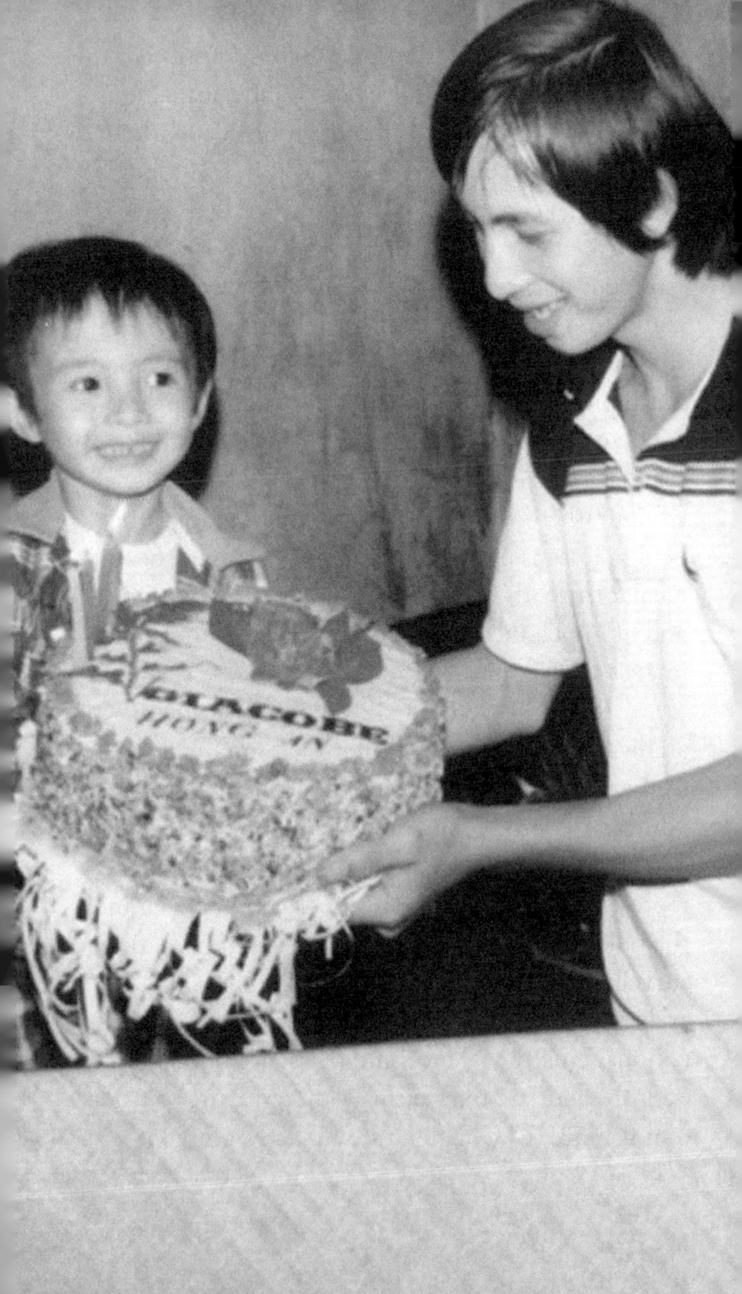
GIACOBBE

The expectation, and the endless consumption of the "pain of others," feeds the colonial indexicality and ever-escalating churn of photographic horror. In daily life, people are constantly immersed in this type of reporting, where the photographic and documentary evidence of elsewhere suffering becomes the norm. Enwezor warns of a paradox where the "documentary can record something that is true but fail to reveal the truth of that something."[6] Both Enwezor and Nash propose that this is where art should insert itself, to disrupt and trouble the many truths that are regularly unseen. By returning to my unexceptional (if not rather awkward) birthday photographs, the benign images of my childhood reveal an unspectacular truth, the truth of administrative compliance and of impossible coercions that those more iconic images fail to capture.

Returning to the family album as a site of archival investigation and interrogation, I will lean to the work of Tina Campt and Jacqueline Hoàng Nguyễn to decode the political violence of exclusion and archival neglect associated with the archival representation of immigrant life. Before delving into the polar opposite, that is, the over-documentation, surveillance, and archival monitoring of people seeking border entry. These forms of institutional and national cruelty, violence, and death are not mutually exclusive, nor are they exclusive to structures outside of my family. In Chapter 3, I will delve more into

6 Enwezor, "Documentary/Vérité," 32.

my own cultural and linguistic abnegations, and the coercive erasures that exist inside the family and the Vietnamese community itself.

In *Image Matters: Archive, Photography, and the African Diaspora in Europe* (2012), Tina Campt notes how image-making exists as "a collective and relational practice of enunciation" for the construction of national identities.[7] To Campt, self-representation is especially important to the visibility and recognition of diasporic and immigrant presence. Campt's discussion on the popularity of family portraiture in the late nineteenth century points to how normative photographs of the European family, and of Europeanness, were conflated with the photography of nationhood and national identity. The way in which family portraits follow racial tropes "family, lineage, respectability, and status were crucial to the representation and creation of middle-class national subjects."[8] Middle-class photography merged with a national project to record and promote the gender norms, racial supremacy, and class aspirations of family albums throughout Europe.[9] Herself returning to archival representations of the family, Campt draws from the photo albums of Afro-German and Afro-European

7 Campt, *Image Matters*, 241.

8 Tina M. Campt, "Family Matters: Diaspora, Difference, and the Visual Archive," *Social Text* 27, no. 1, 98 (2009): 90, https://doi:10.1215/01642472-2008-018.

9 Ibid., 98.

mixed-race families. She points to the ignored and erased presence of integrated and interracial life at the turn of the twentieth century. Contradicting the homogenous representation of middle-class whiteness, many German and European families proudly took photographs with their mixed-race children and grandchildren. Campt disrupts the false construct of a German identity that saw itself as exclusively white and Aryan up until recent waves of late twentieth- and early twenty-first-century migration. These family archives and photo albums record a counter-narrative to the eugenics of European photographic portraiture.

Recognising their capacity to upset dominant national narratives, Campt notes that for someone who is racially different, to partake in the reproduction of photographic tropes established by the European middle-class is in itself radical. To be present in these banal family photographs was a disruptive act which historically contests the white-washing of national identities. Campt proposes that the documentation of these family albums, even in their normative representations of family structures and class, actually accounted for important political documents. "Family photography—as both object and practice—thus performs important forms of semiotic, symbolic, individual, and community labour. Constituting not only the family but also racial, national, gendered, and diasporic belonging."[10]

10 Ibid., 97.

To Campt, the normative performance of the family in these biracial family photos is powerfully loaded and has immense truth-disrupting potential.

Outside of Europe, Jacqueline Hoàng Nguyễn similarly found that the national archives in Canada were exclusively white. Searching for materials and photographs of multicultural and immigrant life following colonisation, Nguyễn found that although economically and socially diverse—Canada was calling itself egalitarian, cosmopolitan, and multicultural (similar to how Australia broadly reprcsents itself)—documentation and acknowledgement of immigrant life in Canada's official archives were practically non-existent. In response, Nguyễn worked with local art centres and organisations to reach out to their immigrant networks, developing a counter archive with Canadian immigrants.

Liz Park, a curator working closely with Jacqueline Hoàng Nguyễn on *The Making of an Archive* (2014–ongoing), speculated about the efficacy of creating such a non-comprehensive project.[11] Contrasting to the orderly and comprehensive methods of collection building by Canada's National Archives, which manifested the systematic erasure of Canadian immigrants, Nguyễn's *Making of an Archive* is undeniably haphazard, unpredictable, and incomplete. Using digital scanners to record

11 Vanessa Kwan, "Jacqueline Hoàng Nguyễn: The Making of an Archive," exh. cat., Grunt Gallery, July 16, 2018, 25.

and return all submitted photographs back to contributors, Nguyễn's process did not assume any pretence at objectivity or comprehensiveness. She relied instead on local and informal networks, word of mouth, and community feedback as the project grew. During this process, Nguyễn received many requests from contributors to have their family photographs added, but not have these materials available for public access. For Nguyễn, archival inclusion did not automatically mean a forfeiture of a right of refusal. Inclusion was offered without the burden of institutional availability, as described by Achille Mbembe.[12] Thus troubling conventional expectations for archival subjects to always be seen, always be accessible and scrutinised, but rarely heard.

The archival turn of Nguyễn's subtle counter-strategy proposes how archives could be made in consultation with people and communities whose archives are being rebuilt. Rather than assuming that all migrants would embrace the opportunity to be finally included, the extractive risk of making national archives more inclusive is just as dangerous. Not only is the neglect of a large portion of Canadian multicultural life negligent, but the lack of consultation and engagement with diasporic communities in how they might want to be included only highlights Jacqueline Hoàng Nguyễn's archival duty of care.

12 Achille Mbembe, "The Power of the Archive and its Limits," in *Refiguring the Archive*, eds. Caroline Hamilton et al., trans. Judith Inggs (Dordrecht: Kluwer Academic Publishers, 2002), 25.

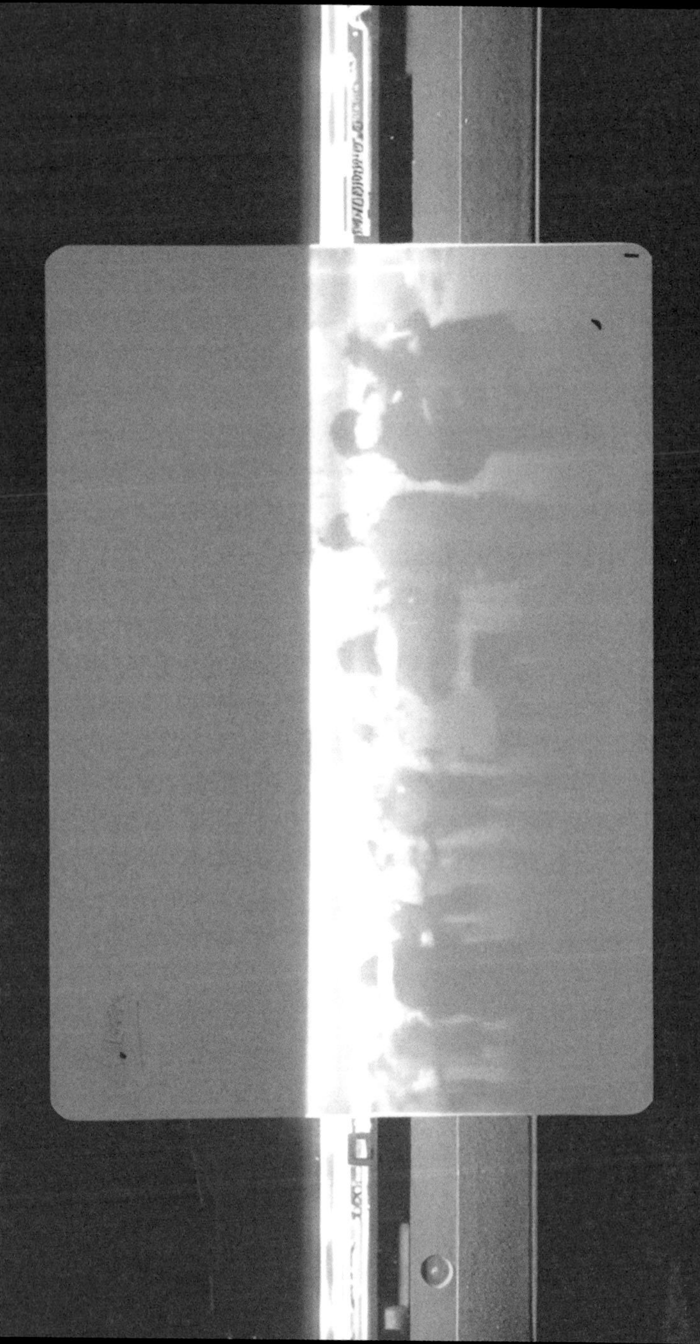

Fig. 14 (p. 147)
Screenshot from project video. Jacqueline Hoàng Nguyễn, *The Making of an Archive*, 2014-ongoing, https://vimeo.com/106758286.

In "An Archival Impulse" (2004), Hal Foster describes the archival impulse of artists who find meaning in the remnants of historic materials. Like the archival work of Campt and Jacqueline Hoàng Nguyễn, Foster describes how "archival artists seek to make historical information, often lost or displaced physically present."[13] The gaps he cites as "lost and found stories" are ripe for artistic excavation. Foster charges that "although the contents of this art are hardly indiscriminate, they remain indeterminant like the contents of any archive," seeming to trivialise the political weight and gravity of the archival impulse.[14] "In this respect the orientation of archival art is often more 'institutive' than 'destructive,' more 'legislative' than 'transgressive.'"[15] Failing to recognise that not all historical gaps can be brought into institutional and archival art, not all archival material should be up for grabs.[15] There are some gaps that are so profound—evidencing the violence of systemic exclusion, erasure, and abuse—that cannot be approached with Foster's perception of an arbitrary archival impulse. Not all cultural experiences of archival materials are the same. For many, the

13 Hal Foster, "An Archival Impulse," *October* 110 (October 2004): 20.

14 Ibid., 5.

15 Ibid.

15 Ibid., 20.

material remnants of historical trauma are so complex and painful that they should never be subjected to Foster's expectation of availability and useability—so easily rendered into the neoliberal appetites of the artworld. Much like the refusal by Chan to render her Weitou language utterly legible to fans of her pop music, the absolute legibility and comprehension of archival trauma should not be assumed. Any archival intervention should be thoroughly interrogated for the real possibility of perpetuating exploitation, abuse, and neglect, as much as providing new opportunities for experimentation, generative enunciation, and self-determination.

Discussing the archival treatment of American slavery, Saidiya Hartman writes about the historic and continued dehumanisation of the "subaltern, the dispossessed, and the enslaved."[16] Even when the oppressed bodies of slaves were included in the written accounts and archives of official documents, they were ultimately rendered and reduced to the racist accounts of slave-owners, European imperialists, and capitalists. Stuck between documentational absence or inclusion as hapless victims of extreme suffering or depravity, the archival narrative of Black American bodies was ultimately a foil for the curiosity and titillation of a European reader. Hartman describes the impossibility of this bind. How can one make any contribution to archives that are so faulty and dehumanising?

16 Saidiya Hartman, "Venus in Two Acts," *Small Axe* 26 (June 2008): 12.

So utterly incommensurate with the lives of your ancestors, your relatives, and inevitably yourself? These archival impulses need to go beyond corrective and institutional restoration. The impulse for archival resistance and reckoning is thus more relevant for Hartman.

Contemplating Hartman's frustrations, Sam Huber sees the impossibility of working within the archival "gaps" of western history, of having to find and "listen for the dominated in the archives of the dominant."[17] Perhaps by looking at what is happening in the contemporary moment, the past might emerge to speak a more accurate truth. In *Wayward Lives, Beautiful Experiments: Intimate Histories of Social Upheaval*, Hartman looks at the representation of Black women who survived and developed alternative solidarities, despite state-sanctioned documentation, terrorisation, surveillance, and punishment. In her book, Hartman applies the archival form to invert archival narratives of Black female deviance into one of defiance. "Under the unremitting pressures of the city, young Black women inaugurated modernity" and progressive lifestyles. The artist as archivist or historian can hold onto these "critical fabulations" that speak a

17
Sam Huber, "Saidiya Hartman Unravels the Archive, In *Wayward Lives, Beautiful Experiments*, Hartman Recovers the Forgotten 'Sexual Modernists' of Twentieth-Century Black Life," *The Nation*, May 1, 2019, https://www.thenation.com/article/saidiya-hartmans-astounding-history-of-the-forgotten-sexual-modernists-in-20th-century-black-life/.

truth to invert and deliberately stand apart from the humiliations and denials of a white version of history.[18]

18 Hartman, "Venus in Two Acts," 11.

Looking more closely at my own family album, I noticed that even within our small collection of photos, there were noticeable gaps. Apart from a few of my parents' wedding photos and three baby photos, most of the archive of letters and photographs retained by my parents covered a period of only four years, between 1986–1989. I queried my Dad, wondering if they had another photo album somewhere else. I was told that no, the reason we seemed to have almost four years of missing photos and documents from 1982–1986 was that our initial set of application forms and immigration documents were lost in the administrative transfer between the Vietnamese Socialist Government in Hanoi and the Australian Federal Government in Canberra.

These documents (so meticulously recorded and compiled) attesting to our identities, heteronormative compliance, migration status, good health, and commitment to the Australian social contract were literally lost in transit. My parents had no other option but to restart the entire process, and produce new material evidence and resubmit their Visa application. Eight years eventually passed. Even by the protracted standards of the Family Reunion Visa Program, this was an unusually long period of separation. Squeezed between the extraordinary documentational demands and administrative negligence of both the Socialist Republic, and the Commonwealth, my parents felt that the loss of all

their documentation was just another administrative mishap, another disappointing trial from the border authorities. After spending eight years of their lives preoccupied with creating documentation for the immigration department, my Mum and I were finally approved the Family Reunification Visa in Australia. At the end of April 1989, my Mum and I boarded a Qantas flight and, landing for the very first time at Sydney Kingsford Smith Airport, I saw my Dad.

For my family, the administrative demands of the immigration department were the main motivation for taking and keeping these photographs. Despite the poverty and limited access to film and camera equipment in post-war Vietnam, it was necessary for both the Vietnamese and Australian governments to thoroughly document their citizens. Vietnam was in a state of post-war upheaval and political reform.[19] The state was fixated on tracking the movements of civilians. Fearing a net efflux of people into the cities and eventually out of the country, the Socialist State maintained authoritarian control to record and monitor the movement of people. Even as a child, I was aware of the lurking presence of a regime through village informants, allocated food rations, and permission certificates to simply cross our provincial borders. Reflecting on Foucault's architecture of power inside the surveillance state, the village officials with their ledgers and registers would covertly monitor movement across the porous borders of Laos, Cambodia, and the Vietnamese coastline.[20]

Documentation, certification, and monitoring were all critical to the controlled movement of citizens.

19
In 1986, the most substantial post-war reform Đổi Mới ~ *New Change* was implemented, allowing for a Socialist-Market economy to emerge in Vietnam.

20
Michel Foucault, *Discipline and Punish: The Birth of the Prison* (Harmondsworth: Penguin, 1979).

I propose that unlike Foster's "Archival Impulse," it was the *archival imposts* endured by my family as people waiting to cross borders that defined how we were treated by the state. Meticulous and coercive record-keeping became part of our daily lives. Documentational monitoring, its reproduction, and upkeep became a self-regulating preoccupation for my family and all the adults around me. Reflecting on Foucault's descriptions of power, Allan Sekula points to how the photographic portrait was an essential tool of identifying criminals and controlling the movement of people.[21] Photography was an essential tool of the surveillance state. Subjects with the criminal intent to escape or transgress borders are followed, detained, and recorded as quantifiable national threats. In this manner, the archive is a disciplinary "extension of that exemplary utilitarian social machine, the Panopticon."[22] Archival documentation, record-keeping, surveillance, and domination was administered as a totalitarian impost on all citizens.

Ironically, the process of applying for the Refugee Family Reunion Visa in Australia eerily paralleled the neurotic documentational demands of a post-war, Socialist Vietnam. As a matter of "National Security," Australia's preoccupation with

21 Allan Sekula, "The Body and the Archive," *October* 39 (1986): 7, https://doi:10.2307/7.

22 Ibid., 9.

border protection and defence was not geared against stemming the efflux of citizens, but militantly fixated on the existential fear of influx from the Asian north and its Oceanic/Moana neighbours—a perennial settler-colonial anxiety of invasion by Asian, Indian, Muslim, and Polynesian people.[23] The burden of proof for entry, evidencing our good health, our humanitarian status, and the authenticity of our relationships had a totalising impact on our lives. The "archival impulse" in my family was to navigate both the archival *imposts* of an anxious Socialist Republic, and a paranoid Commonwealth.[24] The family photo album was never just a repository of family mementos and events, it was to explicitly evidence our humanity and legitimacy within two profoundly suspicious regimes.

Foster's archival impulse is not just about making "historic information, often lost or displaced, physically present."[25] The archival impulse for my family was our urgent need to appease sanctioned power. Powers that would carelessly misplace four years of meticulous record keeping, only to demand another four years without concession.

23 Richard Devetak, "In Fear of Refugees: The Politics of Border Protection in Australia," *The International Journal of Human Rights* 8, no. 1 (January 2004): 103, https://doi:10.1080/1364298042000212565.

24 Ross, "Prolonged Symptoms of Cultural Anxiety," 86.

25 Ibid., 4.

My impulse to revisit our family photo album led me to this knowledge. I had never known about the administrative negligence that extended the separation between my Dad and I for the first eight years of my life. These archival gaps, leading to the estrangement of Father and Child, of Husband and Wife, reveal the cruelty that continues to divide many families still attempting to cross global borders. In Australia, refugee families continue to remain in the administrative and geographic purgatory of indefinite detention, caught between the continuous impossibility of national moral panic and deliberate, legislated neglect.[26]

26 Helena Zeweri and Nadja Eisenberg-Guyot, "Understanding Australia's Offshore Detention Regime, Offshore Detention, Emergent Conversation," *PoLAR: Political and Legal Anthropology Review Online*, October 24-December 15, 2017, https://polarjournal.org/2017/10/24/emergent-conversations-part-7/.

Mbembe points out that archives are produced through a process of deduction and power. As noted in relation to humanitarian migration, archives have the power to determine the parameters of human life and safety. To the state, only certain documents (and therefore, the people that they validate) are deemed as worthy of retention and preservation. Mbembe also notes how "well-established procedures and regulations"[27] of compliance and conformity are mandatory to maintain national security and stability.[28] Over time, the archives generated and the cumulative power retained by the state from these archival processes are enacted through what he calls "dispossessions."[29] The most profound effect of these dispossessions is how archival surveillance and exclusion continue to sanction the punishment of people trying to move legally and illegally across national borders.

Subject to these archival deductions and reductions, humanitarian immigrants are regularly squeezed between being undocumented and over-documented. Mbembe proposes that the state engages in the necro-politics of killing off subjects through documentation and legislation.

27 Mbembe, "The Power of the Archive and its Limits," 20.

28 Devetak, "In Fear of Refugees," 101.

29 Mbembe, "The Power of the Archive and its Limits," 25.

Immigrant bodies continue to be rendered into archival materials, reshaped and co-opted for political gain.[30] This recalls Enwezor's description of death through the documentary turn.[31] The theoretical link between death, documentation, and the archive is most disturbing when viewed through Australia's border policies of indefinite offshore detention.[32] The political and archival impulse of Australia continues to be physically and insidiously enacted on the lives of families waiting in detention centres. Australia's immigration policy is one that overtly engages with the necro-politics of documentation, of repackaging "undocumented arrivals" into "documented detainees." Human life is rendered into archival units for the border-industrial-prison complex. As described by Helena Zeweri and Nadja Eisenberg-Guyot, to be processed and documented by the state does not ensure protection or visibility. Serving as a political deterrent for other "asylum seekers from drowning at sea," these people are sealed-off and off-shored far away from journalistic or legal scrutiny, literally interred and rendered invisible.[33] Individuals seeking asylum, self-representation, and legal representation are ultimately subjected to the administrative imposts and policy

30 Achille Mbembe, "Necropolitics," *Public Culture* 15, no. 1 (2003): 40.

31 Enwezor, "*Documentary/Vérité*," 13.

32 Devetak, "In Fear of Refugees," 102.

33 Zeweri and Eisenberg-Guyot, "Understanding Australia's Offshore Detention Regime," 15.

whims of a Commonwealth that actively pursues the necro-policies of border security.

Although Australians all get a taste of the daily frustrations of embedded surveillance and institutional compliances every time we engage with government agencies like the Health Department, Medicare, the Australian Tax Department, the Electoral Roll, and now my.Gov.au, etc., these archival impositions are perhaps most acutely enacted in this country's carceral and punitive policies. Even when permitted lawful entry, the micro-aggressions, minor social monitoring, and racist reminders of being a perpetual outsider continue to persist. Ien Ang and Stéphanie Cassilde unpack the perennial question of "where are you from?"[34] Faced by many migrants throughout Europe and the colonised Americas and Australia, this question is often deployed (both intentionally and unintentionally) as a loaded reminder of racial non-belonging.[35] Such subtle forms of interrogation are normalised and adopted by everyday gate-keeper citizens. Under these circumstances, Papastergiadis describes how the "ambient fear" instituted by the settler-colony inspires suspicion throughout the populace, where "fear is interpreted as if it were a mechanism for

34
Stéphanie Cassilde, "Where Are You From?" in *The Melanin Millennium: Skin Color as 21st-Century International Discourse*, ed. Ronald E. Hall (Dordrecht: SpringerLink, 2013), 116, https://doi:10.1007/978-94-007-4608-4.

35
Ang, *On Not Speaking Chinese*, 11.

sharpening loyalties and galvanising collective bonds."[36] Instituting a citizen-led policing of non-belonging, perpetual outsiders are afforded little ability to exist without being questioned. Migrant bodies are continuously expected to reassure and attest to their origins and right to be here. One's legal status, employment status, economic productivity, English fluency, religious affiliations, and loyalty to the host country are continuously performed to avoid the humiliation of non-belonging. Despite all the burdens and impositions associated with the necro-politics of documentation and public interrogation, Mbembe proposes a political ultimatum for using archives as a destabilising counterstrategy. If the archive cannot be a site for self-representation, it can under certain circumstances provide a space for contestability, activism, and perhaps even retribution. Therein lies the paradox of the archive. Reliant on proof of evidence, interrogation, and records of dispossession to monitor, exploit, and control people, Mbembe points to how, over time, these archives accumulate a body of evidence of past misdeeds that threaten the moral stability of the state itself. From Australia, Brook Andrew has been working since 1996 to uncover, recover, locate, and return Aboriginal ancestral remains, photographs, other documents, and artefacts from international museums and private collections to their respective family networks and communities.

36 Papastergiadis, *Cosmopolitanism and Culture*, 22.

The legacy and dispersal of these documents and their spirit are themselves powerful fragments that make indisputable the colonial violence inflicted on Aboriginal and Torres Strait Islander peoples and their ancestors. The necro-politics of global colonial archives have not only inflicted death, but diabolically continue to trade in an ongoing legacy of economic benefit and spectacle through their respective collections. Andrew and Jessica Neath write how although profoundly fraught, complex, and traumatic, "legacy images"—the colonial photography of First Nations people—continue to be important objects of ongoing memory and connection for many First Nations people and their ancestors.[37] As Andrew notes, however, many political regimes have also tried to "break familial and cultural memory by destroying photographic records but, at the same time, the persecuted and murdered are diligently photographed in processes of classification and surveillance."[38] As these regimes attempt to bury and destroy the damning parts of their archives, they continue to undermine their legitimacy. Unlike Foster who sees opportunities in the archival impulse to recover and fill in the gaps of history, Mbembe proposes that, "on the other hand, the destroyed archive haunts the state in the

37
Brook Andrew and Jessica Neath, "Encounters with Legacy Images: Decolonising and Re-Imagining Photographic Evidence from the Colonial Archive," *History of Photography* 42, no. 3 (2018): 217.

38
Ibid., 222.

form of a spectre."[39] The absences and gaps left by destroyed archives arguably possess an even more significant threat to the nation state. These hauntings, left with even the slightest fragment of archival violence, are sometimes more enduring than overt and conspicuous documentation of violence and cruelty. It is here that the potential for art, research, poetry, memory, human dialogue, etc. (where the atrocities and violence of dispersed, hidden, destroyed, and silenced archives) finds potency. These gaps can produce a counter presence that undermines the constructed rhetoric and outright denials of the state. The fugitive and compromised archive when left with these gaps and hauntings provides a compelling space for reflection, questioning, and perhaps even retribution and compensation.

Looking back on my own childhood photographs, the unspectacular family photo album reveals much about covert forms of state-sanctioned violence, especially the mala fide deployment of power to arbitrarily and indefinitely separate families. Unlike the iconic photographs of war and trauma that capture images of overt "human suffering … and spectacle," these family archives make visible the archival impost.[40] The missing family photos between 1982–1986 and the years that accompanied the estrangement of my family could never be reclaimed or satisfactorily repaired,

39 Mbembe, "The Power of the Archive and its Limits," 24.

40 Enwezor, "Documentary/Vérité," 31.

despite Foster's claims. My responsibility is to listen to the stories accounting for these gaps. As such, even the administrative mishandling of a set of photographs meant that our Family was indefinitely separated. Navigating the archival negligence of the state, the fact that I appeared in these cheesy photographs, entirely constructed by my parents, reveals another truth. Amidst the archival burden to present ourselves as compliant and normative candidates for reunification, the capacity of families to resist through compliance, even under such impossible circumstances, is evidenced by these remnant photographs. Art-directing, performing, and constructing our semi-biographic life, these photographs simultaneously critique and perform the artifice of normativity: the birthday photo, rendered for the immigration department, is forever contaminated with the incidental pleasure of knowing that this cheesiness captures the latent and pragmatic insubordination that still fuels the creative impulses of my family.

Barriers to HREC Approval

My initial research aim was to also create new documents and archives with my family. My intention was driven by the lack of archival materials we had as a family, including those lost during the visa process. This absence combined with a further lack of home videos, photographs, letters, etc., since our reunion in Australia was impacted by the all-consuming work of resettlement. My Parents at the time were setting up a textile and sewing business during a period of economic deregulation of this industry, and as such, they had little time for family photos or videos.[41] My research provided an opportunity to engage with my Parents and Elders, and finally co-produce some new archival material for ourselves. This seemed particularly urgent as my Elders were beginning to retire and had more time to engage in such pursuits.

Hearing about the procedural indifference of the Australian immigration department from my Dad, I immediately recognised familiar patterns of procedural indifference as I began the process of applying for ethics approval to do work with him and my family as part of this PhD research.

41 Elizabeth van Acker, "Trade Liberalisation and Its Impact on the Australian Textiles, Clothing, and Footwear Industries," *Journal of Fashion Marketing and Management: An International Journal* 2, no. 1 (April 1997): 14, https://doi:10.1108/eb022515.

UNSW requires all research students conducting research with human subjects to obtain formal ethical permission to undertake this research under the UNSW Human Research Ethics Committee (HREC), operating under the Human Research Ethics Advisory Panel (HREAP). The UNSW research protocol (based upon the *National Statement on Ethical Conduct in Human Research 2007*, updated 2018) describes research as a "researcher conducting research with human participants."[42] Such protocol, following a model of research historically developed from the physical sciences, implicitly assumes a separation between the researcher and the people being researched. In the case of my research, these "research subjects" were in fact my family with a subject position described as "people in dependent or unequal relationships" with the researcher (myself).[43] The fact of my being both a researcher and part of the community being researched raised concerns for the ethics committee. Obtaining permissions to conduct research for what was a collaborative and kin-based practice—a project specifically *not* reliant on strict and fixed boundaries between researcher and researched; I considered my family members to be co-researchers and co-collaborators in the project—was administratively troublesome.

42
National Statement on Ethical Conduct in Human Research 2007 (Canberra: National Health and Medical Research Council, 2018), 1.

43
Ibid., 68.

Pursuing approval via one of the defined options, "Pathway 3: More than Low Risk Research—Review by a Human Research Ethics Committee," I was required to satisfy a series of research conventions established by the UNSW HREC. Declaring the value and necessity of my intention to collaborate and produce new documents such as video and photographic materials with my family, I was advised to make my research align with the criteria laid out in the "UNSW Human Research Ethics Application Form (HREA)." Over many drafts and amendments, my "research design" invariably assumed the terminology and focus of the document. My means of archival production, including photography, video, and other audio-visual materials, morphed into "Primary Data Collection Methods." In the process, I had to account for a "viable sample size" to conduct research, taking into consideration what "exclusion parameters" and "relevant characteristics" in order to ensure my "recruitment of Participants" satisfied the "inclusion criteria" for the proposed research. These guidelines felt particularly arbitrary and incongruous to my initial intention of producing archives and making art collaboratively with my family. Nevertheless, each measure had to be addressed to the satisfaction of the UNSW HREC. For example, I had to exclude family members under eighteen years of age but could continue to draw from a diverse group of prospective participants, recruiting members of my family through open call and word of mouth,

ensuring that those who expressed interest would be contacted to discuss their prospective involvement and participation in the research. They would then go through a formal process of screening to ascertain whether they met the parameters of research, ensuring that they were fully informed about the purpose and intent of the research, and only then would I be able to proceed, being satisfied that the potential participant would not be placed at risk by taking part in the project and they understood they could withdraw from the research at any time without negative consequence. Of course, these examples of procedural and ethical ways of working and clarifying important aspects of the research process were not unreasonable, nor were they counter to the ways in which I had already been working with my family. But the systematic and linguistic fulfilment of each and every one of these measures in procedural terms as set out by the UNSW HREC ensured a level of discursive formality and compliancy that felt intrusive and alienating to the very people I was working with and obligated to throughout this process. To fulfil these and other approval criteria, I had to conceptually reframe the artistic parameters of my research and my means of working with my family in ways that could be understood and deemed as ethically compliant to the UNSW HREC.

Stanley Aronowitz in *The Knowledge Factory: Dismantling the Corporate University and Creating True Higher Learning* (2000) outlines the kinds of procedural pervasiveness that universities implement

throughout their ethics processes and protocols. Such procedures unquestioningly uphold a problematic "scientistic separation" between the "object" of research and the privileged "researcher." Aronowitz writes:

> Cartesian epistemology is the master discourse of domination. It posits of subject and object as two quite separate entities, draining the subject of nature and object of culture. They face each other as antagonists; nature is constructed as Other, devoid of any of the presumed qualities of the subject, especially agency.[44]

Historically, academic knowledge was a way to classify and segregate people as either cultured or non-cultured, of those who are part of the master discourse of domination or passive subjects to be dominated and studied. Tehseen Noorani et al. describe this privileged position of the researcher as "Medical Creep" to denote how ethical guidelines in universities continue to be informed by singular and overtly medicalised and paternalistic presumptions of vulnerability and protection—even in distinctly non-medical fields of research such as the visual arts.[45]

44
Stanley Aronowitz, "A Critique of Methodological Reason," *The Sociological Quarterly* 41, no. 4 (September 2000): 714, https://doi:10.1111/j.1533-8525.2000.tb00080.

45
Tehseen Noorani, Andrew Charlesworth, Alison Kite, and Morag McDermont, "Participatory Research and the Medicalization of Research Ethics Processes," *Social & Legal Studies* 26, no. 3 (June 2017): 378-400.

Intended to maintain "ethical conduct," Noorani warns that the inflexibility of these protocols can reproduce paternalistic and "protective" frameworks that may exclude and silence those being "protected" from meaningfully engaging and contributing to the crucial input, output, direction, and agency of the research.[46]

Sofia Villenas notes how the procedural culture of contemporary universities are procedurally biased towards perceived forms of objectivity and separation. To Villenas, these separations often undermine the work of researchers who are producing research with a Minority group of their own background; she calls such researchers a "native ethnographer."[47] This conceptual bind is structurally a non-issue for researchers and academics who are located outside of the communities and cultures they are studying. Researchers who are not kin-related or otherwise bound to the communities they are studying do not have to face the dilemmas researchers with kin and community relations have to face. Villenas claims that this bias ultimately privileges and prioritises so-called forms of "objective" research that enact a "researcher-colonizer position," one not culturally embedded, nor collaboratively produced, and prone to perpetuating the structural hierarchies of conventional academic

46 Ibid., 389.

47 Sofia Villenas, "The Colonizer/Colonized Chicana Ethnographer: Identity, Marginalization, and Co-Optation in the Field," *Harvard Educational Review* 66, no. 4 (January 1996): 712.

research.[48] The fallacy of empirical and unbiased objectivity is regularly challenged by First Nations researchers. Brian Martin emphasises that western standards of objectivity and distance create false binaries that "ignore other metaphysical and epistemological approaches to knowledge acquisition. For example, the importance of lived experience in an Indigenous research paradigm."[49] Martin rejects that such a "notion of objectivity" and separated empiricism is the only viable approach to critical thinking. To him the distinction between researcher and those being researched is not only artificial and arbitrary, but woefully incapable of processing the complex collaborative relationality of Indigenous and non-western frameworks of knowledge production. University ethics processes generally fail to recognise that multiple and diverse communities of people from other cultures and societies may have their own models and frameworks of knowledge production and ethical conduct. First Nations researchers within the academy may well wish to draw upon these models and frameworks in conducting research. By dissolving the hierarchal binary that separates the researcher and research participants, Martin points to how Indigenous research epistemologies can allow researchers, participants, and other entities to

48 Ibid., 711.

49 Brian Martin, "Methodology Is Content: Indigenous Approaches to Research and Knowledge," *Educational Philosophy and Theory* 49, no. 14 (2017): 1397.

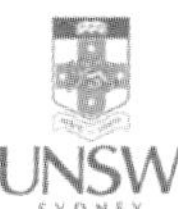

UNSW Human Research Ethics Application Form

More than Low Risk OR Low Risk Research Applications

Supporting Documentation that should be attached to your submission

1. Recruitment Invitations/Advertisements/Verbal Scripts/Social Media Posts/Recruitment Presentations/etc.
2. Letters of support from any organisations/individuals who will recruit on your behalf
3. Screening protocol if the screening process will involve more than asking participants if they meet the inclusion/exclusion stated on the recruitment invitation

8. Consent

Describe how consent from participants will be obtained. In order to address National Statement items 2.2.22, 3.1.23 – 3.1.39 the information at this section must describe:

- The type of consent that will be sought (e.g. verbal/ written/ implied by return of survey etc.);
- how and when you will provide consent materials to your potential participants and why this method of consent is appropriate for the participant population.
- How, when and to whom participants will indicate their consent and how any real or perceived coercion will be avoided during the consent process.

**if the project involves the use of data already collected and the participants have already provided their consent for this to happen, please attach a copy of the original consent form as evidence.

**if you are seeking a waiver of consent, please provide justification. (See the National Statement, Chapters 2.2 and 2.3 for more information).

N.B. A Participant Information Statement and Consent Form (PISCF) is required for all types of consent. Templates are available from the Human Ethics website.

This project will use a written/verbal/implied consent process to seek consent from participants prior to the collection of data.

Written Consent

[How/When the PISCF will be provided] Participants will be provided with the PISCF (e.g. via email, in person) when (e.g. they contact the research team about taking part; they receive the recruitment invitation email as the PISCF will be attached to this email (recommended)).

Participants will be asked to read the PISCF and will have sufficient time to consider their participation because [describe a time gap in times between provision of the PISCF and data collection; explain whether/how the time between provision of the PISCF and data collection is sufficient].

[How participants will contact the researcher(s) to provide their consent] Participants will be advised to contact the researcher(s) if they have any questions, and once they are comfortable providing their consent to participate, will be asked to sign the consent form and return it to the researcher(s) prior to data collection by [e.g. emailing it to the researcher(s); bringing it to the research site on the day of data collection (for an interview study)].

Verbal Consent

Please note that Verbal Consent cannot be used alone. A PISCF for Written Consent must be sent to participants via email, mail or made available in an online format prior to obtaining/recording verbal consent and the data collection process. Please see Guidelines for Collecting Participant Consent for further information.

[How/When the PISCF will be provided] Participants will be provided with the PISCF (e.g. via email, in person) when (e.g. they contact the research team about taking part; they receive the recruitment invitation email as the PISCF will be attached to this email (recommended)).

Participants will be asked to read the PISCF and will have sufficient time to consider their participation because [describe a time gap in times between provision of the PISCF and data collection; explain whether/how the time between provision of the PISCF and data collection is sufficient].

At the time of data collection, participants will be read the verbal consent script by the researcher(s) before the data collection commences. Participants will be asked to advise the researcher(s) if they have any questions.

If the participant verbally provides their consent for the researcher(s) to proceed with the data collection, their consent to participate will be recorded by [e.g. audio recording the consent declaration component of the verbal consent script]

Implied Consent

Fig. 15
Screenshot of a page of the *UNSW Human Research Ethics Application Form* (HREA), UNSW, https://research.unsw.edu.au/forms-and-templates, accessed October 5, 2020.

"co-exist," enabling meaningful "two-way agency."[50] This not only serves to subvert fixed normative frameworks of research practice, but safeguards Indigenous knowledge and protocol. It operates against an otherwise unidirectional potential for exploitation and extraction of knowledge that has become normalised in western academic empirical and imperial knowledge production.

The way in which the UNSW HREC/ HREAP deals with research knowledge is predicated on written agreements centring on informed consent, anonymity of participant identity, and intellectual property. My family, consigned to being research participants in our research project, rather than collaborators or researchers themselves, found their agency limited to their rights to consent (or not), to issues regarding the protection of their intellectual property rights and anonymity (or not). What was available to them as participants were the terms sketched out by a "Participant Information Statement and Consent Form (PISC)": a template provided by the UNSW HREC for all researchers, and was populated by me as the lead researcher, under advice from my supervisors. The process of consent produced via the template conveniently dispenses with the collaborative negotiation and development of its terms and contents with potential participants. The form streamlines the contract between researcher and research participant;

50 Ibid., 1400.

it pre-defines the key terms at stake, rather than inviting a more open-ended conversation about what the participants might want or be concerned about in the process themselves. The terms are pre-given. The form offers opt-in or opt-out options for participation and consent. Conversations that might emerge become proscribed and circumscribed, at least in my experience, having already been defined by the terms, options, and procedural constraints built into the template document itself. These forms tacitly enable a particular type of research method and a particular type of relationship between the researcher and their research subjects. The PISC structuralises a conceptual logic, key definitions, and legal boundaries, all within a benign-looking template document.

To reassure the UNSW HREC that fully informed consent was available to all members of my family and research participants (especially those in Vietnam and those not speaking fluent English), I was asked to provide a form of the "Participant Information Statement and Consent Form (PISC)" in both English and Vietnamese. I was, however, not offered financial support to cover the costs of employing a professional translator. My written Vietnamese is good (as discussed in Chapter 1) but not in this case good enough to undertake the comprehensive nature of this translation. My father volunteered to assist and translate the PISC for me and the other members of our family, thus,

he inadvertently participated in what was technically my administrative duty as a researcher. Fortunately, the HREAP process did not specify who could, or could not, undertake the translation and did not require the translator/s to be acknowledged, named, or identified on the consent form. Thus, as it transpired, one of my "research participants" was the very expert required to translate the academic Vietnamese that the PISC required. This meant that my Dad had also translated the very document he was asked to sign. Perversely, the very process of compliancy necessitated this ambiguous intervention to ultimately conform with the stipulations of the HREC. Thinking through this paradox, the procedure thus inadvertently positioned my Dad on both sides of an otherwise fixed boundary separating researcher from those being researched.

Transposing my Dad's Vietnamese translation into the prescribed template for the university's printed matter, I was asked to parrot the "look" of official university research stationary. Producing this document with my Dad, I was struck by how similar this act of compliance echoed our collaborative family undertaking to perform my birthday photographs. Produced for bureaucratic compliance, these documents—the birthday photograph, and the translated "Participant Research Consent Form"—were accepted as the kind of banal pieces of evidence they ultimately stood for and served to represent.[51] Underlying such benign documents there exists more opaque procedures of bureaucratic formularisation

and structural violence, and, in turn opportunities for the diasporic complicities, collusions, and subversions of a family caught with little choice but to acquiesce. Under these circumstances, the family can never be resolutely defiant nor fully compliant, even if they want to be. As Edward Said notes, the assumptions of vulnerability and incapacity for agency permits the colonial desire of western institutions and nations to sequester and dominate others.[52] So long as systems of domination continue to persist, my family continues to respond through compromised and limited interventions to trouble the exclusionary institutional borders that would otherwise preclude our inclusion and entry.[53]

Submitting my HREAP Ethics Application, it felt disturbing and satisfying to observe how readily the university accepted my Dad's translation of the consent forms. Who had the responsibility for validating the translation or determining its accuracy? Did anyone outside my family read

51
I use the term banal in subtle acknowledgement of Hannah Arendt's *Eichmann in Jerusalem: A Report on the Banality of Evil* in which bureaucratic gatekeeping, or the "tiny cog" defence within the machinery of genocide, is critiqued. Hannah Arendt, *Eichmann in Jerusalem: A Report on the Banality of Evil* (New York: The Viking Press, 1963), 131.

52
Edward W. Said, *Orientalism* (New York: Vintage eBooks, 1979), 44.

53
Matthew Scott, "Edward Said's *Orientalism,*" *Essays in Criticism* 58, no. 1 (2008): 64-81, https://doi:10.1093/escrit/cgm025.

it in Vietnamese? The presumed authority of the PISC translation satisfied the perceived assurance of "informed consent," not unlike my parents' dealings with the immigration department to concoct the necessary documents. Within these archival and procedural frameworks of authenticity and legitimacy, the optics of performing compliance may be more important than the content itself. In the end, one of the final hurdles for my UNSW HREC approval was to update the font and style of my forms to the most current formatting template. Having endured the documentational and structural imperatives of the HREC, it seemed rather appropriate that the stylistic appearance of official documentation ultimately ensured my research was approved.

What my work with my Father and our family archive highlights is how institutional documentation requires tacit, compliant, sometimes coercive, and otherwise ambiguous forms of collusion. The archival imposts that we had to undertake collectively have material impacts and consequences for the types of knowledge we can produce and access. This does not mean that complying and engaging with these institutions are ultimately defeating. Through our creative navigation of these archival imposts, we can still produce critique and knowledge with the limited options we find ourselves squeezed into. There is always a capacity to trouble the established infrastructures of institutional imposition, even by simply being present as proposed by Campt. By subtly and persistently inserting ourselves into these

spaces, we do not have to forfeit our humanity nor our identities as we seek entry across borders and into academia and the artworld. There is always a desire, as well as doing what is required by the immigrant family, to create our own forms of resistance—both because of and despite the infrastructures of power that affect us as outsiders. Paradoxically, the same archival burdens that blunt our capacity to fully access self-representation provides us with the motivation to confide in the family and collude in alternative strategies towards imperfect forms of self-determination.

Having to navigate and exist between the arbitrary separations of researcher-research subject, outsider-insider, entrant-defector, citizen-noncitizen, the distinctions between submission and resistance, compliance and refusals are never easy or clear. As Paul C. Taylor notes, agency, self-representation, and self-determination under these circumstances can never be assumed because the individuality of non-westerners is either not considered or deliberately disregarded altogether.[54] By analysing the archival strategies of my peers from the Vietnamese diaspora, I can develop a clearer understanding of how contemporary diasporic approaches to the archive might engage with the limited forms of self-representation available to us.

Nguyễn Thị Thanh Mai, a Huế-based video and installation artist from Vietnam, situates contemporary archive-making in response to the border politics of colonial and post-war conflict. As part of her project *Day by Day* (2014), Nguyễn spent time with Vietnamese villagers near Tonlé Sap Lake, Siem Reap, in Cambodia. Following the closure of colonial borders established by the French occupation of Indochina, these ethnic Vietnamese

54 Paul C. Taylor, *Race: A Philosophical Introduction* (Cambridge: Polity Press, in association with Blackwell Publishing, 2004), 34.

[INSERT any other organisational letterhead and the name of the School/Organisation/Centre]

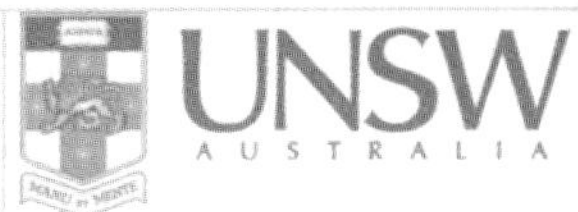

PARTICIPANT INFORMATION STATEMENT AND CONSENT FORM

[INSERT Participant Group (if applicable)]

[INSERT Title of project]

[INSERT Chief Investigator Name]

Guidance: The information provided in this document is a guide only. Please revise the wording in this section as necessary. The information provided in blue italics must be removed from the document before it is submitted to the HREC/HREAP. Please delete].

1. **What is the research study about?**
   You are invited to take part in this research study. The research study aims to *[INSERT a brief description of the purpose, aims and significance of your research study in plain English].* You have been invited because *[INSERT reason for invitation], and your contact details were obtained from [Insert how their details were obtained].*

2. **Who is conducting this research?**
   The study is being carried out by the following researchers: *[INSERT name of CI, PI and the student investigator], [INSERT School/Faculty or Organisation], [INSERT telephone]*.
   Research Funder: This research is being funded by *[list the name/s of funding organisation/s].*

3. **Inclusion/Exclusion Criteria**
   Before you decide to participate in this research project, we need to ensure that it is ok for you to take part. The research study is looking recruit people who meet the following criteria:
   - *[INSERTthe inclusion criteria]*
   - *[INSERTthe inclusion criteria]*

4. **Do I have to take part in this research study?**
   Participation in any research project is voluntary. If you do not want to take part, you do not have to. If you decide to take part and later change your mind, you are free to withdraw from the project at any stage.

   If you decide you want to take part in the research study, you will be asked to:
   - Read the information carefully (ask questions if necessary);
   - If you would like to participate, sign the consent form and;
   - Take a copy of this form home with you to keep.

5. **What does participation in this research require, and are there any risks involved?**
   Guidance: The information provided at this section needs to tell participants what they will be expected to do during their involvement in the research. Please delete any information that is not relevant to your project.

   If you decide to take part in the research study, we will ask you to complete the following tasks:

   [Completion of a Questionnaire]
   The research team will ask you to complete [INSERT an online or a paper based] questionnaire. This questionnaire will ask you questions about [provide a description of the questions to be asked], it should take approximately [insert approx time] to complete.

   We don't expect this questionnaire to cause any harm or discomfort, however if you experience feelings of distress as a result of participation in this study you can let the research team know and they will provide you with assistance. Alternatively lists of services are provided in the contact details below to assist you if necessary.

Fig. 16
Screenshot of a page of the UNSW *Participant Information Statement and Consent Form* (PISC). UNSW, https://research.unsw.edu.au/document/participant-information-statement-and-consent-form-template-pis-and-cf-form-template, accessed October 5, 2020.

families (having lived along the Mekong River for centuries) found themselves inside Cambodia. Made up of approximately 400 households, the villagers are stateless and excluded from education, healthcare, and social services reserved for recognised Cambodian citizens. These families remain unrecognised and administratively invisible to both current Cambodian and Vietnamese governments. During an artist residency in Vietnam in 2018, Nguyễn Thị Thanh Mai described to me that the most significant prejudice enacted on these villagers was documentational neglect. Stateless and without any form of photographic identification and paperwork, these people were prevented from accessing basic social services and participating in civic life. In her work, Thanh Mai developed a project among the villagers to photograph each other, self-issuing and self-producing laminated personal identity (ID) cards. Although not legally recognised by either Cambodia or Vietnam, these cards became a way for people to start the process of self-identification. Thanh Mai spent extended periods of time working with the villagers, taking around a portable camera, printer, and laminator, they would approximate the tropes and bureaucratic apparatus of the identity card. Collectivising the process of generating documentation, the villagers came together, trying to recall and verify bits of personal information such as birthdates and anniversaries that the state had refused to collect from them. This work drew on both social and administrative forms of productive

archival and memory-making. Consolidating social discourse to replicate the procedural protocols of state documentation, Nguyễn Thị Thanh Mai and the villagers point to the selective indifference and neglect of border peoples throughout Southeast Asia.

In another chance encounter, I meet Hoàng Trần Nguyễn at an artist's talk in 2019 in Melbourne. Like Thanh Mai, I learnt how Hoàng was also engaged in forms of archival activism. In an effort to retain the bilingual status of Footscray Primary School in the suburbs of Melbourne, Hoàng Trần Nguyễn was generating an archive of parent-teacher letters, mail outs, and digital advocacy materials to inform the community about the gradual dismantling of minority language learning programs.[55] The Mother Tongues curriculum, started in 1985, was part of the Victorian Department of Education's cultural policy.[56] Over time, the large Vietnamese-speaking population in Footscray has been progressively displaced by recent gentrification and large-scale property redevelopment projects threatening the cultural and economic diversity of

55
Footscray Primary School remains one of a handful of public schools in the state of Victoria running a bilingual curriculum. The school maintains a Vietnamese and English program that serves a large Vietnamese-speaking community in Footscray.

56
Serving many non-English-speaking immigrants and their broader communities in Victoria, the Mother Tongues program was a unique state-funded education tool that was never taken up by any other state government throughout Australia.

these suburbs. With changing student demographics, the school's principal decided to unilaterally cancel Footscray Primary School's language program, citing a lack of community interest, despite not doing any community consultation.

Hoàng's practice is squarely located in the preservation of minoritarian language whilst recognising the importance of documentational and archival presencing. Far from being disinterested, like-minded parents, teachers, and the local Vietnamese community in Melbourne organised by Trần Nguyễn through the Footscray Primary School Bilingual Immersion Group began producing documentation and building up an archive of the massive community support for retaining the heritage language programs at Footscray Primary School. The FPS Bilingual Immersion Group organised letter-writing nights, parent-teacher meetings, a social media campaign, printed posters, and produced a series of educational videos and interviews that recorded and documented the concerns of the parents and community. The visibility of speaking directly to camera and the vocal willingness of people who wanted to have their voices recorded all signed up in support. This archival project around the language program disputed the absence and lack of community interest claimed by the school principal.

These archival materials were important pieces of evidence when collated and sent to the State Education Minister James Merlino, who quickly reinstated the program at the end of 2016.

Bản xác định những thông tin và đơn đồng ý của tham dự viên.

ĐỀ TÀI: ***Sự gần gũi của xa cách***

Những hợp tác trong gia đình như là một sách lược của người di dân nhằm giữ gìn và làm sống lại những ký ức đã thu thập được qua việc cố gắng truyền bá tài liệu, qua sự diễn tả của chính mình hoặc qua phong cảnh.

Một công trình nghiên cứu PHD của Hồng Ân James Nguyễn.

1. Nghiên cứu, học tập về điều gì?
Bạn được mời tham dự vào việc nghiên cứu học tập này với mục đích:
1/ Bằng cách thu thập để tạo dựng film và hình ảnh (trữ liệu có từ gia đình) được lưu lại và chỉ được xử dụng cho những người trong gia đình.
2/ Thu thập để làm ra những nghệ phẩm mới (tuyển chọn từ những trữ liệu kể trên như là một nguồn sáng tạo) để trưng bày cho công chúng _ tại những nơi trưng bày nghệ thuật dành cho công chúng hay cho tư nhân _ qua những xuất bản nghệ thuật trên mạng và tại những nơi trưng bày.
3/ Phân tích những tiến trình nghiên cứu và những tài liệu công cộng trong khuôn khổ kiến thức bậc PhD _ dùng cho những ấn bản có tính cách hàn lâm trên mạng.

Bạn được mời vì bạn đã tỏ ra thích thú tham gia vào công trình nghiên cứu này, qua việc bạn để lại địa chỉ liên lạc và tự ý tỏ ra thích tham gia vào việc nghiên cứu học hỏi.

2. Ai là người hướng dẫn việc ngiện cứu này?
Việc học tập được thực hiện bởi những nghiên cứu sinh sau đây:
Hồng Ân James Nguyễn
USNW Art & Design, Oxford St & Green Rd. Paddington, NSW, Australia 2021
Mobile: +61 414 389 057
Người bảo trợ: Công trình nghiên cứu này được bảo trợ bởi Phân Khoa Nghệ thuật Hội Họa thuộc Trường Đại Học New South Wales Úc.

3. Nguyên tắc bao gồm và miễn trừ
Trước khi bạn quyết định tham dự vào công trình nghiên cứu này, chúng tôi cần biết chắc chắn là điều đó phù hợp để bạn tham dự. Công trình nghiên cứu học tập đang tìm cách đào tạo những người hội đủ những điều kiện sau đây:
- Trên 18 tuổi.
- Nam, Nữ hay không lưỡng tính.
- Phải có liên hệ huyết tộc hay pháp lý với Hồng Ân James Nguyễn.
- Phải được chọn từ những khuôn khổ, thứ bậc khác nhau về nghề nghiệp và kinh nghiệm sống.
- Biết đọc biết viết, có đủ trình độ để hiểu những từ ngữ như: nghiên cứu, mục đích, kết quả và mục tiêu của công trình.
- Dù gặp trở ngại trong việc xử dụng Anh Ngữ, nhưng phải nói lưu loát và đọc thông thạo tiếng Việt.

4. Tôi có bị bó buộc phải tham gia vào công trình nghiên cứu học tập này không?

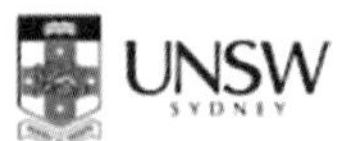

UNSW Art & DESIGN

Bản xác định những thông tin và đơn đồng ý của tham dự viên.

ĐỀ TÀI: Sự gần gũi của xa cách

Những hợp tác trong gia đình như là một sách lược của người di dân nhằm giữ gìn và làm sống lại những ký ức đã thu thập được qua việc cố gắng truyền bá tài liệu, qua sự diễn tả của chính mình hoặc qua phong cảnh.

Một công trình nghiên cứu PHD của Hồng Ân James Nguyễn.

1. **Nghiên cứu, học tập về điều gì?**
   Bạn được mời tham dự vào việc nghiên cứu học tập này với mục đích:

   1. **Bằng cách thu thập để tạo dựng film và hình ảnh (trữ liệu có từ gia đình) được lưu lại và chỉ được xử dụng cho những người trong gia đình.**
   2. **Thu thập để làm ra những nghệ phẩm mới (tuyển chọn từ những trữ liệu kể trên như là một nguồn sáng tạo) để trưng bày cho công chúng _ tại những nơi trưng bày nghệ thuật dành cho công chúng hay cho tư nhân _ qua những xuất bản nghệ thuật trên mạng và tại những nơi trưng bày.**
   3. **Phân tích những tiến trình nghiên cứu và những tài liệu công cộng trong khuôn khổ kiến thức bậc PhD _ dùng cho những ấn bản có tính cách hàn lâm trên mạng.**

   Bạn được mời vì bạn đã tỏ ra thích thú tham gia vào công trình nghiên cứu này, qua việc bạn để lại địa chỉ liên lạc và tự ý tỏ ra thích tham gia vào việc nghiên cứu học hỏi.

2. **Ai là người hướng dẫn việc ngiên cứu này?**
   Việc học tập được thực hiện bởi những nghiên cứu sinh sau đây: Hồng Ân James Nguyễn
   UNSW Art & Design, Oxford St & Green Rd. Paddington, NSW, Australia 2021 Mobile: +61 414 389 057
   Email: honganjames.nguyen@unsw.edu.au

   Chinh Nghiên cứu sinh: phó giáo sư Jennifer Biddle
   UNSW Art & Design, Oxford St and & Greens Rd, Paddington, NSW, Australia, 2021 Telephone: +61 (2) 8936 0751
   Email: j.biddle@unsw.edu.au

   Người bảo trợ: Công trình nghiên cứu này được bảo trợ bởi Phân Khoa Nghệ thuật Hội Họa thuộc Trường Đại Học New South Wales Úc.

Fig. 17 (pp. 188-189)
Screenshots of *Participant Information Statement and Consent Form, application number HC180430*, Nguyễn Ngọc Cư. (Left Translation) and James Nguyen (Right Formatting), 2018.

The struggles of this language program continue, however. Amidst the state-wide lockdown of Victoria during a second-wave resurgence of the COVID-19 pandemic in August 2020, the same school principal, again without any community consultation, announced that the Vietnamese Mother Tongues program would be replaced by an Italian language program on the school website. Aiming to pit one minority language group against another, this strategy is part of an ongoing dismantling of minority languages and cultural recognition in Victorian schools. Building on the parent-led archival materials produced in their 2016 campaign, Hoàng Trần Nguyễn with other parents and community members have responded with plans to reorganise a new campaign. The FPS Bilingual Immersion Group highlights the precarity of immigrant communities who are forced to encounter culturally dismissive and non-consultative governance structures amidst the continuing gentrification of neighbourhoods, a lack of community consultation by administrators, and the erosion of multilingualism that continues to occur even at the very early stages of education in Australia.

These strategies of archival self-determination by artists from the Vietnamese diaspora continue to expand and provide the political nuance that informs the contemporary archival practices of artists working in Australia, Canada, and the Indo Pacific region. Their local concerns have particular global and universal relevance in speaking up against state

neglect and institutional erasure in a contemporary context. Ranging from the work of Jacqueline Hoàng Nguyễn, who created an alternative immigrant archive in response to Canada's whitewashed institutions, to the work of Nguyễn Thị Thanh Mai in the fishing villages of Cambodia, and Hoàng Trần Nguyễn's work with the parents and teachers in the Melbourne suburb of Footscray, the archival approaches of diasporic Vietnamese practitioners across the world is diverse and dynamic. In coming into contact with these practices, these diasporic ecosystems of archival practice have helped me to situate the collaborative work I do with my family. The alienation instituted by administrative and procedural segregation in the university and the ongoing violence of Australia's immigration system feel less despairing when situated against the archival agency and activism of these artists. Among our broader diasporic landscapes, I continue to see the many ways in which archival production provides alternative means of political resistance and presence-making beyond more overt and sensationalised representations of violence and dread. Instead, these artists continue to confront a range of contemporary diasporic concerns that speak against institutional neglect, contemporary border violence, and ongoing forms of gentrification that shape the global experiences of the Vietnamese diaspora.

In a similar, but very different way, my return to the family photo album and my dealings with the UNSW HREC allowed me to bring our

intergenerational and institutional experiences into the present. Studying the past archival activities of my family has revealed strategies still relevant to my current academic research and practice. The family as a site of archival resistance must be conversant with the expanded family of artists dealing with the politics of diasporic presence. It is from these intimate and local relations that the plurality of resistance can coalesce. Chin-Tao Wu notes how these simultaneous dispersals of the local might accrue to decolonise and decentralise the hegemony of the global—which she equates to a form of westernisation.[57] The ways in which artists continue to work through collaborative and social forms of archival production to evidence their encounters with institutional violence remains especially important. Not only do these practices need to be incorporated into contemporary writing and critique beyond identity politics, but the human knowledge embedded in the experience of violence and inequality is something that is universally applicable.

57
Chin-Tao Wu, "Worlds Apart," *Third Text* 21, no. 6 (2007): 731.

Fig. 18 (p. 193)
Installation detail of printed sample ID Cards from the exhibition titled *Day by Day*. Nguyễn Thị Thanh Mai, courtesy of the artist, 2014.

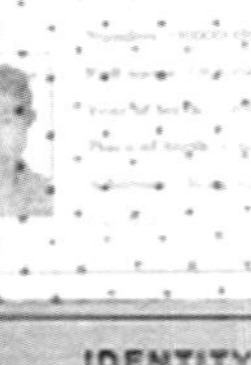
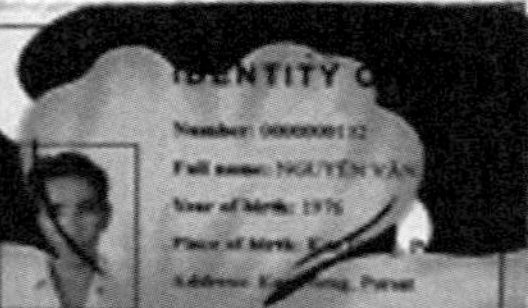
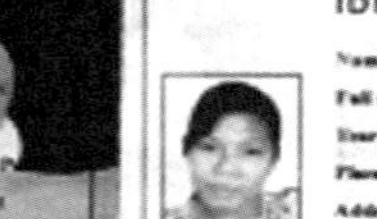
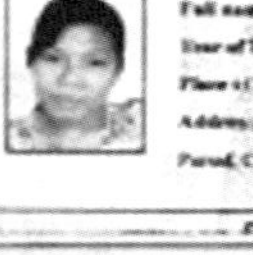
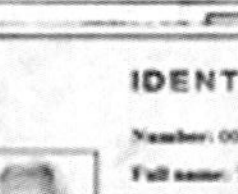
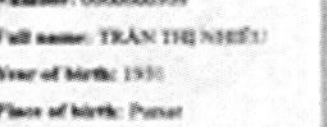
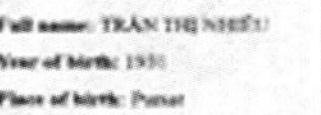
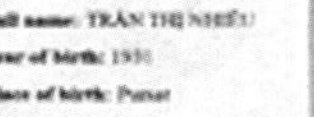
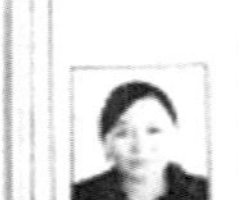
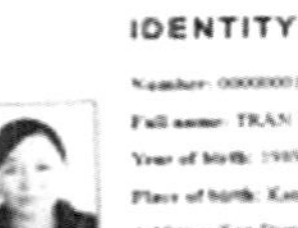
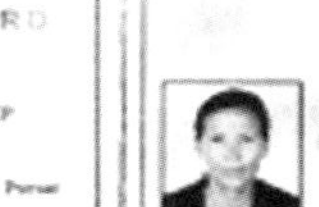
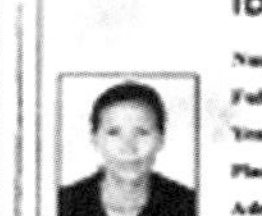
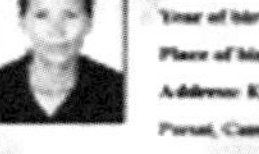
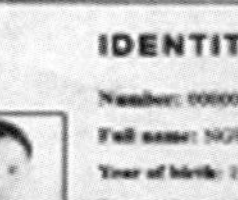
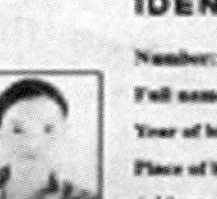
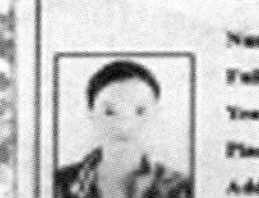
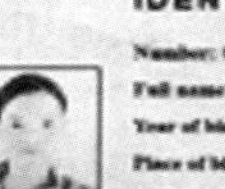
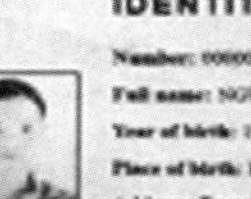
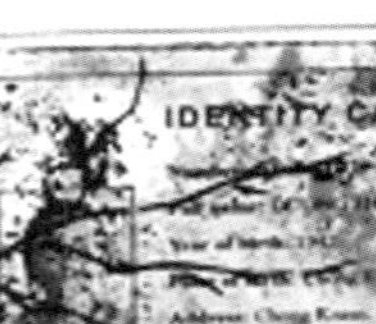
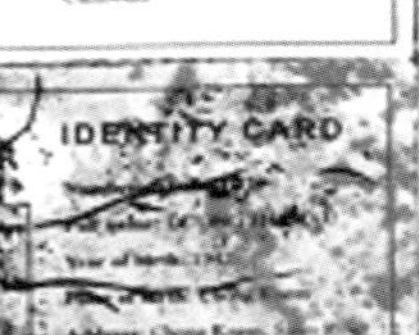
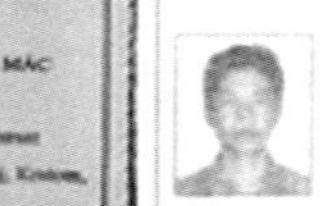

Upon receiving advice from the HREAP Executive that I was finally granted the official approval to continue my research with my family, I decided to do some basic administrative housekeeping, reorganising, and clearing out of my university inbox.[58] Having freshly purged my emails of all the regular university-wide bulletins, I noticed a mass email sent by the Deputy Vice-Chancellor with the subject heading: "DVC Inclusion and Diversity."

The email notified recipients that "The Division of Inclusion and Diversity was established in August 2017 to oversee the equity, diversity, and inclusion (EDI) initiatives outlined in the UNSW 2025 Strategy." Everyone was invited to the Roundhouse on Kensington Campus to celebrate the achievements of the first year of the Division. Accompanying this invite was an image of aspirational diversity. Bathed in sunlight and walking as a united squad, six students move towards the camera. The image is composed of two students wearing glasses, two in a black-and-white striped shirt, two in a light grey shirt, and two in a black shirt. The aesthetically balanced wardrobe backgrounded the visual diversity of the

58
This PhD research and thesis was conducted in full compliance with the UNSW HREC (UNSW Human Research Ethics Committee): project no. HC180430, including all terms and conditions associated with this approval.

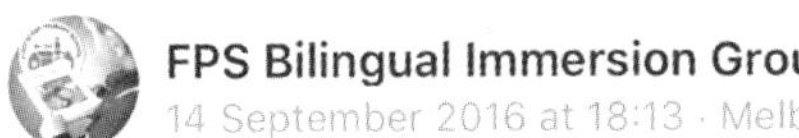

VIDEO 1: As a parent I asked others from the school what they valued about the bilingual program at FPS. Here's what some said - Hoang Nguyen

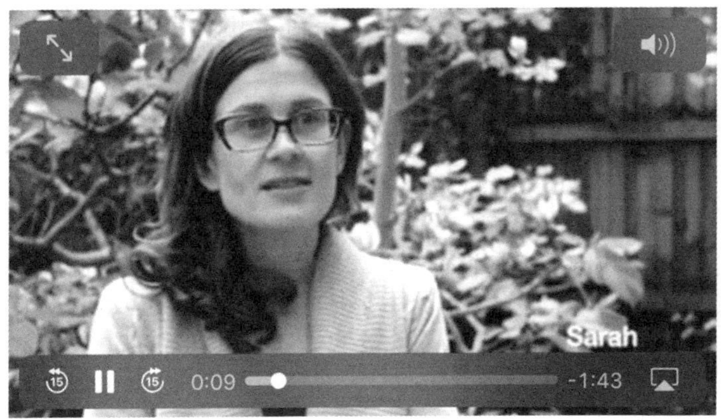

Fig. 19
Screenshot of Facebook page and video released by the *Footscray Primary School Bilingual Immersion Group*, Hoàng Trần Nguyễn, 2016-ongoing.

students: two of Asian descent, one accompanied by a guide dog, and a wheelchair user. The awkward-looking group had an air of composed diversity, almost as convincing as the photos that were staged by my parents of me with my birthday cake. Symptomatic of the constructed imagery of diversity in higher education are the associated scripts of "diversity," "inclusion," and "equity." Having just endured the patronising, inflexible, and unaccommodating process of HREC approval, this sunny representation of diversity and inclusion felt not quite right. Rather than addressing the underlying infrastructures of institutional bias, or perhaps acknowledging the problematic frameworks of human research that prevent open access and participation, the university seemed more invested in fulfilling the optics of inclusion. By disseminating and building up this self-congratulatory archive of publicity and self-promotional diversity rhetoric, the university was actively engaged in a pre-emptive strategy against any criticism of structural inflexibility and bias.

In the years since Ahmed published *On Being Included (Racism and Diversity in Institutional Life)* (2012), many Australian universities, including UNSW (where I have conducted this research), have steered their prospectus towards implementing strategies of inclusion. Like Ahmed, Yvonna Lincoln forewarns of the widespread marketing of diversity and inclusion in the university, whereby its corporate

culture has pushed the tertiary system to commodify and espouse a language of opportunity, inclusion, and generic diversity.[59] Revealingly, in the UNSW ten-year strategic plan towards 2025, the Deputy Vice-Chancellor of UNSW highlights how the university had:

> implemented initiatives and programs, with measurable outcomes [that] form the basis of UNSW's social engagement objectives:
>
> - UNSW's *Disability Action Plan (DIAP)*.
> - Individual grant opportunities for *Equity, Diversity and Inclusivity (EDI Grants)*.
> - A *Facing Equality Photography Exhibition*.
> - Promoting UNSW Diversity Champions—passionate individuals who drive change in their respective diversity areas: gender, flexible work, cultural diversity, LGBTIQ+ and disability.
> - An annual UNSW *Diversity FEST.*
> - The UNSW *Respect Survey* conducted between 18 April–17 May 2019 to share experiences in relation to harassment, bullying, discrimination, sexual misconduct and related topics.[60]

These initiatives outline the University's diversity strategy around promoting inclusion. Apart from the DIAP, these "measurable outcomes" are clearly centred on individual pursuit. Deferring to the achievements of individuals (including individual small grants and promoting diversity champions), the university conveniently avoids reflecting on its own structural accountability. Ahmed is particularly sceptical of the incorporation of zeitgeisty terms like "inclusion," "diversity," and "equal opportunity," into these strategic plans. The university sector's attachment to what she calls the "language of diversity" reveals more about an attachment to language rather than actual measures that take on the challenging work of systemic change.[61] "If diversity creates the impression of addressing something without addressing anything, diversity is used as a way of managing impressions."[62] To Ahmed, these words, more often than not, deflect underlying structural dysfunction.

59
Yvonna S. Lincoln, "The Political Economy of Publication: Marketing, Commodification, and Qualitative Scholarly Work," *Qualitative Health Research* 22, no. 11 (November 2012): 1451-59, https://doi:10.1177/1049732312457713.

60
"Equity, Diversity and Inclusion," UNSW 2025 Strategy, accessed May 28, 2020, https://www.edi.unsw.edu.au/about-us/strategy-2025.

61
Ahmed, "Doing Diversity Work in Higher Education in Australia," 746.

62
Ahmed, *What's the Use?*, 148.

In the policy document *UNSW 2025 Strategy—Our Strategic Priorities and Themes,* the University Chancellor David Gonski AC states: "UNSW has always been a university with a strong sense of social responsibility, so it is right that the 2025 Strategy emphasises our commitment to promoting equity, diversity, and social justice."[63] His aspirational mission is admirable but offers little detail, diagnostics, or measurable outcomes regarding what is meant by social responsibility, equality, diversity, and justice. The Chancellor is more intent on glossing over any historic failures, even claiming some archival righteousness: one in which the University has apparently always pursued a path guided by a strong sense of social responsibility. This messaging completely denies Aronowitz's charge that the corporate university is inevitably built on "the master discourse of domination."[64] These ubiquitous mission statements and press releases are by no means unique to UNSW; they are a staple for many other Australian universities. For example, a year after I had received HREC approval, the previous year's Harmony Day at UNSW was converted to

63 UNSW Australia, *UNSW 2025 Strategy, Our Strategic Priorities and Themes* (Sydney, NSW: UNSW Marketing Services, 2015), https://www.2025.unsw.edu.au/sites/default/files/uploads/unsw_2025strategy_201015.pdf.

64 Aronowitz, "A Critique of Methodological Reason," 714.

65 "UNSW Diversity Fest," UNSW Events, accessed May 28, 2020, https://www.events.unsw.edu.au/event/unsw-diversity-fest.

"a week-long celebration of inclusiveness," heralding the arrival of Diversity FEST 2019 into my email inbox.[65] A snazzier version of DIVERSITY WEEK 2010, I was reminded that only a decade before, Ahmed had cited a similar event at the University of Queensland.[66] Even though these events punctuate the annual calendars of universities throughout Australia over the last decade, it feels like little has changed at a structural level.

Interestingly, the image of diverse students used in the DVC Inclusion and Diversity email in 2018 made a repeat reappearance, promoting the "Diversity Showcase" at "Diversity Fest" in 2019.[67] The programmatic recycling of these images reveals how diversity continues to be replicated and disseminated. As such, UNSW continues to draw from its archival stock of promotional materials to reproduce these constructed events. As Ahmed points out, tokenistic diversity for the university is not only a textual preoccupation; it is also visual.[68] Recycling these images reveals familiar patterns of diversity washing.

Quite unexpectedly, a month following Diversity FEST 2019, the university announced that the contract for the Director of Indigenous Programs at UNSW Art & Design would be terminated.

66
Sara Ahmed, *On Being Included: Racism and Diversity in Institutional Life* (Durham: Duke University Press, 2012), 32.

67
"Diversity Showcase," UNSW Eventbrite Invite September 26, 2019, organised by UNSW Careers.

68
Ahmed, *What's the Use?* 150.

This role played an essential part in the faculty's work towards providing support, community networks, and academic outcomes for First Nations students. Working in this role, Wiradjuri woman and curator Tess Allas had contributed to the careers, cultural, and intellectual life of students, artists, and staff at UNSW for over a decade.[69] The sudden termination of Allas' appointment—with no explanation given by the University as to why—reminded many in the faculty of their own precarity as contract employees. Such events underscore the vulnerable nature of both tertiary and diversity work. It felt dubious that the University was actively promoting a week-long festival highlighting diversity and inclusion whilst providing no accountability and explanation for why they were removing the position of the Director of Indigenous Programs in the Art & Design department without guaranteeing an equivalent replacement. Exuberant adjectives used during Diversity FEST like "inspirational," "connection," and "celebration" felt especially grating for the many students and staff who organised protests around a "Stand with Tess" campaign. A large number of Australian and international First Nations artists including Girramay, Yidinji, and Kuku-Yalanji man Tony Albert, Kamilaroi, Kooma, Jiman, and Gurang Gurang man Richard Bell, and Aotearoa/Australian artist with Samoan heritage Angela Tiatia called for all artists to boycott the UNSW Galleries. This was accompanied by a petition of signatures demanding the University reverse its decision and start to take

diversity work seriously. What complicated this situation was that the University and its leadership vehemently made no concessions to any of these artist-led demands. As the months passed, some of these artists (many close friends and colleagues of mine) became impossibly squeezed by the inflexible unwillingness of the institution to budge, and the compounding commitments, responsibilities, and cost burdens of having spent months and years of making work in preparation for exhibition at the UNSW Galleries. Apart from those who could not boycott UNSW because of immediate graduating exhibitions and assessment, a number of First Nations and Moana artists themselves eventually exhibited works at UNSW Galleries in early 2020 as part of the multi-site exhibition *Wansolwara: One Salt Water*. Curated by UNSW Gallery Director José Da Silva, Léuli Eshraghi who independently curated *O le ūa na fua mai Manu'a* (also at UNSW Galleries), and Mikala Tai (at that time the director at 4A Centre for Contemporary Asian Art), this project brought together the largest exhibition of contemporary Moana and Pasifika practices in Australia outside of the Asia Pacific Triennial.[70]

69 Joanna Mendelssohn, "Asset Stripping," *The Art Life*, October 7, 2019, https://theartlife.com.au/2019/asset-stripping/.

70 Gina Fairley, "Review: *Wansolwara: One Salt Water*, UNSW Galleries (NSW)," *Artshub*, February 15, 2020, https://visual.artshub.com.au/news-article/reviews/visual-arts/gina-fairley/review-wansolwara-one-salt-water-unsw-galleries-nsw-259778.

DVC Inclusion and Diversity 25/7/18
Invitation to the Equity, Diversity an...
Equity, Diversity and Inclusion Town Hall The Roundhouse | Monday 20 A...

DVC Inclusion and Diversity

Invitation to the Equity, Diversity and Inclusion Town Hall

RESEARCH READS 25 July 2018 at 6:47 pm

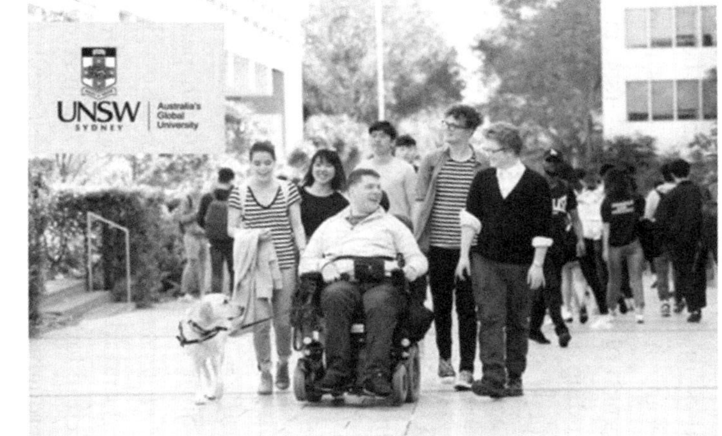

Equity, Diversity and Inclusion Town Hall
The Roundhouse | Monday 20 August, 2:00 - 3:00pm

With so few opportunities to showcase the diasporic voices from the Pacific region, these artists had the impossible task of choosing between a sustained boycott or to exhibit in solidarity with their community of curators and cultural peers. Against the context of such hard-won artworld opportunities to present the practice of Moana artists in Australia, the moralistic capacity to aggressively withdraw and boycott from powerful institutions like UNSW for an indefinite period of time felt like that might itself be another form of privilege. Uncomplicated moral resoluteness is rarely available for most artists. Discussing the limitations of protest and institutional critique in relation to Hans Haacke and Andrea Fraser, Aruna D'Souza points out the difficulty of moral resolve when engaging with institutions of power. D'Souza notes that although there are creative opportunities to redirect the abusive instrumentalisation of museums, even artists involved in institutional critique, like Haacke and Fraser, are fully aware:

> precisely that there is no "outside" to the art world; artists cannot exist in an antagonistic relationship to the institution of art because artists are integral to the institutions of art … And so it follows that even protesting a museum exhibition is still a form of participation since the gesture takes meaning from its relation to the art world.[71]

The struggle of artists against these institutions is one thing, but the moral culpability of powerful institutions, on the other hand, feels particularly cynical when places like UNSW consistently deploy the rhetoric of liberal and progressive values like diversity, whilst working behind the scenes to undermine the work and value of key diversity workers, readily squeezing staff and artists into increasingly impossible moral positions.

71
Aruna D'Souza, "What Can We Learn from Institutional Critique?" *Art In America*, October 29, 2019, https://www.artnews.com/art-in-america/features/hans-haacke-new-museum-retrospective-institutional-critique-63666/.

Fig. 20 (p. 204)
Screenshot of email sent and received on July 25, 2018 in the university email inbox of Hong An James Nguyen. *DVC Inclusion and Diversity email,* original image unattributed by UNSW, 2018.

Thinking about my own friends and peers who were caught up in the position of having boycotted the University, then over time having to support their communities and exhibit with UNSW Galleries, I had to reflect on my own participation inside these spaces. Unrelated to the boycotts, I remembered a problematic experience my family had encountered when we presented *The Pants of Eva (Eva)* for the "Academic Symposium for the Forced Migration Research Network" at UNSW (2017). The performance involved myself, my Aunty, Mum, and Dad slowly converging through the crowd at a symposium opening event. In this performance, we each stood atop two white plastic chairs. Starting without announcement we would quietly recount a version of my Aunt's story of failed escape from Vietnam. Speaking in both Vietnamese and English our voices would gradually escalate as we came into the centre of the space. Culminating with us yelling at one another, we would compete to finish the story, before abruptly leaving.

The vocal disruptions, the elevation on the chairs, the sudden temporality of the performance, and our white clothes (a regular costume we use for these family-based performances) allowed my family and I to have visual presence at the centre of the crowd. These white performance uniforms reference the legacy of 1970s western conceptual and body art where white shirts or uniforms were

regularly adopted by establishment performance artists like Gina Pane, Marina Abramovic, and Bruce Nauman to heighten their performance gestures on black-and-white photography and film/video recordings. This trope of European-American performance art was subsequently critiqued by artists like Lorraine O'Grady in works such as *Untitled (MIIe Bourgeoise Noire)* in the 1980s.[72] The photographic documentation of O'Grady hijacking the white debutant archetype of the artworld with an untouchable full-length dress and white gloves "in full regalia, with fellow artists and friends, her head thrown back in full-throated laughter," vividly captures what D'Souza describes as O'Grady's physical rupturing of the art world's exclusion of her Black body.[73]

72
In 1980, Lorraine O'Grady performed *Untitled (MIIe Bourgeoise Noire)* wearing an evening gown made up of 180 pairs of white dinner gloves and a white whip. Entering an art party at JAM (Just Above Midtown) in Manhattan, O'Grady whipped herself and spoke poems of protest which acknowledged slavery and the exclusion of Black artists and perspectives from the mainstream New York artworld. The gloves implied the hands-off labour and pure aesthetics of bourgeois contemporary art that maintain this historic system of white domination and oppression. "Untitled (MIIe Bourgeoise Noire)," MoMA Learning, accessed May 28, 2020, https://www.moma.org/learn/moma_learning/lorraine-ogrady-untitled-mlle-bourgeoise-noire-1980-832009/.

73
Aruna D'Souza, "A Feminist Diary," *Canadian Art* 35, no. 4 (2019): 60.

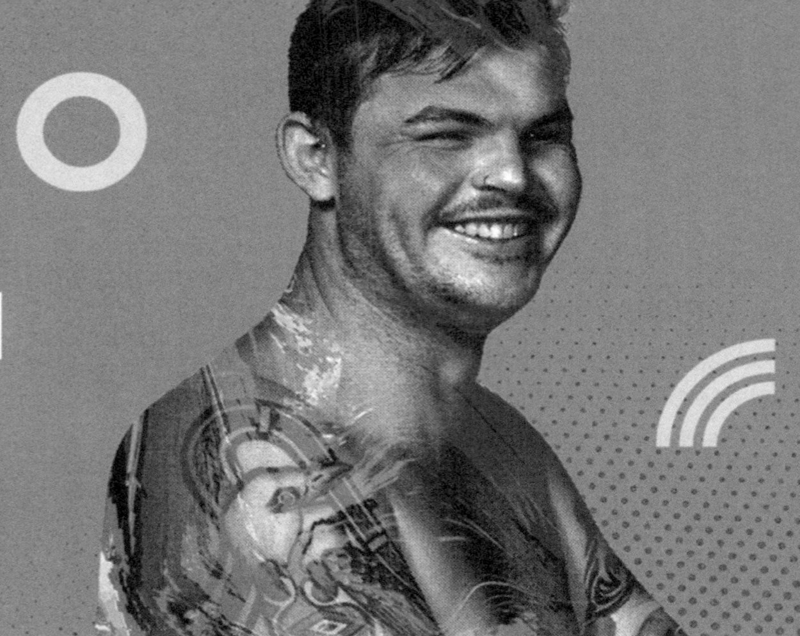
DIVERSITY
FEST 2019
A WEEK-LONG
CELEBRATION OF
INCLUSIVENESS
23–27 SEPTEMBER
Jake Fing | UNSW student | he / him / his
Diversity Fest is here!

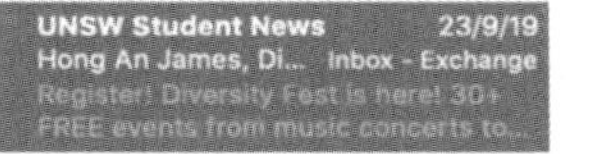

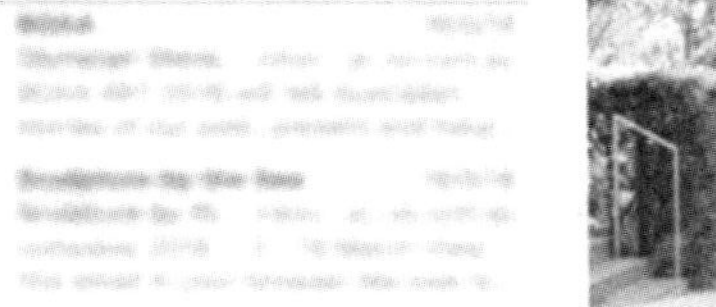

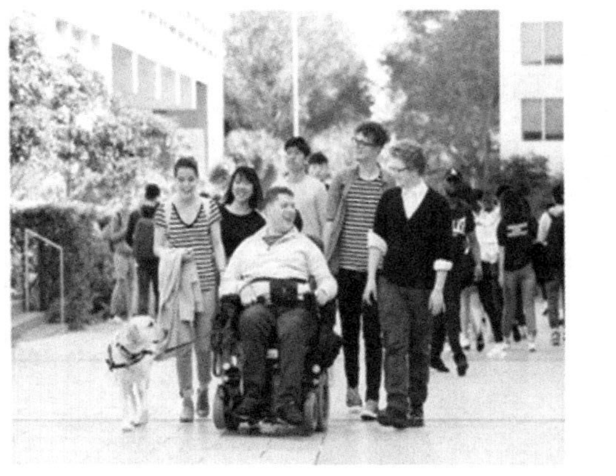

Diversity Showcase

A showcase connecting UNSW staff, students, academics, industry experts and alumni across the diversity spectrum. This Thursday!

Learn more and register.

My family's performance is indebted to these histories and counter-histories of performance and body art, presenting a more recent comment on ways in which we too, as immigrant outsiders, are only ever permitted a brief moment of incursion into these art events, left to "shout" our migrant testimonies at audiences.

The first time we performed this work was at the opening of the 2016 Sydney Contemporary Art Fair. We were part of the program of performances and installations that the fair had curated along its commercial enterprise. Amongst the music, pop-up bars, and over-capacity art stands, our performance was part of a series of happenings with people darting in and out of the way as the spectacle of an art fair opening. For the performance at the UNSW Galleries, we were curated into an academic symposium around the topic of forced global migrations—part of the university's PLuS Alliance Program. The audience here mistook our performance for perhaps a piece of relational aesthetics, and unlike the raucous novelty and entertainment at the fair, the performance at the UNSW Galleries ended with a number of audience members approaching my family, seeking direct engagement as we performed. Feeling obliged, my Mum and Dad ended up talking to the audience rather than leaving the space as planned. This interesting delineation was ultimately shaped by the unexpected curiosity of people attending the

symposium. Talking with my friend, Melbourne-based artist Phương Ngô about his ten-day durational performance *Article 14.1* (2019) at the Museum of Contemporary Art Australia (MCA), interrogating the administrative violence enacted on refugees seeking asylum in Australia, we discussed how physical encounters of immigrant bodies and our storytelling to audiences were particularly fraught.[74] In his performance, Ngô found himself, like my Mum and Dad, automatically taking on the responsibility and burden of attending to the needs of the audience. In the predominantly white museum, Ngô noted that the minority performer was implicitly expected to address the interests and curiosities of the audience, rather than the other way around. D'Souza has noted a similar experience of casual American institutional racism. During the opening of MASS MoCA's 2017 expansion, D'Souza had noted how the massive extension to the exhibition and studio spaces were the reserve of predominantly white artists, recruited and run by white curators, and inevitably for white audiences.

74
Phương Ngô's live performance was part of *Primavera 2018*, which explored the question: why is diversity important today? His performance paid tribute to his father's boat journey and the journeys of other refugees coming to Australia. He told me of the additional psychological burden of not only performing this durational work, but also being accosted by a constant stream of audience members who saw these refugee stories as an opportunity for them to off-load on their own anxieties and sense of powerlessness at not being able to help or engage from a distance.

The diverse population demographics that the museum should have served as a public institution was, however, cynically only brought in just for the opening celebrations:

> It wasn't that blackness was erased from the opening festivities, rather it was made to serve its usual function in a liberal institution: to act as a cover for the museum's almost exclusive investment in whiteness. Blackness was present as spectacle, as performance, as entertainment—but wasn't afforded the primary thing MASS MoCA has to offer: namely, real estate. Strip away these fleeting performances and what remains is a monument to white art, a point that was painfully apparent when I revisited the building after the celebrations were over.[75]

Beyond parading otherness as entertainment, the responsibility that institutions have, to invest in the training, challenging, and education of their predominantly white audiences to the exclusion of other communities remains perfunctory. It is unsurprising that these inevitably white audiences continue to be endangered by their own unintended racial blunders and mishaps which harm both themselves and the minority artists and patrons that have

75 Aruna D'Souza, "White Space, Black Spectacle at MASS MoCA," *MOMUS*, June 29, 2017, http://momus.ca/awhite-space-black-spectacle-mass-moca/.

STAND
WITH
TESS

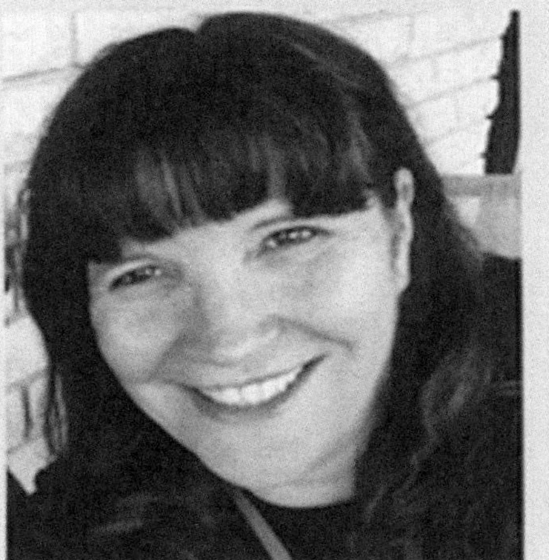

to endure their lack of training within these spaces of unequal power. With these experiences in mind, I was again reminded of the complicated politics of making art from inside spaces like the university. The discomfort of being included and implicated in these unequal infrastructures remains particularly troublesome, especially when the family you work with is also drawn into such problematic and fraught interactions.

Having invested a significant amount of time and energy into gaining entry into the university and getting UNSW HREC approval to do research with my family, it was difficult to come to terms with the contentious devaluation of "diversity work" as described by Ahmed. Unlike many of my peers who had booked their graduation exhibitions in the UNSW Galleries (because of limited exhibition spaces throughout Sydney), or had previously signed contracts for upcoming shows there, I had, prior to the artists' boycotts, been in conversation with my supervisors about pursuing only online and off-site examination for a non-Sydney-based assessment of my PhD. The groundswell on campus to boycott the UNSW Galleries only made my intentions easier. I was able to outwardly avoid presenting my examination at UNSW Galleries "in solidarity with Allas" whilst continuing to complete my thesis for UNSW and be examined off-site. I am, and still continue to benefit from my relationship with the community of artists, academics, workers, and administrative staff who make up UNSW

Art & Design. Much like my own compromised navigation of the UNSW HREC approval process, the capacity to not exhibit my assessment at UNSW Galleries was ultimately a pragmatic privilege rather than a moral choice. Being examined on-or-off-site would still mean my tacit acceptance of UNSW's structural violence. Reflecting on this, my decisions, however compromised or convenient, would likely have little political impact. Coincidentally, then-current pandemic conditions had inevitably moved the majority of all assessments online and to off-site iterations anyway. But again, these reflections emphasise how subtle forms of complicity, allegiance building, and compromised refusals are so important when working inside institutions that continue to utilise inclusion as an exercise in rhetoric, rather than one that seriously engages with structural change.

Fig. 21 (p. 209)
Screenshot of email September 23, 2019 in the university inbox of Hong An James Nguyen. *UNSW Student News email,* with featured students, including Jake Fing a UNSW Law Student who was a joint recipient of the Spirit Award for Law, 2019.

Fig. 22 (p. 210)
Screenshot of email sent on September 26, 2019 in the university inbox of Hong An James Nguyen. *UNSW Student News email, Diversity Showcase details:* UNSW John Niland Scientia Building, Kensington, 2019.

Fig. 23 (p. 214)
Screenshot of Instagram tile on *standwithtess1 Instagram account.* Original campaign poster and image unattributed, posted on October 10, 2019.

In an attempt to construct an archive with my family, we had intended to produce new materials and contribute to the University as a trusted institutional repository of knowledge and discourse. By making artworks together, the aim was to create new knowledge and be represented not only in public art galleries, but also in the academic realm (through exhibition and discourse). Finding examples of other artists from the Vietnamese diaspora, I wanted to understand their various archival approaches. The works of Phương Ngô, Jacqueline Hoàng Nguyễn, Hoàng Trần Nguyễn, and Nguyễn Thị Thanh Mai, although geographically dispersed, were responding to very contemporary experiences of minoritarian archival exclusion and neglect. Through the compulsion to create alternative and collective forms of archival self-determination, these artists used both the documentary form and archival methods to draw attention to processes that would have been largely neglected and unseen. Instead of producing new archives, my own work with my family began when I returned to my old family photo album. Realising that I was part of the photographic contrivances of my parents, who were making documents specifically for the immigration department, I learnt about the administrative negligence that was imposed on my family. Drawing from this knowledge, I instantly recognised patterns of epistemic power and inflexibility as I sought

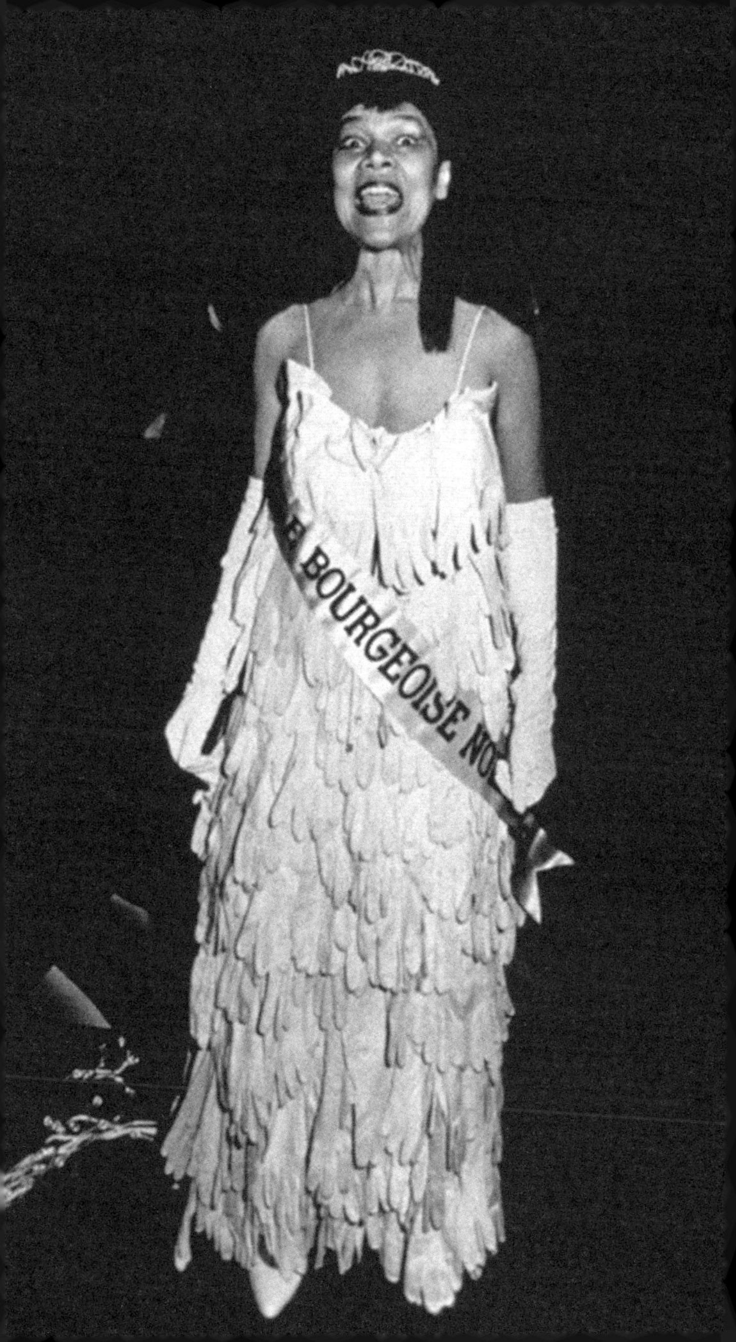
BOURGEOISE

UNSW HREC approval to do research with my family.

What actually transpired from the UNSW HREC application process was my recognition of the procedural and paternalistic ways in which higher research is conducted. These institutional impacts actually resulted in a shift in how my family approached these archival imposts. In the end, I did not necessarily rely on producing any new material to add to the archive we already had. What was more important was directly engaging with the rhetoric of the university and working with my Dad to navigate the documentational demands on us as "vulnerable" research subjects. The material archive that did emerge was one driven by compromise and collusion. My Dad's Vietnamese translation of the Participant Information Statement and Consent Form, like my birthday photos, was contingent on meeting the expectations of external gatekeepers—the UNSW HREC and the Department of Immigration respectively.

Fig. 24 (p. 218)
Lorraine O'Grady, photographic documentation of performance *MIle Bourgeoise Noire shouts out her poem*, The New Museum, New York, 1981. Photos by Coreen Simpson and Salima Ali, http://lorraineogrady.com/slideshow/mlle-bourgeoise-noire/.

Nguyen Thi Kim Nhung is my aunty on my mother's side.

She attempted to on five occasions and failed
flee Vietnam by boat every time.

the highlands,
from she could neither
Coming, swim nor navigate the coast,
but like countless others, she would try again and
again to
escape.

On one occasion, she left with her younger brother. After a few days journeying they quietly arrived in the homes of some fishing villagers. They were immediately led into the mangroves. They were told to hide and wait in the trees for small fishing rafts to pick them up and ferry them at high tide to a larger boat.

Hiding until sunrise, no rafts came.
in the mangroves

People called out that they had been busted! thinking she would not
get caught if she headed
away from all the others, my
taking aunty found herself in a little clearing

deeper
and
deeper   Realising too late she had stepped into
steps.
a sinking mudpit.

At the risk of being caught, some of her fellow escapees ran
back with sticks and branches. Laying these down in a crisscross
pattern. An older man whose name she no longer remembers, managed
to crawl out and grab a hold of her.   It must have taken at least half an hour,
but he and the others managed to slowly pull her out.

It then dawned on my aunty that having runaway at night, she was wearing elastic waist pyjamas.
So she tried her hardest to hold onto her pants as she was being pulled out,
but the elastic   gave   way   and   her pants   were left   behind.

exhaustion
In her moment of   embarrassment,   and humiliation,
her younger brother threw her his shirt.
Tying it around her waist,
the group clambered out of the mangroves and were quickly rounded up by the patrol guards.

Nine months later, she was released. Every now and then when she runs into people who were in prison with her,

they would still call her Eva, having crawled out of the garden half-naked.

By investigating the historic neglect and exclusion of diasporic narratives beyond overt representations of trauma and tragedy, research into how personal archives are made has led me to reconsider firsthand the violence embedded in the documentation of the immigrant family. Like the ongoing separation of families sanctioned by Australia's border policy, the university continues to struggle with the inherent bias that separates academic excellence and cultural experience. The violence of not understanding that the knowledge embedded in the family is epistemically equal and potentially more meaningful than the rhetoric built into "academic excellence" is colonial, racist, and arrogant. If the university continues to wear the language of inclusion and diversity without addressing what Ahmed deems as the necessary work to dismantle and shift underlying issues of systemic exclusion and racism, then it continues to expose not only itself, but its faculty, staff, the student body, and its publics to precarious and morally fraught situations.[76]

By applying the multiple knowledge systems and wealth of experience gained from minoritarian, First Nations, and immigrant dealings with archival neglect, surveillance, and exclusion, artists can shape our understanding of the very infrastructures of power that impact our everyday lives. Caught between the archival impasse of being neglected

76 Ahmed, "Doing Diversity Work in Higher Education in Australia," 747.

or being over-documented, and of facing recurrent forms of coercive paternalism and exploitation, artists working with archival self-presencing through "a collective and relational practice of enunciation" are essential to contemporary discourse.[77] In the end, this chapter articulates how self-determination can exist in understanding the work of my peers and developing a deeper appreciation for the documentational burdens that my family has had to endure. By articulating our strategies for navigating these recurrent patterns of exclusion, a more critical understanding of archival practice can be constituted through our families and networks.

77 Campt, *Image Matters*, 241.

Fig. 25 (pp. 220-221)
English language script (for James Nguyen and Nguyễn Ngọc Cu) as part of a live performance spoken in both Vietnamese and English at the Sydney Art Fair and UNSW Galleries. *Pants of Eva* by Nguyễn Thị Kim Nhung, Nguyễn Thị Kim Dung, Nguyễn Ngọc Cu, and James Nguyen. Performance Poetry and Text courtesy of the artists, 2016.

CHAPTER 3

Troubling Tongues

After my Mum and I arrived in Australia, my parents started a textiles business on the industrial side of Governor Macquarie Drive in the Sydney suburb of Chipping Norton. This was the early 1990s and establishing a textiles business to knit polo-shirt collars and fabric, and then sewing these into garments in a one-stop shop was an ambitious and risky undertaking. It so happened that this business venture coincided with the Labor government's second wave of economic reforms, which started with the floating of the Australian dollar in 1983, followed by tariff cuts to labour-intensive manufacturing sectors including the textiles, clothing, and footwear industries.[1] Deregulating these sectors eventually produced net gains in the broader economy, especially for banking and mining.[2] However, there was immediate economic fallout in traditionally lower paid, lower skilled manufacturing sectors that had once employed many immigrants and non-fluent English speakers.

1
Acker, "Trade Liberalisation and Its Impact on the Australian Textiles," 14.

2
Laura Berger-Thompson, John Breush, and Louise Lilley, "Australia's Experience with Economic Reform, Treasury Working Paper," The Macroeconomic Group, Department of Treasury, Langton Crescent, Parkes ACT 2600, Australia, October 2018, https://treasury.gov.au/sites/default/files/2019-03/p2018-t332486-economic-reform-v2.pdf.

Unable to compete with cheaper imports from China and Southeast Asia, our family business had to drastically cut costs. We ended up moving into the factory, sleeping in the alcove above the office. Two units down from us, a Chinese family also moved in to save money and keep their tool-box manufacturing business afloat. As tariffs for imported clothing and textiles were lifted, local orders for polo-shirts dipped. Eventually, the family business became increasingly reliant on my Mum's sewing skills. In addition to helping sponsor her younger Sister Nguyễn Thị Kim Nhung (Dì Nhung ~ *my Aunty Nhung*), over from Vietnam, both my Mum and Aunty to this day continue to do piecework. Continuing to do the majority of the sewing and assembly work, it fell on my Mum to, piece-by-piece, pay off the debt accrued by the business, enabling my family to kickstart our own micro-economic transition. When they finally closed the factory, Mum continued to do piecework at home in the garage. This work paid for my school fees, uniforms, and excursions. She also sent Dad back to university to qualify as a social worker.

These shifts in the global economy had a trickle-down effect on our family life, and as with any transition, there were winners and losers. My Dad, my younger Brother, and I all gained the privileges of English literacy and tertiary qualifications. My Mum, and to a lesser extent my Aunty, emerged from this process with profoundly bad English. Forgoing English classes upon arrival to support the family

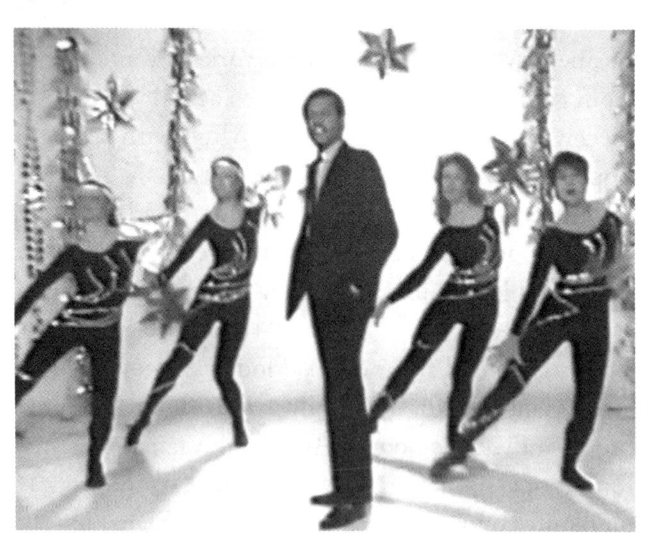

Fig. 26
Screenshot of online video, *Hoa Cài Mái Tóc,* Performed by Quốc Anh *(Paris By Night, Volume 1)*, 1983. https://www.nhaccuatui.com/video/hoa-cai-mai-toc-quoc-anh.CrlXcsxxID.html.

business, Mum's relentless piecework prevented her from gaining the language skills to actually leave piecework. These constraints left Mum with few opportunities to engage with the culture she had resettled into. But compelled to understand the world around her, she started to write Vietnamese poetry whilst fulfilling orders on the sewing machine.

In this chapter, I focus on a period of economic and social transition for my family as part of our ongoing process of resettlement in Australia. Against the tumult of assimilation, I now recognise its impact on family connections, culture, and language. I am only now beginning to recognise the power of linguistic resistance and dialogue as I start the work of back-translating the work my elders (i.e., Mẹ ~ *Mum*, Ba ~ *Dad*, and Dì Nhung ~ *Aunty Nhung*). With the guidance of my Mum and Aunty, I learnt about the feminist and orthographic traditions of the Vietnamese folk script Chữ Nôm 𡨸喃 before being converted to a Romanised script. I will discuss how reconnecting with the canonical work of Vietnamese women poets and our encounter with Chris Xu's *Letters for Black Lives* opened up new dialogues about our diasporic role in the settler-colony.[3] These encounters within my family inadvertently echo Spivak's provocation of whether the "subaltern can

3
Chris Xu, *Letters for Black Lives*, Google.doc, July 26, 2016, https://docs.google.com/document/d/1qwon6Q-h3YC2n_vZGKIVxZxEhXG8ZQah4IVCMQzGaUk/edit.

speak" with nuance and clarity.[4] Through this process, both Mẹ and Dì Nhung were deeply aware of their own particular settler-colonial subjectivities as refugees and non-English speakers.

Responding to broader dialogues on decolonisation and reclaiming our "wild tongues," both Mẹ and Dì Nhung engaged me in intergenerational translations to foreground new settler-colonial perspectives. I experienced this firsthand through my Mum's poetry, and my Aunt's desire to say an Acknowledgement of Country on the lands of the Wurundjeri and Boon Wurrung in Vietnamese. For Dì Nhung, her decision to *not speak* and defer to English, the original language of the coloniser was a significant act of decolonial resistance and agency. Such minoritarian interventions demonstrate the capacity for the Mother tongue to trouble the politics of assimilation and domination that muzzles new immigrants from speaking openly about our complicity in the same systems of racism, misogyny, and prejudice that we are also subject to.

Beyond the compounding biases of external power, the Vietnamese community and the diasporic family itself should be re-examined. In the final chapter of this thesis, I again draw on the methodologies of translation, language-brokering, and dialogue to engage in collective self-reflection as we continue to make art as a family.

4 Spivak and Morris, "Can the Subaltern Speak?" 45-48.

Paris by Night, Bootleg by Day

The economic reforms of post-war Socialist Vietnam under the 1986 Đổi Mới ~ *New Change* (previously mentioned in the footnotes of Chapter 2) and the Hawke–Keating era of mass deregulation and globalisation of Australian industries (1983–1996) coincided with my family's resettlement from Vietnam to Australia. These overlapping economic upheavals, coupled with our suburban readjustment to a new way of life, found an unusual, but necessary comfort in the televisual productions of the Vietnamese diaspora. During this time, representations of Vietnameseness were few and far between. Save for the occasional foreign correspondence, travel documentaries, or the racist and sensationalised bulletins of Vietnamese gangs and drug dealers, or Hollywood Vietnam War movies, media representations of Vietnamese people were rare. I will contextualise the enduring temperament of this period, focusing on concepts of belonging and non-belonging within the shifting media language of pop culture, entertainment, and cinema.

I begin with the Vietnamese-language production *Paris by Night* (1983–ongoing) a diasporic variety show that provided an idiosyncratic and almost universal point of connection for many Vietnamese dispersed across the world. Instantly recognisable to many Vietnamese speakers, *Paris by Night* is produced by Thúy Nga Productions and

remains the most iconic of the various Vietnamese-language and exile-led musical variety shows since the 1980s.[5] With the colonial baggage of being founded in France, the producers of *Paris by Night* shrewdly moved the entire production company and enterprise to the major diasporic hub of Orange County, California, where many post-war Vietnamese refugees had established themselves a sizeable community and economy. Tina Nguyen and Stuart Cunningham describe how many Vietnamese refugees facing profound isolation in their various host countries of resettlement, working long hours in low-skilled and low-paying jobs, found a cheap and accessible cultural point of connection in these types of direct-to-video variety shows.[6] Idealising traditional Vietnamese culture and folk music, intercut with one-act plays, slapstick sketch shows, karaoke, and increasingly extravagant musical numbers, the variety show encapsulated the emotional spectrum of everyday struggles, their exuberances, and endless absurdities. Describing these diasporic productions as escapist and self-soothing, Ashley Carruthers reiterates the profound

5 Other production companies that are less well known include ASIA productions of *Đêm Saigon (Saigon Nights)*, and Mey productions of *Hollywood Nights, Khánh Hà*, and *Diễm Xưa*.

6 Tina Nguyen and Stuart Cunningham, "The Popular Media of the Vietnamese Diaspora," *Media International Australia* 91, no. 1 (May 1999): 131, https://doi:10.1177/1329878X9909100113.

effect of these Vietnamese productions for people dealing with the daily alienation of being dislocated and excluded from participation in their host societies as non-fluent English speakers.[7] Beyond nostalgic representations of Quê Hương ~ *the Mother-Land*, these shows deliberately appropriated and evolved with the music, fashion, and tastes of American mainstream culture but always through a distinctly Vietnamese lens. Drawing on pop-cultural references like Michael Jackson, hip hop, and K-pop, the aspirational and cultural mashups of these shows reflect the social and economic desires of their Vietnamese-speaking audiences.[8]

Re-encountering the scratched and pirated VHS clips of *Paris by Night* in the pub/karaoke/mash-up artworks *Working Class Man* (2009), *Like a Version* (2009), and *We Built This City* (2009) by artist Hoàng Trần Nguyễn at the exhibition *National Anthem* (2019) at Buxton Contemporary in Melbourne, I was reminded of how my own family, and many other Vietnamese people I know, had endlessly retaped and passed on these VHS recordings. The hand-to-hand trafficking of the latest *Paris by Night* releases established a transnational network of

7 Ashley Carruthers, "Saigon from the Diaspora," *Singapore Journal of Tropical Geography* 29, no. 1 (March 2008): 69, https://doi:10.1111/j.1467-9493.2008.00320.

8 Ashley Carruthers, "Rethinking the Vietnamese Media Relation," *Australian Journal of Communication* 22, no. 1 (1995): 54.

diasporic exchange and redistribution: with a suite of video compilations, cassette tapes, and karaoke CDs expressing the pop and televisual nostalgia of a lost homeland and the aspirational excesses of a new life, constantly passed from friend to neighbour, between the United States, Australia, Canada, and throughout our diasporic networks. Hoàng Trần's videos had the decayed and archival appearance of VHS piracy, accompanied by a soundtrack spliced with video clips and lyrics of classic Australian rock anthems like Jimmy Barnes' *Working Class Man* from the same era. The artist's youth, like my own, was simultaneously a mash-up of popular Australian and Vietnamese-American culture.

In our family textiles factory, a pirated soundtrack of veteran *Paris by Night* singers like Khánh Ly, Hương Lan, Phượng Mai, and Quốc Anh was played over the hum of knitting and sewing machines. Like so many other Vietnamese kids, I would outwardly reject these songs, and the campy sketches and cheesy glitz that accompanied the music. But despite my suburban snobbery, I still would prefer the over-the-top productions of *Paris by Night* to the patronising demonisation of Vietnamese people on Australian broadcast TV and cinema. For me, the chaotic variety show with its camp and casual misogyny was oftentimes cringeworthy, but always far more relatable as an unapologetic representation of diasporic Vietnameseness.

Away from the world of *Paris by Night*, popular audio-visual and screen representations of Vietnamese people at the time were either non-existent or plain offensive. When Vietnamese people did appear on screen, they were there to fulfil the racial and political prejudices and imperatives of the Australian mainstream. One of the most well-known representations of Vietnamese people within the canon of Australian cinema is Geoffrey Wright's film *Romper Stomper* (1993). Starring Russell Crowe and Jacqueline McKenzie, the film traces a fictional story of a neo-Nazi gang in the working-class suburbs of Melbourne. Following the dismantling of the White Australia Policy and its dreaded dictation tests, the arrival of Asian settlers setting up local businesses in Wright's film is disturbing and disruptive to the Anglo-European make-up of the inner suburbs.[9]

9
According to the National Museum of Australia, the White Australia Policy was enacted on December 23, 1901, implementing the Immigration Restriction Act and other bills. The Act gave immigration officers the power to make any non-European migrant sit a fifty-word dictation test. This was initially given in any European language, and after 1905 in any prescribed language. As the language chosen for the dictation test was at the discretion of the immigration officer, it was easy to ensure failure for any migrant deemed undesirable, either because of their country of origin, possible criminal record, medical history, or if they were considered to be morally unfit. Extremely small numbers of non-white migrants were ever allowed to pass. The test was administered 1359 times prior to

As described by Carruthers, the presence of Southeast Asian and Vietnamese refugees reignited fears that "white Australian identities would be swamped by the penetration of racial Others into their 'proper' territory … in working-class suburbs of Melbourne" and beyond.[10] The enduring representation of the Asian Other as weak, unheroic, voiceless, and inchoate victims, yet somehow a perennial threat to the supremacy of White Australia and its way of life (even when it is a dystopian skinhead way of life), remains a constant trope "reflected in the scene where vengeful Vietnamese youths storm a warehouse in which the neo-Nazi gang is holed up. Here, the image of tens of Vietnamese streaming into the building unmistakably conjures up the traditional paranoid image of the 'yellow hordes.'"[11]

1909, with only fifty-two people granted entry to Australia. After 1909, not a single migrant who sat the language test passed. Dismantling of the policy was begun by the Holt government in 1966, and the Whitlam government implemented the Racial Discrimination Act in 1975, which ended the racial barriers to immigration imposed by the White Australia Policy. "White Australia Policy," Defining Moments, National Museum of Australia, last accessed May 28, 2020, https://www.nma.gov.au/defining-moments/resources/white-australia-policy.

10 Ashley Carruthers, "Suburbanasia!: Ways of Reading Cultural Difference in the Mainstream Australian Media," *Media International Australia*, no. 77 (August 1995): 87.

11 Ibid., 90.

Inflicting cinematic violence against victimised Vietnamese-Australians, whilst simultaneously playing into the racial vilification of these people as faceless "hordes," Wright valorises the violent masculinity and individuality of the neo-Nazis against the faceless hordes of Vietnamese gangs.[12] Wright's film showed how Vietnamese people are perennially rendered as generic plot devices. Unlike the cheesy depictions of ourselves in *Paris by Night*, Vietnamese people are elsewhere consigned to a sequence of plot-points to drive the character development of the white protagonists. *Romper Stomper* dramatises Australia during a particular time. But even as it purports to critique one of the most overt and violent forms of racism—extremist Australian skinheads—the film nevertheless perpetuates a staunchly colonial racialisation of the Asian Other. These stereotypical representations of Vietnamese people as weak but ultimately an existential threat to Anglo-identity is described

12 What Ashley Carruthers describes as "Yellow Hordes," others have also talked about using its partner term "The Yellow Peril." Ien Ang writes that these racist terminologies in Australia have a particular inflection and urgency to the national colonial consciousness, which is geographically inflected by its condition of being an island-continent, isolated, and conceptually "empty" for Anglo-colonial settlers. Placing the anxiety of Asian invasion continually at the doorstep of the national psyche, Ang describes this as "Racial/Spatial" anxiety.

Carruthers, "*Suburbanasia!*, 87.
Ang, *On Not Speaking Chinese*, 11.

by Ross as "the historical and cultural unconsciousness of an anxious settler nation."[13] The settler psyche, it seems, is perennially most afraid of being overrun and resettled by a racial other.

Diasporic self-representation is uniformly curtailed in the settler-colony. Rendered as unimportant plot devices, Vietnamese presence in the media and on Australian movie screens regularly reinforce the racial biases and hierarchies of the settler-colony. However, even in the case of self-produced, self-styled, and self-distributed media, the representation of Vietnameseness by the Vietnamese diaspora through popular variety shows like *Paris By Night* are themselves largely preoccupied with only Vietnamese concerns. Limited to a romantic nostalgia for the homeland, or a capitalist fantasy that desires to be accepted and integrated into American popular culture, these Vietnamese songs, skits, and stories we tell ourselves are ultimately self-contained and narrow. These images of ourselves, although made for and by us, largely disregard our own racial biases, and rarely challenge the settler-colonial inheritance of the American/Australian dream, and so on. Ultimately not so different to *Romper Stomper*, *Paris By Night* ultimately upholds the structural biases of the settler-colony, albeit in a more self-focused way.

13 Ross, "Prolonged Symptoms of Cultural Anxiety," 86.

Both Jacqueline Lo and Bundjalung, Muruwari, and Kamilaroi artist Brian Martin have considered the structural logics of migrant-settler positionality. Lo looks to artists such as Jason Wing and John Young to open up the complex discourse of what it means to encounter Asian representations in Australia. Aboriginal-Asian artists like Biripi and Cantonese man Jason Wing have produced works that account for the cultural hybridity between their Aboriginality and Asian heritage in spite of the White Australia Policy. Lo notes how Asian-Aboriginal encounters had preceded the Anglo-colonisation of Australia. Young's work, on the other hand, straddles the profound modernity of globalised migrancy, homeland, and diasporic archives. Young combines photographic imagery, representational painting, and the gestures of modernist abstraction to express his cultural dislocation and hybridity.[14] Martin has expressed a hesitancy with the cosmopolitanism of diasporic self-representation. On Young, Martin writes:

> it may be argued that his work looks at the difficulty in defining cultural centeredness and connectedness, especially in relation to his own diaspora. But Young's work maintains a relationship with the symbolic and the imaginary that perpetuates a state of amnesia

> from within a representational mode … to the deferral of meaning that is offered in the postmodern space of this practice.[15]

Compared with Young, who appropriates western formalism to articulate his own diasporic dislocation, Martin is resolutely against the artist Imants Tillers and the institutions that have supported Tillers' appropriation of Aboriginal imagery and knowledge systems under the guise of post modernism:

> This challenge is what has informed the work of Tillers in reference to his own diaspora and position of being a migrant to Australia. The context of Australia's history is one that could rightfully be defined as one of theft, and Tillers' work which operates under the morphological banner of postmodernism and appropriation can be said to illustrate this notion. This is demonstrated by the elusive and contentious title of his exhibition *Not yet post-Aboriginal*.[16]

To Martin, the immigrant and diasporic experience does not exempt waves of recent settlers from facing the colonial predispositions of self-representation.

14 Ibid., 222-231.

15 Martin, "Immaterial Land and Indigenous Ideology," 60.

16 Ibid., 66.

Both Lo and Martin argue for a critical recognition that migrant settler-colonialism as part of the colonial project. This is the case for myself and my family. As we make ourselves present in the artworld, we must be alert to the specifics of diasporic settler-coloniality.

In this section, I will briefly return to the work *On the Border of Things* with Cậu Ái ~ *my Uncle Ái* or Nguyễn Công Ái. Gaining some media exposure in the broader Vietnamese community in Australia for our work, I go on to focus on my collaborations with Mẹ ~ *my Mum* or Nguyễn Thị Kim Dung and Dì Nhung ~ *my Aunty*, Nhung or Nguyễn Thị Kim Nhung. Their literary interventions have inevitably shaped my understanding of the Vietnamese community, as well as the role that language and critique play in implicating the family and our broader communities into decolonial discourse.

As I was working on the first performance of the project *On the Border of Things (Part 1)* with Cậu Ái, SBS Radio, a national multilingual broadcasting service, reached out for an interview: Thế hệ thứ Hai (Bài 131) James Nguyễn—từ dược sĩ đến nghệ sĩ[17] ~ *The second generation (Segment 131) James Nguyen—from pharmacist to artist.* On air, I discussed how I was trying to reconnect and rebuild my relationship with my Uncle. Delving into his seasonal work in fruit-picking and market gardening, I talked about how I had used art in the form of performance, video, interviews, etc., to engage and work with my Uncle.

17 Kim Anh, "Thế hệ thứ Hai (Bài 131) James Nguyễn-từ Dược sĩ đến Nghệ Sĩ," SBS Tiếng Việt, last modified April 16, 2018, https://www.sbs.com.au/language/vietnamese/audio/the-he-thu-hai-bai-131-james-nguyen-tu-duoc-si-den-nghe-si.

Addressing a national Vietnamese-speaking audience, my past as a pharmacist was noted by the interviewer. Contrasting this to my Uncle's seasonal work, my background in pharmacy and now a PhD candidate had a particular status when clarified to the listener. After being on air, my parents received numerous phone calls from friends congratulating them on my interview. The feedback was mostly about how listeners were impressed by my ability to speak and respond in basic conversational Vietnamese. Unlike many past interviewees from the 1.5th or 2nd generation, I addressed the Vietnamese-listening audience in a broken Vietnamese they could recognise and understand.

In her book *On Not Speaking Chinese*, Ang points to the impossibility of living between the Chinese and English language, and multiple the layers of domination, erasure, and social shaming that oscillate between neither being Chinese enough nor western enough.[18] To Ang, the linguistic impasse of not being able to speak Chinese yet presenting as ethnically Chinese is inherently complex. My experience of language dislocation differs slightly from Ang, as I was born and immersed in the Mother tongue of my birth yet primarily educated in English-speaking Australia (thank-you eight year Family Reunion Visa Process). My intermediate retention of the Mother tongue and fluency in the adopted tongue is often experienced by the 1.5th generation.

18 Ang, *On Not Speaking Chinese*, 24.

Thanh Hai Le Cao describes the condition of being part of the 1.5th generation as specific to overseas-born migrant children, including Vietnam-born children who migrated between the ages of five and twelve years. Like myself, these children had arrived in their host countries throughout the 1980s and 1990s.[19] This specificity disrupts the clean distinction between adults who leave versus children who are born and fully immersed in the dominant culture and language of the host country. Unlike Ang, I have ended up with the ability to be erratically bilingual, regularly code-switching between my Mother tongue and naturalised Australian-English. Despite retaining my birth language, my speech and literacy is suspended at the level of an eight-year-old, comically inflected by a distinctly out-dated Vietnamese inherited from my parents. As my Vietnam-based Cousins have relentlessly made fun of, I speak Vietnamese like I just stepped out of the 1970s. Fluency in my Mother tongue, however practiced, still betrays the peculiarities of stunted linguistic isolation and a residual infantilisation that is immediately recognised as odd to naturalised speakers, that is, the broken Vietnamese of a Việt Kiều ~ *an Overseas Vietnamese*. It is from this idiosyncratic position that I can only partially deploy what Anzaldúa calls a "wild tongue," helping my

19 Thanh Hai Le Cao, "Crafting a New Self in Diaspora: A Study of the 1.5 Generation of Vietnamese Americans," PhD diss., University of Kansas, 2013, 2-3.

family to mediate and broker the English language.[20] Anzaldúa emphasises how important it is to hold onto the bastardised languages and accents of whatever tongue you have, and not to be shamed into becoming estranged from this linguistic heritage. When I read this, I felt like Anzaldúa was directly addressing me—describing people raised or born into linguistic submission, educated by a dominant language, and instructed to feel shame every time I spoke imperfect English. Conversely, my clumsy wild tongue, when heard by Vietnamese listeners, is often tolerated with affection. Hearing the 1.5th or 2nd generation speak broken Vietnamese garners a sense of pride and recognition—akin to my own fondness for the kitschy *Paris by Night* VHS tapes playing in the background. Many who heard me on the radio asserted that I was a thằng trai ngoan ~ *a good son*, who had không quên tiếng của quê hương ~ *not forgotten the language of the homeland*.

Performing to meet the expectations of my elders, I was fully aware of the power and status of my bilingual, if somewhat clumsy tongue. Like the highlighting of my past career as a pharmacist, deploying my linguistic skills gave my views a level of legitimacy, and more importantly, an idealised image of a good Vietnamese migrant. My privilege as a young man, doing academic research, qualified in both fine arts and pharmacy, yet still capable of holding onto the Vietnamese language, was perceived

20 Anzaldúa, *Borderlands = La Frontera*, 33.

as respectable.[21] This clearly contrasted with other members of my family who spoke "bad" English and ultimately were perceived by their diasporic compatriots as linguistically inept, getting by on low-paid seasonal or piecework—that is, uncomfortably reflecting a non-model minority.

21
The social pressures and burdens placed on Asian people as model minorities is a form of contingent racism according to Kiang, et al. See Lisa Kiang, Virginia W. Huynh, Charissa S. L. Cheah, Yijie Wang, and Hirokazu Yoshikawa, "Moving Beyond the Model Minority," *Asian American Journal of Psychology* 8, no. 1 (2017): 2. https://doi:10.1037/aap0000070.

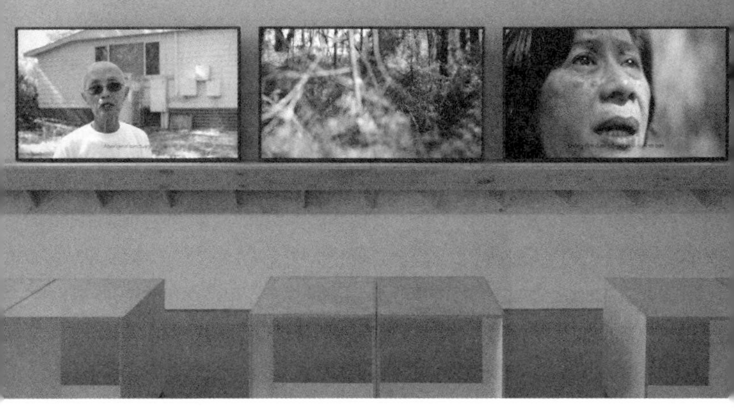

Fig. 27
Portion 53, installation view, *The National*, Museum of Contemporary Art, Australia, Sydney. Nguyễn Thị Kim Dung, Nguyễn Ngọc Cư, Kezia Yap, and James Nguyen, photographed by Zan Wimberley, 2019.

Later that year, SBS Radio approached me again for a follow-up interview during National Reconciliation Week. In a different segment *Hạt giống yêu thương (198) Nghệ sĩ James Nguyễn và nỗ lực hòa giải với người Thổ dân*[22] ~ *Seeds of Love (Segment 198) Artist James Nguyen on efforts to reconcile with Indigenous people.* In this program, we discussed my research project *Portion 53* (2019). This artwork was conceptualised as a series of moving-image recordings made with my family as we revisited the site of my Dad's first arrival in Australia at the Easthills Migrant Hostel. The work was intended to present refugee resettlement as part of a longer history of settler-colonisation in Australia. In a conversation about how Vietnamese people could engage with the broader national discourse of Indigenous Sovereignty and Land Rights, I spoke to the radio interviewer about reading Heather Goodall and Allison Cadzow's book *Rivers and Resilience: Aboriginal People on Sydney's Georges River* (2009). From their research, I learnt how the Easthills Migrant Hostel was built on land stolen from the D'harawal/Tharawal people in 1949 following

22 Emma Tran (Hương), "*Hạt Giống Yêu Thương (198) Nghệ Sĩ James Nguyễn và nỗ lực hòa giải với Người Thổ Dân,*" SBS Tiếng Việt, last modified June 1, 2018, https://www.sbs.com.au/language/vietnamese/audio/hat-giong-yeu-thuong-198-nghe-si-james-nguyen-va-no-luc-hoa-giai-voi-nguoi-tho-dan.

the Second World War.[23] The interview included, for the first time, a public broadcast of my Mum, Nguyễn Thị Kim Dung, reciting a Vietnamese poem she had written.

Detailing the twentieth-century removal of D'harawal/Tharawal families from their land, my Mum's poem told Vietnamese listeners the story of how the Australian military had expelled these families, much like how many post-war diasporic Vietnamese were expelled from *their* homelands following the fall of Điện Biênh Phủ and Saigon.[24] The conceit my Mum embedded in her poem was that this narrative of dispossession was written entirely in Vietnamese. People hearing the poem would likely assume that she was describing her own refugee narrative, presencing a testimony of her own displaced subjectivity. However, as a Vietnamese speaker, she was using poetry in an attempt to conceptualise the alienation of seeing her own complicity in Australia's ongoing settler-colonisation.

23 Heather Goodall and Allison Cadzow, *Rivers and Resilience: Aboriginal People on Sydney's Georges River* (Sydney: UNSW Press, 2009), 135–184.

24 The Battle of Điện Biênh Phủ in 1954 marked a significant turning point in Vietnamese history. It is perceived by many as the decolonial turning point, when the French Union's colonial Corps Expéditionnaire Français en Extrême-Orient was defeated by the Việt Minh. This event set off the mass migration and internal displacement of hundreds and thousands of Vietnamese. George F. Stanley, "Dien Bien Phu in Retrospect," *International Journal* 10, no. 1 (1954): 38. https://doi.org/10.2307/40198089.

Being granted asylum and refuge in Australia, her presence was ultimately a manifestation of continuing forms of Aboriginal erasure, in this case, D'harawal/Tharawal families being displaced from the surrounding "multicultural" suburbs of Sydney:

Lâu lắm không dám về nơi ấy
Vùng đất nhuộm giòng máu tổ tiên
Có giòng suối ngọt thơm ngon
Có muôn đồng cỏ hoa vàng thương thương
Có ngôi nhà nhỏ xinh xinh
Có cha có mẹ họ hàng gần xa
Có muôn vàn ký ức tuổi thơ
Hái hoa, đuổi bướm bên đường
Nâng niu mái tóc cha già sớm hôm

Rồi một chiều hoàng hôn tím đỏ
Một đoàn lính rầm rầm bước tới
Người xua người ra khỏi nơi chốn ấy
Bước đi ngoảnh lại muôn vàn xót xa
Kìa ngôi nhà lá đơn sơ
Hằng đêm yên giấc trong tay mẹ hiền

Khi xa rồi bỗng thì nơi ấy
Từng dãy nhà vòm mọc lên như nấm
Ngạo nghễ cười đè nát chòi xưa
Cảnh đã lạ, cả người cũng lạ
Họ đem vào nhiều người mới lạ
nói không cùng một ngôn ngữ

Sau những lúc tàn chinh chiến
Lính đi rồi người còn ở lại
Xây phố thị trên mảnh đất thân thương
Sầm uất lắm
Đông đúc lắm nhưng toàn người xứ lạ
...
33 năm sau ngày bạn rời nơi ấy
Chúng tôi được vào mảnh đất yêu thương của bạn
Không cầm được nỗi xót xa vì nghĩ tới bạn
Xin muôn đời tri ân tổ tiên mảnh đất thanh bình này
Xin đa tạ

Kim Dung người tỵ nạn CSVN

So long since, but not daring to return,
A place dyed by the bloodlines of ancestors.
A sweet river, fragrant water,
Fields of green and yellow blooms,
A humble home
A father, mother
Relations near and far.
These souvenirs of a childhood—
Picking flowers, chasing butterflies
Plucking greying hairs in the early afternoon.

One late evening, a dusky purple red.
A squadron of soldiers did advance
As one was pushed the other shoved.
Reeling from this place, this distance aches,
A simple home displaced.
Waiting each night to rest in a mother's arms.

How easy is it then, to be erased?
As row upon row of corrugated huts,
sprout up like mushrooms.
A resounding laughter, our homes are lost
In their place, a strange and brand-new vista.
Stranger still, the people
Speaking uncommon tongues.
The soldiers moved on once war was quelled.
Leaving it for the newcomers
arriving in waves to build and industrialise,
A new settlement filled
with crowds of elsewhere people.

…

33 years since your removal,
My family came,
housed on this patch, of your beloved soil.
I don't have to think so far, to feel a loss,
and think how my new life, owes much to your
ancestors
Granted a peaceful refuge here.
My gratitude.

Kim Dung Nguyễn a refugee from the Socialist Republic of Vietnam
Translation with James Nguyen

As curator Abigail Moncrieff argues in *The National* exhibition catalogue, my Mum's poem articulated "a sequence of displacements and erasures, enacting a kind of territorial tabula rasa in which prior histories and settlements are wiped away."[25] The poem appeals to the Vietnamese listener that we and other new settlers should not merely adopt the colonial tabula rasa of resettlement to conveniently ignore the Indigenous dispossessions of our host country:

> Cảnh đã lạ, cả người cũng lạ
> Họ đem vào nhiều người mới lạ
> nói không cùng một ngôn ngữ

> *a strange and brand-new vista.*
> *Stranger still, the people*
> *Speaking uncommon tongues*

The multicultural narrative of suburban Sydney becomes a continuous set of erasures by toàn người xứ lạ ~ *elsewhere people*. The poem compresses time, describing ageing and losing one's memory. There is a narrative pivot at a mere 33 năm sau ngày bạn rời nơi ấy ~ *years since your removal*. Transient reveries of childhood: hái hoa ~ *picking flowers* and đuổi bướm ~ *chasing butterflies*, quickly turns to Nâng niu mái tóc cha già sớm hôm ~ *Plucking grey hairs in the early*

25 Abigail Moncrieff, "James Nguyen," in *The National 2019 : New Australian Art*, ed. Genevieve O'Callaghan and Faith Chisholm (Sydney: Art Gallery of New South Wales, Carriageworks, Museum of Contemporary Art Australia, 2019), 122.

afternoon, when the saprophytic decomposition of bodies and buildings mọc lên như nấm ~ *sprout up like mushrooms*. The speed at which the landscape changes outlines the abruptness of colonisation and erasure. My Mum speaks of the daily jostling, sầm uất lắm ~ *the very busy lives* of new migrants. Người xua người ~ *People push and shove* to resettle and create a kind of totalising amnesia in the suburbs. Describing a numbness from the personal trauma of losing your home, one that conveniently distances you from those who themselves were rời nơi ấy ~ *severed from this place*, making way for your arrival.

My Mum received some indirect negative responses after her poem was aired on Vietnamese national radio. A male family friend relayed his opinion of Mum's work to my Aunty. He said, "why should she, a pieceworker, be writing any poetry?" While I was a "thằng tiến sĩ" ~ *a PhD scholar,* my Mum was simply "ới dơi ơi, bà ấy mà …" ~ *oh, that woman.*[26] Her words on settler-colonialism were perceived as a piece of incoherent amateur babbling to be dismissed because they weren't uttered by a credible academic like myself. By now, my Mum's artistic and intellectual capacity had been called into question by both this family friend, and, indirectly, by the university's HREC—which assumed that her low-English proficiency was an indicator of intellectual vulnerability which required special institutional attention. Not speaking good English,

26 This person had assumed that I had completed my PhD.

not holding an Australian tertiary degree, and, worse still, continuing to do low-paid piecework, Nguyễn Thị Kim Dung was transgressing and overstepping her immigrant station as a low-skilled, non-fluent English speaker, and Mother.[27]

Instead of defending my Mum, my Dad began to reflect similar sentiments to those of our male family friend. He mentioned that her words were lộn xộn ~ *haphazard* and không theo hình thước thơ ~ *not following any conventional poetry*. Questioning the legitimacy of my Mum's work made it especially hard for our family to continue discussions concerning the political provocations of her poem. When we did return to Easthills to record and film the work *Portion 53* in early 2019, we had a difficult time creating meaningful dialogue as individuals responding to an already troubled site. Unlike most projects in the past where my family readily conversed and were engaged in productive dialogue together, there emerged a deliberate aesthetic of separation and estrangement within the work itself.

What we ended up making together was a three-channel triptych. The first screen is a medium-shot portrait and monologue. My Dad directly addresses and speaks to the camera in English (subtitles cycling between English and Vietnamese). Speaking in front of the only building left standing from the Easthills Migrant Hostel, he recounts

27 My Mother Nguyễn Thị Kim Dung was a lecturer in Early Childhood Education at Truòng Đại Học Đà Lạt ~ *the University of Dalat* in Vietnam before she came to Australia.

his arrival at this very particular hostel and how everything had changed over time. He also refers to how he had "heard about the Aboriginal" families and military presence before the Migrant Hostel was built.

In contrast to this, the third screen is a close-up of my Mum looking off-camera into the distance. She recites her poem in Vietnamese (subtitles cycling between Vietnamese and English). The focus is on her voice to camera. There is no direct eye contact, and the displacement of her gaze off-screen suggests internal thought and reflection, rather than a direct address.

The second screen, positioned between my parents, contains my own observations of the landscape. Focussed on my manual and tactile activation of detritus found onsite. My hands pick-up, tap, and rub together pieces of polystyrene among a verdant background of invasive asparagus weed.

A soundtrack created from site-visits and recordings made by me and my friend, Malaysian-Australian artist Kezia Yap, plays across the three channels. The inescapable drone of cicadas in high summer and scraping polystyrene become almost unbearable. The dissonances drawn from the site foreground the individual conflicts and disagreements between my Dad, my Mum, and myself, betraying the real-life complexity of diasporic contestations and family disagreements. These conflicts are as much present in our proximity when working together, but also our distance due to differences of opinion.

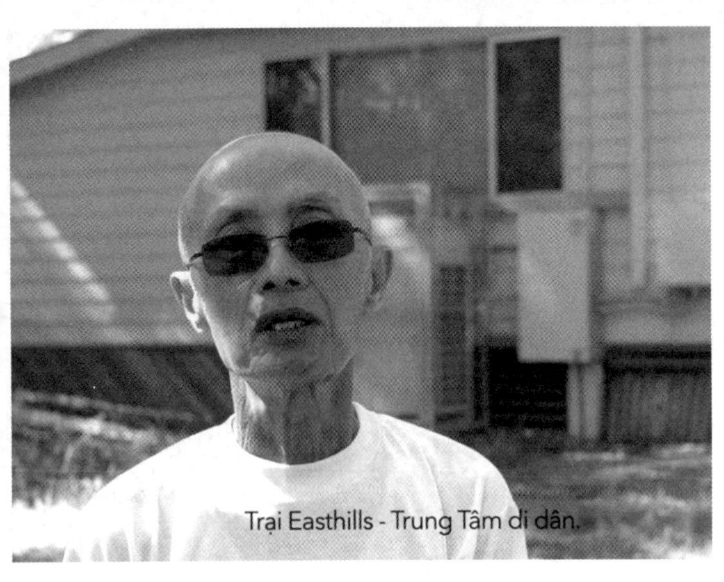

Fig. 28
Channel 1, Screenshot of Dad talking to camera, subtitles in Vietnamese, *Portion 53*, installation view, *The National*, Museum of Contemporary Art, Australia, Sydney. Nguyễn Thị Kim Dung, Nguyễn Ngọc Cư, Kezia Yap, and James Nguyen, 2019.

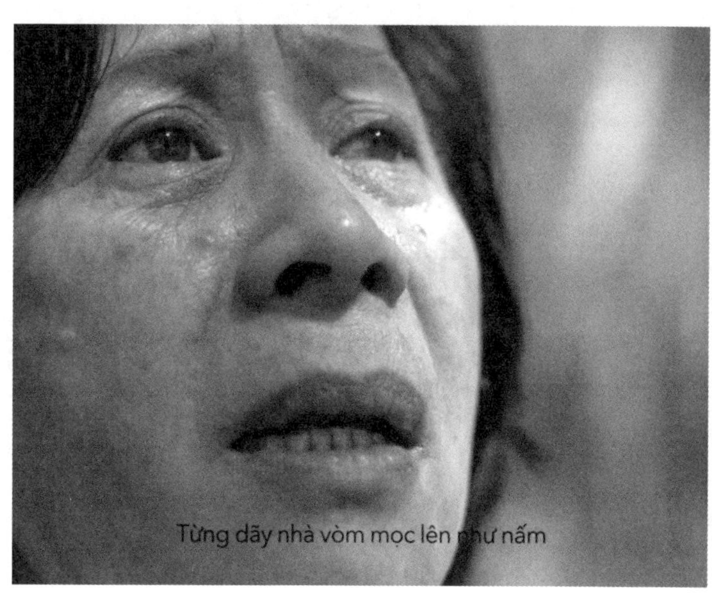

Fig. 29
Channel 3, Screenshot of Mum reciting poetry, subtitles in Vietnamese, *Portion 53*, installation view, *The National*, Museum of Contemporary Art, Australia, Sydney. Nguyễn Thị Kim Dung, Nguyễn Ngọc Cư, Kezia Yap, and James Nguyen, 2019.

My Dad's criticism and *othering* of my Mum's poetry continued to be particularly troubling.[28] In *Transnationalising Vietnam*, Kieu-Linh Caroline Valverde describes how the Vietnamese community in the United States is subject to a dual domination of racial and cultural exclusion from both the United States, and the extraterritorial Socialist government in Vietnam. Extrapolating from these pressures, the subtle hostilities towards my Mother by Vietnamese men around her, including my Dad, exerted a *triple* domination. The tension between my Dad and his male friends, and the women in my family (my Mum and Aunt), actually affected our ability to work and communicate easily with each other. The gendered divisions and hierarchy in the Vietnamese-Australian community was apparent in my own family and our network of friends and neighbours. Carruthers describes the dominant Việt Kiều Yêu Nước ~ *Patriotic Overseas Vietnamese* in Australia as being vocally intolerant of any dissenting voices that challenge their normative and regularly misogynist paradigms of cultural compliance.[29]

28
As described by Debra Bergoffen and Megan Burke: Simone De Beauvoir in *The Second Sex* is driven by the concept of gendered *Othering*, which has been integral to discourse on colonised and marginalised people like the elderly, etc. Exploitation is premised on placing man as the standard or absolute subject, and the Other as a non-essential and inferior counterpart. See Debra Bergoffen and Megan Burke, "Simone de Beauvoir," *The Stanford Encyclopedia of Philosophy*, ed. Edward N. Zalta (Summer 2020 Edition), https://plato.stanford.edu/archives/sum2020/entries/beauvoir/.

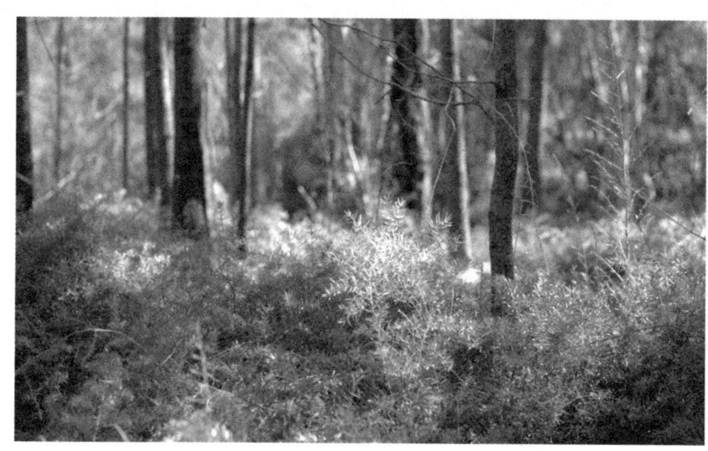

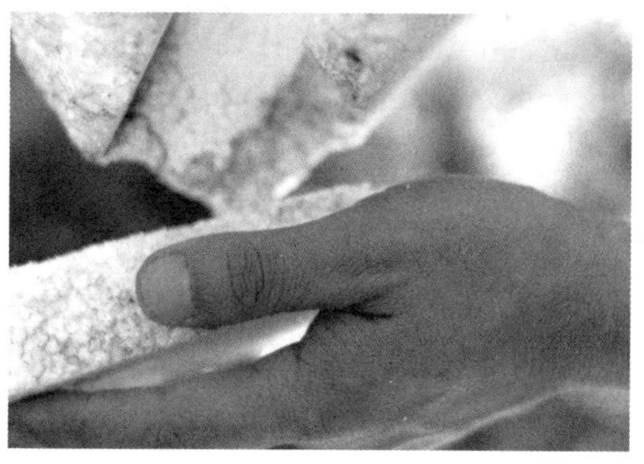

Fig. 30
Channel 2, Screenshot of asparagus weed growing between Casuarina trees, subtitles in Vietnamese, *Portion 53,* installation view, *The National*, Museum of Contemporary Art, Australia, Sydney. Nguyễn Thị Kim Dung, Nguyễn Ngọc Cư, Kezia Yap, and James Nguyen, 2019.

Fig. 31
Channel 2, Screenshot, rubbing polystyrene together, *Portion 53,* installation view, *The National*, Museum of Contemporary Art, Australia, Sydney. Nguyễn Thị Kim Dung, Nguyễn Ngọc Cư, Kezia Yap, and James Nguyen, 2019.

The policing and undermining of my Mother as merely a pieceworker, sought to moderate her according to their conventional gender norms and expectations.[30] It appears that these heterogenous forms of domination, shaped by misogyny and normative compliance, continue to regulate the conditions for when and how Vietnamese women are permitted to speak in their own communities and families. Cherríe Moraga's critique of intersectional sexism describes the hierarchy of these community-based prejudices. These diasporic interactions are shaped by complex forms of oppression which are multi-layered, cascading, and enforced in ways that are pervasive, but not always easily discernible.[31] Ironically, by provoking my Dad and the ire of a number of men around her, my Mum's poem revealed a latent sexism. Talking with my Mum, she describes how these forms of intersectional oppressions, although real, did not stop her from writing poems whilst doing piecework. The industrial sewing

29 Ashley Carruthers, "National Multiculturalism, Transnational Identities," *Journal of Intercultural Studies: Rethinking Migration and Diversity in Australia* 34, no. 2 (April 2013): 214-28, https://doi:10.1080/07256868.2013.781984.

30 Jessica Schiffman, Laura O'Toole, Margie Edwards, and Margie L. Kiter Edwards (eds), *Gender Violence: Interdisciplinary Perspectives* (New York: New York University Press, 2007), 39.

31 Cherríe Moraga, "La Guerra," in *This Bridge Called My Back: Writings by Radical Women of Color*, ed. Cherríe Moraga and Gloria Anzaldúa (New York: Kitchen Table Press, 1983), 27-34.

machine that kept her from learning English and cut short her career ambitions was also a desk for her writing. Invisible and disregarded by everyone around her as a mere pieceworker, she is inevitably left to her own devices. When the kids had been put to bed, Nguyễn Thị Kim Dung would stay up to read aloud her drafts, reshaping, and crafting notes she had jotted down on scraps of pattern-making paper. As I slept, I had no idea that she was writing or madly sewing to meet the next bulk delivery of garments. The estrangements imposed on my Mum had overtime motivated her to start writing as a break from the drudgery of piecework. As she later told me, invisibility meant she could avoid the distraction of friends and gossip—whereas she could simply practice her craft. She expressed some of these sentiments in a poem titled "Hao Dại Với Thằng Ngốc" ~ *Wild Flowers and the Fool.* This short poem describes how Đem hao dại vào nhà và nó sẽ héo ~ *bringing wild flowers into the house and they will wilt.* These undomesticated blooms are beautiful because of the harsh conditions they were used to, these wild flowers only thrive and are most beautiful when left alone.

... nào yêu

... ý nghĩa ở trẻ

... đây đủ không? ⓒ

... cảm thấy yêu ①

... nhưng người nuôi mới

... ăn [illegible]

... phải [illegible] thì lại

xem cảm nhận đó ăn

của trẻ đối & lúc nào có [illegible]

nhận khi ② ③

[illegible], thì cho đến khi chào bay

đi và cảm nhận

và đồng thời để nghiên cứu

[illegible] khi nó thì đói [illegible] thế

cảm nhận ra sao?

đơn ra . ① bảo đảm

may ra là phải người nuôi những

[illegible] đầy đủ không? ④ mà sao

còn vậy?

Có hay quá! cái lọ gì của NG [illegible] khử

[illegible] khởi nhé, [illegible] còn phải suy nghĩ

+ theo tinh thần của các bạn ko thấy

ở chỉ các cụ thích "dông dài", mà các bà mẹ

mới cũng đang "dông dài"!

cả các bà mẹ mới cũng thích dông dài nữa

để stress [illegible] sẽ

mới [illegible] điều biết cần điều dinh phục [illegible]

bao giờ — có vẻ đúng rồi

4.15 PM

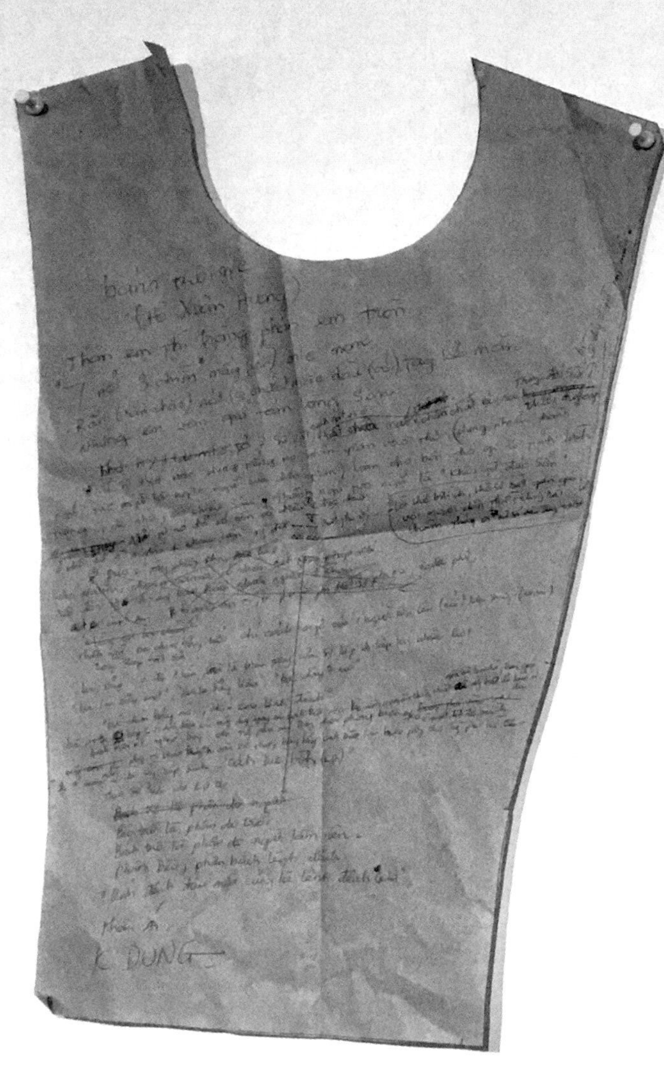
K. DUNG

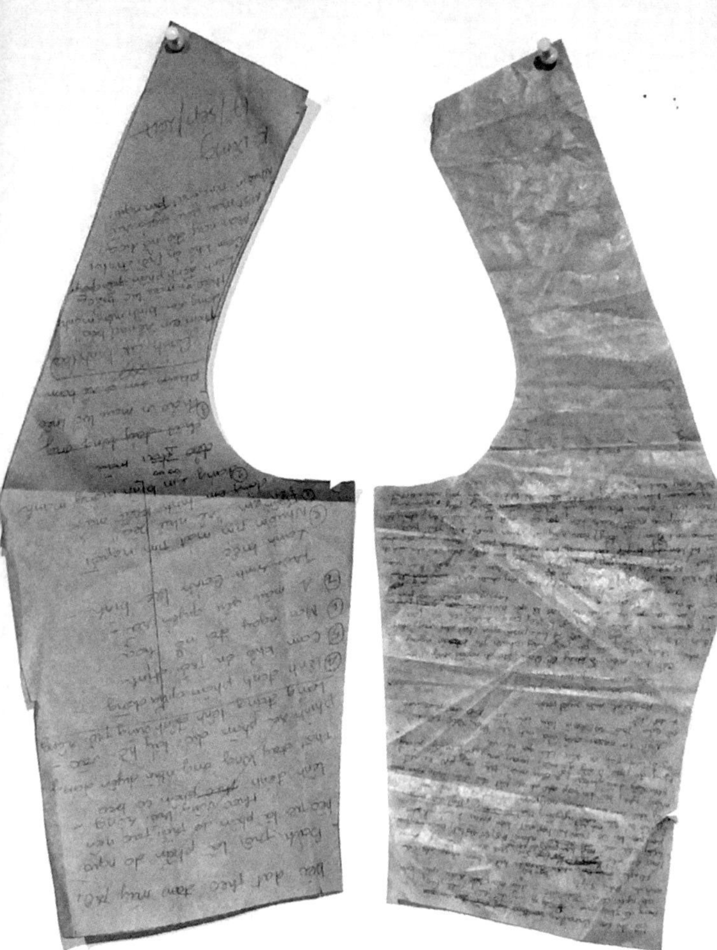

43 ENSUA
4 bịch
3 mũ – 1 lưỡi trai 2 lớp
1 đôi giày ũng
1 cái áo gai con koala
trong túi có 2 đôi vớ
1 cái đồ chơi xe sẵn có 2
cục tẩy mini cỡ lg –
thịt chiết 1 tuần 2
3 hộp
2 xà bông DOSE (5 cái)
Face body cho hồng
pack 5
2 kem dưỡng này
2 kho mây
bàn chải đánh răng.
PP127510
1 tuýp cho hồng
1 hộp lớn cho chính
kho mắt chính + tuần 1
SELF

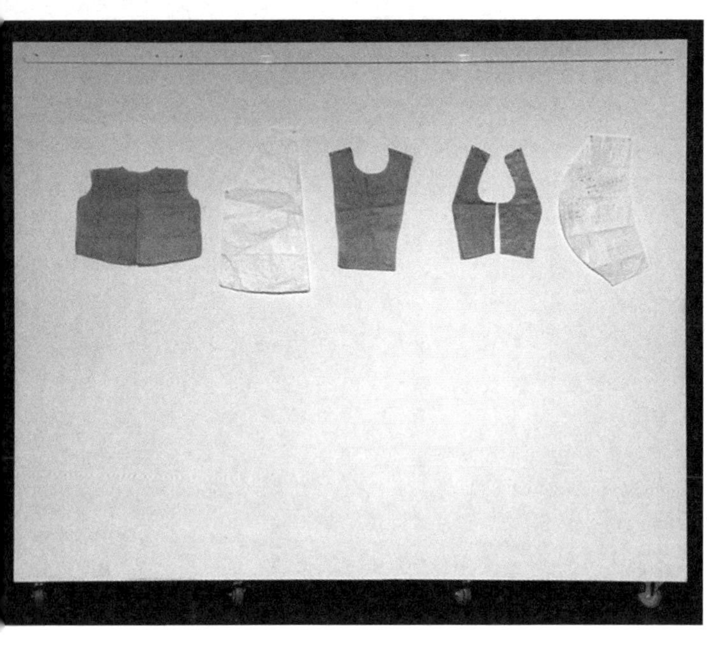

Figs 32-33 (pp. 267-270)
Photograph (detail) of an example of *Draft Poetry and Notes* by Nguyễn Thị Kim Dung, written on a piece of pattern-making paper, 2000s-ongoing.

Fig. 34
Photograph, examples of wall mounted *Draft Poetry and Notes* by Nguyễn Thị Kim Dung, written on pieces of pattern making paper, 2000s-ongoing.

Reflecting on these gendered estrangements, I could not help but recall how Vietnamese-Australian artist Mai Nguyễn-Long was treated by members of the Vietnamese community at the Casula Powerhouse in 2006. Cheerfully titled *I Love Phở*, her exhibition was a tongue-in-cheek and probably ill-judged word play with the Vietnamese beef noodle soup, Phở. The violent reaction to her work *Phở Dogs* was swift and brutal. Around that time, the Vietnamese community was still raw from the 2004 SBS Television protests, seeking to block the broadcasting of content produced by the Socialist Republic of Vietnam on Australian TV.[32] Added to this, the sensational news of Australia's first political assassination.[33]

32 Claiming "to better serve the needs of the Vietnamese community in Australia," SBS Television decided to broadcast Vietnamese-language programs direct from Vietnam in 2004. With little consultation, SBS Television failed to comprehend the political temperament of the Australian Vietnamese community. Older generations who could recall the trauma of fleeing their homeland mobilised with the Vietnamese Community in Australia (VCA) to organise a vocal grass-roots campaign to block these daily news broadcasts. Carruthers, "National Multiculturalism, Transnational Identities," 218.

33 Gill H. Boehringer, "Who Killed John Newman?" *Alternative Law Journal* 29, no. 3 (June 2004): 145–46, http://doi:10.1177/1037969X0402900309.

Aspiring Vietnamese politician and club owner Phương Cảnh Ngô was finally charged in 2001 of murdering (by joint enterprise) Labor politician John Newman back in 1994. Against this context of anxiety and hyper-defensive zeal, the Vietnamese community in Australia did not take well to Mai Nguyễn-Long's creative wordplay. Juxtaposing the national cuisine Phở with the loaded symbolism of a pack of papier-mâché dogs was profoundly offensive to many in the community. Calling someone con chó ~ *a dog* and the compounding racist trope of Vietnamese people eating dogs was seen as perpetuating a stereotype. Consistent with the titling of this thesis as Chó Bò, an approximate Vietnamese homonym for ~ *trouble,* Nguyễn-Long's choice of cultural imagery, including painting contested national flags onto her *Phở Dogs*, was perceived as triggering and troublesome.[34]

Nguyễn-Long consequently faced a series of death threats, along with overtly sexist vilification and public intimidation as her exhibition toured Australia. These events made visible the vitriol, latent misogyny, and political rawness within the Vietnamese community. In fear for her own safety, Nguyễn-Long self-censored her work, covering her *Phở Dogs* with a black cloth. Nguyễn-Long later wrote in 2008:

> It is with great sadness that I have decided to cover the entire installation of *Phở Dogs* with a black sheet, as if a shrouding,

> a mourning, a death-ness, a frustrated silence with mysterious and alien bumps. This is a gesture to acknowledge the suffering of the Vietnamese Community concerned, and at the same time the suffering of all peoples who cannot speak out in the world, and who are censored in their own societies.[35]

Nguyễn-Long therefore acknowledges the traumas and "bumps" of the Vietnamese diaspora, using the blanket of censorship as a metaphor to articulate her encounter with the triple domination and troubles of her own community.

34
These flags included the US star-spangled banner, with the yellow, three-striped flag of the Former Democratic South, and the official yellow star and red flag of the Socialist Republic of Vietnam.

35
Mai Nguyễn-Long quoted in Hao Pham, "Pho Dog Fuss," *Peril Magazine*, January 11, 2009, https://peril.com.au/back-editions/edition06/pho-dog-fuss/.

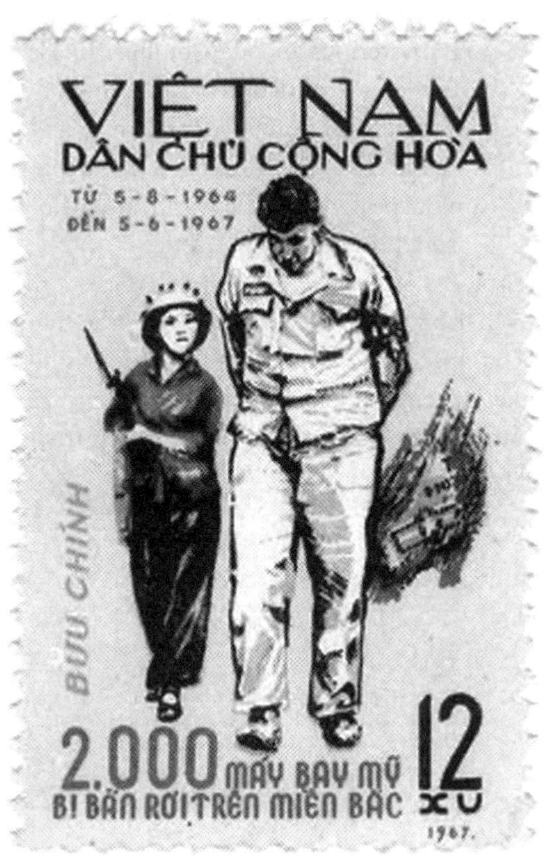

Fig. 35
O du kích nhỏ, a Socialist Republic of Việt Nam Stamp, depicting a photograph taken of North Vietnamese guerrilla Kim Lai capturing helicopter mechanic William Andrew Robinson, held for seven years as a POW in North Vietnam in 1973. This popular image often accompanied the poem above in Vietnamese primary school books during the 1980s.

Remembering these events, I asked my Aunty about what the male family friend had told her about my Mum, and how she personally felt about these patronising responses to my Mum's poetry. In addition to this, I wanted to know how these compounding cultural dismissals had affected their lives as immigrant women.

Instead of answering these prosaic questions, Dì Nhung ~ *Aunty Nhung* curtly recited a poem to me, one I had never heard before. She told me to record it on my phone, and read up on Bà Hồ Xuân Hương and Bà Huyện Thanh Quan:

Bước tới đèo ngang bóng xế tà
Cỏ cây che đá lá chen hoa
Lom khom dưới núi điều vài chú
Lác đác bên sông chợ mấy nhà
Nhớ nước đau lòng con quốc quốc *[5]
Thương nhà mỏi miệng cái gia gia *[6]
Dừng chân đứng lại trời non nước
Một mảnh tình riêng ta với ta

Listening back to the recording of my Aunty reciting this poem, I transcribed and roughly translated it into English:

Stepping onto a mountain pass, a shadowy sunset
Grass covering stones, leaves pushing
against flowers
Hunched down low below the mountain,
a few boys
Lapping at the riverbank, a market with so
few homes
Yearning for water as the con quốc quốc *bird*[36]
Homesickness, the mouth aches with outpouring
cái gia gia
Stop your step to find the sky full of fresh water
This fragment of love solely for me, for myself.

I noticed how this, and my Mum's poem for *Portion 53*, similarly opens up with the picturesque. They share similar scenes of "picking flowers, chasing butterflies," and "humble homes," as a loneliness creeps into the "evening." Various motifs imply the

36
The call of con quốc quốc ~ *the White Breasted Waterhen (Amaurornis phoenicurus)*, which is a water bird endemic to India and Southeast Asia. In this poem, its call is a phonetic call for home and nation (quốc gia) and a reference to agricultural practices in tilling the soil with a *hoe*-in reference to its bill, which probes and digs up insects in the marshes (quốc đất). The link below is the quốc quốc call of the bird: https://upload.wikimedia.org/wikipedia/commons/b/b5/AmaurornisPhoenicurusCall.ogg.

sadness of being separated from home. In this poem, the sunset is described as a bóng ~ *shadow*, that xế tà ~ *tears at the hem of your clothes*. Motherhood, childbirth, and child-rearing are equated with the wrapping and tearing of cloth and the torn shadows at sunset. Young boys and men are hunched and buried under the mountain; the markets lay bare. The mountain pass is therefore a moment of reflection on a long journey. Either returning to a home that is no longer there, or leaving home for some other place, is never clarified. Recalling my Mum's poem, home is a place where you không dám về nơi ấy ~ *do not dare return*. Ideas of nationhood and belonging reverberate through both poems. There is a recurring motif of nước *(shorthand for water, country, and nation)*. In this poem, the onomatopoeic combination of *con quốc quốc* [*5] with *cái gia gia*[*6] becomes a conflation con-cái ~ *offspring*, and quốc-gia ~ *the nation*.

Entering this Vietnamese transcription into Google confirmed that the poem was written by Bà Huyện Thanh Quan (1805–1848). She followed a generation of women poets led by Bà Hồ Xuân Hương. These women and many others wrote poetry during times of profound conflict and political upheaval in Vietnam. Both playing a part in the linguistic renaissance of the local folk-script Chữ Nôm 𡨸喃. This preceded the Vietnamese language being deemed the langue vulgaire by French colonists and missionaries who systematically Romanised the entire script in the 1890s.[37] The sorrow and loneliness of women living through exile, displacement, and

loss is inevitably bound to the loss of their children, families, and homelands. However, what concludes Bà Huyện Thanh Quan's journey along the mountain pass, is that, despite everything around her, the thing that remains for her is mảnh tình ~ *a fragment of love*: that is, the fragments of poetry that remains riêng ta với ta ~ *solely for me, for myself*.

As I read about these canonical poets, I realised how the Vietnamese linguistic renaissance venerated both the poetry of men *and* women. During this crucial period, Bà Hồ Xuân Hương (1772–1822), often referred to as the Grandmother of Vietnamese poetry, wrote numerous well-known four- to eight-line quatrains which made her famous. The Grandfather of Vietnamese poetry, Ông Nguyễn Du (1765–1820), by contrast wrote a 3254-line epic titled *Truyện Kiều ~ Tale of Kieu*. Both writing poetry in the distinctive and renewed Chữ Nôm 𡨸喃, Bà Hồ Xuân Hương and Ông Nguyễn Du made popular the orthographic transition of Vietnamese writing from the imperial Han Confucian Chinese script of administration—Chữ Nho 字儒. Their poetry ultimately shaped a new national vernacular, integrating both their individual and contrasting styles into the oral language of Vietnamese people to this day. What appealed to both non-literate and literate Vietnamese were the often sexually charged

37
Dinh-Hoa Nguyen, *Vietnamese Lexicography*, 1987 (non-journaled text)(ERIC Number: ED302082, https://primoa.library.unsw.edu.au/permalink/f/11jha62/TN_eric_sED302082).

and scathing critique of authority in the works of these foundational poets. Poetry specialist and translator John Balaban notes that the Bà Hồ Xuân Hương canon, with its sonnet-like Lu-Shih style structure, was no less popular than Ông Nguyễn Du. Despite the patriarchal Confucian society around her, Bà Hồ Xuân Hương and other women took on great personal risk[38] to openly criticise the domination of their bodies and the decimation of their homelands by incompetent male authority figures around them.[39] The linguistic wordplay and imagery from this period are so steeped in Vietnamese oral culture that I could recognise and appreciate how it was echoed in Nguyễn Thị Kim Dung work.[40] As with the description for nhà thơ ~ *a house of letters, or a poet*, she too belonged to a canon, a *house*, and a tradition of Vietnamese feminist poetry.

By not giving me a direct answer to how the patriarchy had affected the lives of Vietnamese women, my Aunty offered instead a double lesson in Vietnamese poetry. One that can be traced back to the orthographic renaissance of our foundational Chữ Nôm 㚱喃 script. Having to translate Bà Huyện Thanh Quan's poem, and learning about the canonical

38
Ibid., 5.
39
Donna Seaman, "A Conversation with John Balaban," *Triquarterly* 114 (Fall 2002): 153.
40
John Balaban, "About the Poet: Ho Xuan Huong," *The American Poetry Review* 29, no. 5 (September 2000): 4-6.

influence of Bà Hồ Xuân Hương on the Vietnamese language, my Aunty made me realise how my own lack of awareness was symptomatic of the routine dismissal and diasporic marginalisation of women's work. As described in my Mum's poem, the daily struggles of new immigrants, Người xua người ~ *the push and shove of people*, is not simply the difficult jostlings of resettlement. Noting the subtle aural similarity to Người xưa người ~ *the past/out-dated/obsolete disconnect between people,* my Mum makes clear the profound estrangement and separations from cultural literacy. Perhaps, one of the most brutal forms of violence that can be inflicted on displaced peoples is the stripping away of their language and everything that is intrinsically connected to the Mother tongue. Immersed in the canon of Anglo-European literary traditions from the Australian education system, my so-called literacy is perhaps a profoundly narrow and western one. Beyond basic language-brokering for my family, being estranged from the literary traditions and rich linguistic wealth of Vietnamese meant that my literary canon, history, and psyche has never been entirely mine. Resettlement and assimilation have not only caused me to be rời nơi ấy ~ *severed from* my birthplace, but has also prevented me from appreciating the true depth of my literary and linguistic inheritance. Ignorant of the feminist traditions of Vietnamese poetry, my own linguistic failure could not recognise the true and intrinsic value of the very people and linguistic traditions immediately around me.

My Mum, however, reminded me to refrain from holding on to hypothetical and romantic notions of an alternative literary immersion. The traditions that she and my Aunty had been raised in were a product of a particular time and political period. My own Vietnamese literary memory was profoundly different to theirs. What had I retained from the brief primary school years of a post-war Vietnam? Vividly, I started to recall and recite without hesitation Tố Hữu's 1967 state endorsed poem:

> *O du kích nh*ỏ giương cao súng,
> Thằng Mỹ lênh khênh bước cúi đầu.
> Ra thế! To gan hơn béo bụng.
> Anh hùng đâu cứ phải *mày râu!*

> *O little Guerrilla, raise up her gun,*
> *The American loser hangs his head.*
> *And So! Your fearless liver, bigger than*
> *his fat stomach.*
> *Heroes do not need to trim their beards.*

The complex reminders of the disruptions of war, coupled with the disruptions of education and diasporic estrangement from the literary traditions of the Mother tongue, points to the impossible bind of linguistic displacement. What I have inherited as a 1.5 Vietnamese expat has its particular idiosyncrasies and inflections. This is something I am only now recognising because of these interactions with my family.

In continuing to speak and write her poetry in Vietnamese, my Mum's refusal to engage with the broader expectation of linguistic assimilation and learning good English can be further understood in terms of Anzaldúa's work. Refusing to be humiliated by not speaking the dominant tongue, my Mum kept writing poetry in Vietnamese at night as she did piecework on the sewing machine. Drawing directly from Anzaldúa, Mignolo describes how people who speak English as a second language have to ultimately accept their apparent linguistic inferiority—foregoing the shame of their "wild tongue" to comply with the norms that continuously humiliate them.[41] For Mignolo, the colonial recruitment of colonised subjects has to convince them of their linguistic subservience; where "your inferiority is a fiction created to dominate you."[42] This is the inferiority of a "vulgar tongue" subjected to an "official tongue" as discussed in Chapter 1, established in academia and elsewhere as the literary dominance and superiority of Romance and Latin languages above others. Anzaldúa, however, is not satisfied with simply recognising the impacts of

41
Walter D. Mignolo, "Geopolitics of Sensing and Knowing: On (de)coloniality, Border Thinking, and Epistemic Disobedience," *Postcolonial Studies* 14, no. 3 (September 2011): 275. https://doi:10.1080/13688790.2011.613105.

42
Ibid., 276.

linguistic oppression. She insists that we act on the urge to speak aloud, to be troublesome, to overstep, and transgress the constraint of domination: "I will no longer be made to feel ashamed of existing. I will have my voice: Indian, Spanish, white. I will have my serpent's tongue—my woman's voice, my sexual voice, my poet's voice. I will overcome the tradition of silence."[43] Epistemic disobedience to speaks one's own language is a refusal to silence, a refusal of compliance and perceived incoherence. To Anzaldúa, a "wild tongue" divulges the many forms of structural oppression deep in colonialism and the patriarchy. To speak a wild tongue is to engage in decolonial feminism.[44] María Lugones notes that coloniality seeks to silence the intersectionality of both race *and* gender. The persistent attempts at colonising immigrant women and their speech are again always present but can never be totalising—even when their language is physically ripped out of their mouths. Like Anzaldúa, Lugones points out the importance of refusal and survival as having been "continually resisted and being resisted today."[45] Here, to enact decolonial continuity is to face a multitude of cascading dominations. It is the capacity to consistently resist the structural, gendered, and diasporic marginalisation as you are doing piecework, deftly overlocking pockets and collars to fulfil yet another garment order.

Exhibited as part of *The National 2019* exhibition, a biannual exhibition of contemporary Australian art practice held across three major

Sydney institutions—MCA, Carriageworks, and the Art Gallery of New South Wales—my Mum's poem in the installation for *Portion 53* found particular resonance with other immigrant women, including Soo-Min Shim. In her piece *The Land Between Us* (2019) for the Australian art publication *Running Dog*, Shim describes how my Mum's poem "acknowledges the dialogue between Indigenous and Asian communities, subverting the black-white partitioning of race relations."[46] This compelled her to similarly speak and write in her first language, starting a decolonising conversation with her own Mother:

> Stumbling through forgotten Korean, I try to ask her about citizenship and what she knows about First Nations sovereignty. But my clumsy tongue trips and falls over the clipped endings and nasal tones. And yet in English, I can only do so much to address the displacement my own community has perpetuated.

43
Anzaldúa, *Borderlands = La Frontera*, 40.

44
María Lugones, "Toward a Decolonial Feminism," *Hypatia* 25, no. 4 (October 2010): 748, https://doi:10.1111/j.1527-2001.2010.01137.

45
Ibid.

46
Soo-Min Shim, "The Land Between Us: On James Nguyen's Portion 53," *Running Dog*, June 7, 2019, https://rundog.art/the-land-between-us-james-nguyen-portion-53/.

… (그런데 (끊임 없는 중국의 한국 침략과 지속되고 있는 미국의 제국주의는 물론) 일본이 한국에 대해 한 행동에 대해서는 많은 토론이 존재하고 있습니다. 우리는 식민화를 이해하고 있습니다 – 처음에는 그것을 견뎌내야 했고 그리고 세대 간의 트라우마 [*Intergenerational Trauma*] 와 신식민주의 [*Neo-colonialism*] 를 이해하고 있으며 또한 식민화는 결코 끝까지 않았다는 것을 이해하고 있습니다. 고투와 몸부림은 서로 다르고 완벽하게 인접하고 있지는 아니하더라도 그럼에도 불구하고 우리는 자유와 자주를 향한 몸부림을 이해하고 있습니다. 우리는 또한 생존과 저항을 위해 투쟁했으며 우리의 원주민 언어와 관습과 의례를 보호하기 위해서 투쟁했습니다. 우리는 보다 좋은 동맹국이 되기 위해서 이러한 이해를 선용해야 합니다.)[47]

For Shim, it is through one's own language that the complex process of articulating the colonisation of culture can be conceptualised and challenged. Drawing from the successive colonisation of Korea by Japan, China, and the United States, Shim argues that the struggle to protect Korean cultural heritage should be resonant with Korean immigrant support for Indigenous Sovereignty in Australia. Moreover, through engaging with the provocations of Nguyễn Thị Kim Dung's poem,

47 Ibid.

Shim seeks the decolonising feminism of cross-cultural and inter-diasporic annunciations and knowledge-making—this time, through intimate conversation with her Mum and her own "clumsy tongue." By reclaiming language through family relationships, and finding solidarities outside of her own community, Soo-Min Shim's feminism, like that of my Mum's, is centred on decolonising and troubling the diasporic self.

Letters for Black Lives Transla ×

docs.google.com/document/d/1qwon6Q-h3YC2n_vZGKlVxZxEhXG8ZQah4lVCMQzGaUk/edit

Letters for Black Lives Translations 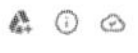

File Edit View Tools Help

Request edit access 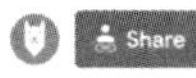

Letters for Black Lives

Letters for Black Lives is a set of crowdsourced, multilingual, and culturally-aware resources aimed at creating a space for open and honest conversations about racial justice, police violence, and anti-Blackness in our families and communities.

We wrote a letter in 2016, which you can read here along with how this project came together.

Here are the finished translated 2016 Letters (and Readings):

Available translations in Arabic, Bahasa Indonesia, Bahasa Malaysia, Bengali, Portuguese, Chinese (Simplified), Chinese (Traditional), Hindi, Hmong (Green dialect), Hmong (White dialect), Farsi, French, Japanese, Khmer, Korean, Russian, Spanish, Tagalog, Tamil, Telugu, Thai, Urdu, Vietnamese.

And here's some background on how this all began:

Fig. 36
Screenshot of Google.doc landing page. *Letters for Black Lives (Online Google.doc)*, courtesy Chris Xu and collaborators, July 6, 2016.

These examples of immigrant feminisms form connections that share uncomfortable solidarities. Regularly, language-brokering and knowledge-sharing along these networks produce strategies across cultural, linguistic, intergenerational, and economic divides. Contemporary Black activists like Mikki Kendall have called for new feminist counter movements to distance themselves from what she views as mainstream white feminism. Kendall proposes that presencing space for *Hood Feminism* (2020)[48] reduces the ability for mainstream feminists to get away with "sidestepping their own discomfort with race."[49] Self-reflection, self-criticality, and building uncomfortable connections across diverse cultural needs and challenges becomes the priority when engaging in dialogue.

An interesting example of a collaborative online project of language-brokering and translation that interrogates endemic racism within Asian immigrant communities is Chris Xu's 2016 *Letters for Black Lives*. A freelance ethnographer based in New York, Xu felt the limitations of their poor command

48 Mikki Kendall, *Hood Feminism: Notes from the Women that a Movement Forgot* (New York: Viking, 2020).

49 Vicki Borah Bloom, "The Future of Feminism: PW Talks with Mikki Kendall," *Publishers Weekly* 266, no. 52 (December 2019): 99, http://search.proquest.com/docview/2329489570/.

of Chinese. Unable to speak and talk to their elders about the Black Lives Matters movement, they posted an English-language file on a Google.doc titled *Letters for Black Lives* to address their parents and elders about supporting their Black colleagues and friends against police brutality and anti-Black racism within the Asian-American community. Reaching out to their network of Chinese speaking friends and colleagues, Xu asked if more fluent speakers and interpreters could help them to translate their letter. What transpired was an expanded social response, forming a self-organised outpouring of care and linguistic effort. Working across multiple minoritarian languages and variant dialects, their network of peers shared this document with other peers. Collaboratively, friends and strangers took on the work of translating Xu's letter (articulating their solidarity with #BlackLivesMatter) into over fifty languages. Initially intended for the elder members of their family who could not read or speak fluent English, Xu's letter became a tool for starting difficult conversations about anti-Black racism by POC and immigrant communities and families across the world.

Sent a link to the Google.doc by my friend Xi Liu from New York, I took time out in late July 2016 with my Dad to proof-read the Vietnamese version of the document. Making a few minor adjustments as part of a collective body of tracked changes, we took a step back, and with my Mum, talked about the political content of the letter that

we had just helped edit in Vietnamese. The impact of Xu's appeal to their own family ended up facilitating many more conversations about race and racism against Black Lives amongst immigrant families. The ability to make an editing contribution, and to then engage in conversations about the power of translation and racism beyond our own encounters with it, was a meaningful way to engage with my own Ba and Mẹ. Activating these moments of conversation with non-English speaking immigrant parents and elders, *Letters for Black Lives* was underpinned by the drive to reconcile a loss of language with the need to engage our families in difficult conversations. The immediate sharing and collective recording of these documents into videos for promotion and communication with non-text literate non-English speakers was driven by a desire to contribute to contemporary social movements, rather than just be passive and silent observers on the sidelines of anti-Black racism.

These emerging diasporic strategies, which seek to reconnect and rebuild dialogue with family despite our multiple and profound estrangements and depleted language skills, point to the continuing relevance of language-brokering for intergenerational migrant dialogues and political activism. The collaborative effort of translation manifests a distinctive form of feminism that seeks to reconnect and incorporate multiple approaches and perspectives to unpack the brutalities of political disconnection and cultural estrangement.

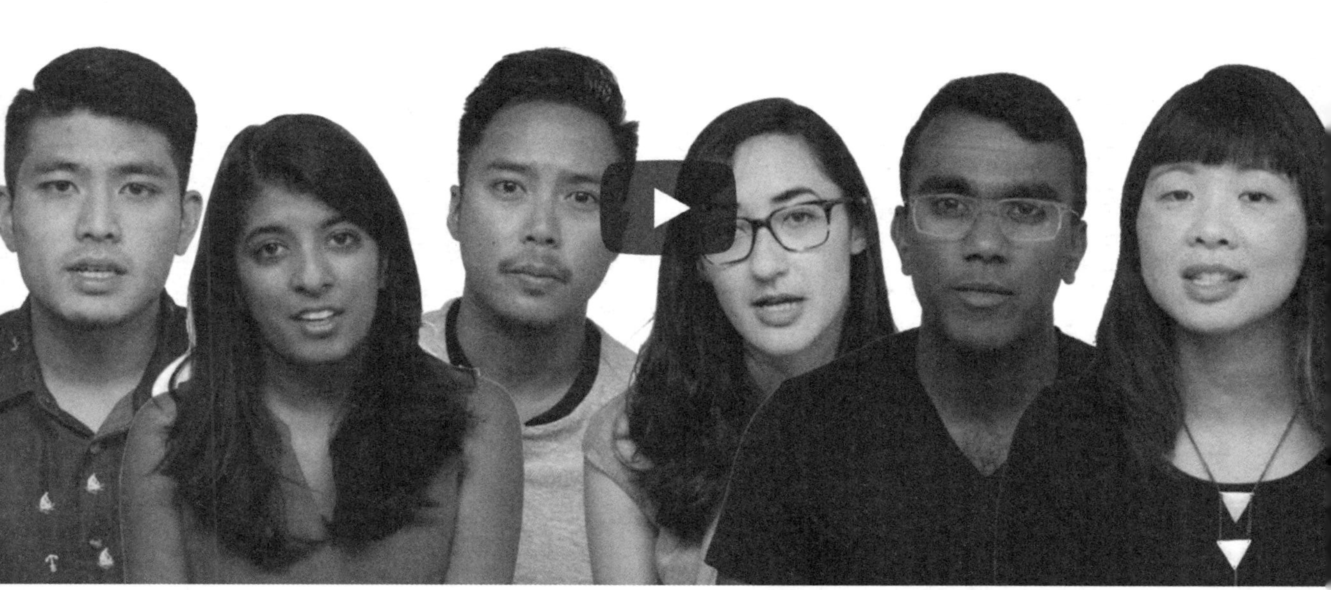
Letters for Black Lives | Inaugural ENG Letter
LETTERS FOR BLACK LIVES
Watch later
Share

In her critique of white feminism, Susan Koshy points to the work of Chandra Talpade Mohanty[50] and Trinh T. Minh-Ha[51] to describe the historic frustrations felt by feminists of colour with mainstream feminism.[52] Mohanty claims that frequently, western feminism presents Third-World women as backward and passive victims, unable to articulate their own needs, and unable to organise themselves to coherently engage with discourse and deliver effective solidarities. Xu's *Letters for Black Lives* openly acknowledges their own personal deficiencies (especially around language and cultural connection), but Xu's feminist response was to bring multiple immigrant communities and networks together to overcome their personal limitation.

50 Chandra Talpade Mohanty, "Under Western Eyes: Feminist Scholarship and Colonial Discourses," *Boundary* 212, no. 3 (April 1984): 333-358, https://doi:10.2307/302821.

51 Minh-Ha T. Trinh, *Woman, Native, Other: Writing Postcoloniality and Feminism* (Bloomington: Indiana University Press, 1989), 106.

52 Susan Koshy, "The Geography of Female Subjectivity: Ethnicity, Gender, and Diaspora," *Diaspora* 3, no. 1 (Spring 1994): 69-84, http://doi:10.1353/dsp.1994.0000.=.

Fig. 37 (p. 294) Screenshot of website video link, *Letters for Black Lives (Online Content)*, 2016. https://lettersforblacklives.com/dear-mom-dad-uncle-auntie-black-lives-matter-to-us-too-7ca577d59f4c.

These strategies contest the representation of minoritarian feminism as beleaguered, victimised, quaint, and ineffective. Mohanty concludes that "these distinctions are made on the basis of the privileging of a particular group as the norm or referent," and the rest as invisible.[53] Similarly, Minh-Ha exclaims that the underlying ethnographic and colonial ideologies that support "feminism in such a context may well mean 'westernization.'"[54] Minh-Ha is critical of the type of feminism that develops and benefits from claiming racial supremacy without acknowledging its own colonial culpability. Westernisation, for Xu and their contemporaries (myself included), has been a significant cause of division and estrangement in our own families. This has led to a profound state of disconnection with our elders. Becoming westernised was once offered to refugees and immigrants as a way to assimilate and integrate into what was taught to us as far more safe, secure, and superior than our own societies. But over time, as we struggled to integrate, especially as recent settler-occupiers, we have come to realise that our westernisation was part of the problem.

The national independence movements of former European colonies (including Vietnam) following the Second World War meant that

53
Chandra Talpade Mohanty, *Feminism Without Borders: Decolonizing Theory, Practicing Solidarity* (Durham; London: Duke University Press, 2003), 22.

54
Minh-Ha, *Woman, Native, Other*, 106.

many parts of the "Global South" were actively "de-westernising" from former European colonial masters. According to Mignolo, the US seized on this opportunity to assert economic and political influence across the Middle East, Africa, Latin America, Southeast Asia, the Pacific, and parts of Europe by leveraging investment and economic recovery programs through a process of US-led "re-westernisation."[55] Mignolo's sweeping Macro-economic narratives, although compelling, fail to recognise the complex micro de-westernisations and re-westernisations of diasporic life. As demonstrated in *Letters for Black Lives*, the migrant dynamic is profoundly complex, being hyper-local, and hyper-transnational. The mass displacements of diasporic peoples throughout the twentieth and twenty-first century simultaneously confirms and contradicts Mignolo's macro concepts of re-westernisation and de-westernisation. For example, the arrival of Vietnamese after the dissolution of the White Australia Policy has contributed to the ongoing diversity and de-westernisation of this largely Anglo-dominated nation. Within our families, however, the resettlement of thousands of Vietnamese refugees meant that many of us have inevitably become westernised. Our loss of language, separation from family, and separation from a dominant Vietnamese

55 Water D. Mignolo, "The Global South and World Dis/order," *Journal of Anthropological Research* 67, no. 2 (2011): 180, https://doi:10.3998/jar.0521004.0067.202.

culture are, in turn, leading many Vietnamese-Australians to find ways to de-westernise within persistent colonial frameworks still fixated on the politics of nostalgic re-westernisation—to politically reclaim, reassert, and reframe the benefits of western civilisation.[56] These dynamic interactions mean that the trajectories of decoloniality and de-westernisation are never predictable. Within the slippery diasporic spectrum of de-westernisation and re-westernisation, refugees, migrants, and our families now share multiple broken languages, including imperfect English. There is also a basic level of technological literacy and digital fluidity.

56 Australian Prime Minister Scott Morrison had allocated AUD $6.7 million in 2020 for a replica of the ship *Endeavour* to circumnavigate Australia and celebrate 250 years of Captain James Cook's "discovery of the continent in 1770." Calling this a "re-enactment," Morrison had to clarify that he was only referring to "retracing" the east coast leg of the journey. It was actually Matthew Flinders who, in 1803, completed a maritime circumnavigation of Australia, something that Cook never managed or even intended to do. https://www.abc.net.au/news/2019-01-22/endeavour-replica-to-sail-around-australia/10734998. Additionally, the Ramsay Centre (worth AUD $3 billion in 2017) has continued to invest tens of millions of dollars to build new partnerships with Australian universities and have bipartisan support from both Labour and Liberal involvement in order to facilitate and provide scholarships and research funding into the "benefits of Western Civilisation." https://www.afr.com/politics/federal/paul-ramsay-donation-paves-way-for-new-centre-to-study-western-civilisation-20171117-gznuba.

For Vietnamese-Australians, Vietnamese-Americans, Vietnamese-Canadians, Vietnamese-Aotearoans, and other diaspora, we are perhaps politically and socially more troublesome and uncontrollable than ever.

By changing the conversation, rather than just changing "the terms of the conversation,"[57] we flip Mignolo's macro-economic worldview of dynamic westernisation as inevitably capitalist and anti-life. How westernised diaspora are de-westernising continues to come into focus, including: reconnecting with family, calling for the safety and life of our Black and Blak colleagues and friends, relearning our languages, and building up new solidarities amongst our global and digital peers.[58]

57 Mignolo, "The Global South and World Dis/order," 183.

58 The term "Blak" was first used in the early 1990s by artist Destiny Deacon in her exhibition *Blak lik mi.* and *Blakness: Blak City Culture* (1994). Jack Latimore for Reconciliation Australia describes Blak as Deacon's linguistic intervention. "Growing up, Deacon always heard white people calling Aboriginal people 'black c---s.' So she wanted to take the 'c' out of Black … It still signifies urban, contemporary Indigeneity, but has also become important in differentiating the Blak experience from the racialised experiences of non-Indigenous communities of colour. Blackfella or Blackfulla is now often used for the same purpose, but Blak also carries with it connotations of actively engaged, critical-political conscience, which Blackfella or Blackfulla, arguably, doesn't always convey. The concept and relational use of Blak also continues to emerge, which adds to its dynamism." https://www.reconciliation.org.au/blak-black-blackfulla-language-is-important-but-it-can-be-tricky/.

Instead of trying to redefine or locate patterns of de-westernisation, projects of collective intent and the linguistic translations that underscore the spirit of *Letters for Black Lives* and demonstrate emerging and practical forms of diasporic action.

Bringing these various arguments back to Blak and Indigenous politics in Australia, Quandamooka woman Aileen Moreton-Robinson in "Whiteness Matters: Implications of *Talkin' Up to the White Woman*" (2006) reflects on her acclaimed book—first published in 2000—calling on white feminists, as well as the entire white establishment, to take active steps towards doing the difficult work of decolonising (and perhaps also de-westernising) themselves. She challenges those who have the privilege to relinquish power to actually do so. That is, to cede theoretical as well as actual space to Blak Indigenous women:

> White women are not represented to themselves as being white; instead they position themselves as variously classed, sexualised, aged and abled. The disjuncture between representation and self-presentation of both Indigenous women and white feminists means that the involvement of Indigenous women in Australian feminism is, and will remain, partial. This partiality in practice requires white feminists to relinquish some power, dominance and privilege in Australian feminism to give Indigenous

> women's interests some priority. To do any less means that the subject position "middle-class white woman" will remain centred as a site of dominance participating in maintaining the racial order in Australian society.[59]

Moreton-Robinson has little patience for passive forms of feminism that are only interested in "listening to, hearing and remembering Indigenous women's voices."[60] These are inadequate substitutes for the actual work of decolonising the self, and from this, the work of interrupting the institutions of privilege and power that mandate the blatant racism and sexism that contemporary Australia continues to reproduce.

Reflecting on making and exhibiting *Portion 53* with my family, the work of self-interrogation and opening up dialogue within the Vietnamese community about our settler-colonial subject position is indeed a slow and difficult process. Even within the intimacies of the family, our work demanded endless conversations about immigrant-perpetrated racism, sexism, and power which itself continues to shift unpredictably. We are only at the beginning of this process. Much like the narrator in Bà Huyện Thanh Quan's poem on the mountain pass, my family has

59 Aileen Moreton-Robinson, "Whiteness Matters: Implications of *Talkin' Up to the White Woman*," *Australian Feminist Studies* 21, no. 50 (July 2006): 246, https://doi:10.1080/08164640600731788.

60 Ibid., 250.

just stepped onto the precipice to accept that we are forever người xứ lạ ~ *elsewhere people*, as strangers and uninvited guests living on Aboriginal and Torres Strait Islander Land. My Mum's poem reminds us that Cảnh đã lạ ~ *the strange vistas* that we now find ourselves in should be recognised for their brutality, their beauty, and the continuing settler-colonisation that we as resettled refugees are implicated in.

The troublesome and troubling condition of partaking in the coloniality of contemporary Australia is all too familiar to the troubles that we ourselves have tried to escape. Reflecting on Moreton-Robinson's provocation, my family must extend beyond its own troubles and consider the troubles of those around us. Under such circumstances, it becomes very difficult to just "sit with the trouble," as proposed by Haraway. To do so would mean just passively accepting our part in the enduring forms of colonialism, misogyny, and racism of Australia. We need to somehow take ownership of the profound troubles of being here, but displaced from elsewhere. As a family, we have to regularly reassess our positionality within the context of the host country, as much as reflecting on that country's profound effect on us. Equality is ultimately something shared and continuously maintained with others. As we develop the knowledge to recognise the entrenched troubles of our new home, how do we then keep ourselves from replicating the troubles of the settler-colony?

Nguyễn Thị Kim Nhung and an Acknowledgement of Country

During a rehearsal for *On the Border of Things (Part II)*, for Next Wave Festival in 2018, I was focused on sorting out work with Dì Nhung ~ *Aunty Nhung* and Cậu Aí ~ *my Uncle*, and our encounter with Telstra and the NBN. A few weeks before the opening at the festival, my Uncle got cold feet and became particularly anxious about performing in public. Having written the piece with me and his Sister, Cậu Ái decided to pull out of the performance. I was happy to do a solo version, but Dì Nhung, who had often performed with me, volunteered to step in and play the part of her Brother. As part of the comedic conceit of this new adapted performance, Dì Nhung and I would apply colourful Vietnamese opera-type make-up to each other, with my aunty sporting a moustache and assuming the role of Cậu Aí.

Dealing with these last-minute changes, on top of recording Công Aí for the soundtrack and voiceover, I realised that I had completely neglected to sort out the Acknowledgement of Country. Should I perform this before or after the soundtrack started? Or before we applied our make-up?

Distracted by last-minute changes, I just wanted to lock down the Acknowledgement of Country and get it out of the way. Demonstrating just how routine these acknowledgement protocols had become, I proceeded to treat it as a pragmatic exercise.

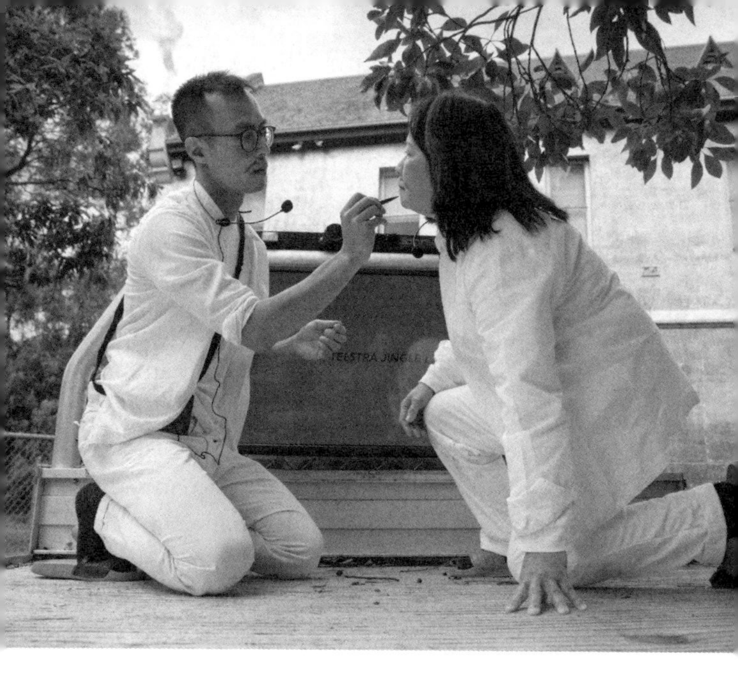

Fig. 38
On the Border Of Things (Part II) at Next Wave Festival. Nguyễn Thị Kim Nhung, Nguyễn Công Aí, Hayley Forward and James Nguyen, performance photography by Ghosh Snehargho, 2018.

This exemplified what Moreton-Robinson called a "rhetorical strategy" for a type of "reconciliation that continue[s] to make Indigenous people the focus of the problem."[61] Feeling the time pressure of the performance, I was making sure that my perfunctory demonstration of "reconciliation" was met, whilst internally processing the Acknowledgement of Country as a problem that I needed to "solve." In "Rethinking the Practice and Performance of Indigenous Land Acknowledgement," Stó:lō man Dylan Robinson, Mohawk woman Kanonhsyonne Janice C. Hill, Anishnaabe (Ojibway) man Armand Garnet Ruffo, settler woman Selena Couture, and Ojibwe/Swampy Cree and English/Irish woman Lisa Cooke Ravensbergen argue that to "move beyond the mere spectacle of acknowledgement as a public performance of contrition, we must take into account acknowledgement's site and context specificity," requiring the investment of time, thoughtfulness, and self-evaluation beyond lip service.[62] At the plenary presentation, the panel were asked whether:

> The acknowledgement of Indigenous lands and waterways elide[s] the acknowledgement of other forms of structural and epistemic violence within the specific contexts we work in as academics and artists? How might acknowledgement be aligned with a politics of recognition that is a continuation of settler-colonial logics rather than a break from them?

> What must occur for acts of acknowledgement to transform into actions that effect Indigenous sovereignty?[63]

But before I could even proceed to engage with any of these necessary questions, my Aunty straight-up asked why I had unilaterally decided to perform the Acknowledgement of Country *for* her? I was taken aback. Dì Nhung told me that instead, she would perform the Acknowledgement of Country herself. She also preferred to do it in Vietnamese. To my Aunty, addressing the audience in her Mother tongue was not just linguistically easier, but would help her to directly address any Vietnamese speakers who might be in the audience, giving them, and any First Nations people present, a level of recognition within the protocol. This signified that not all settler-colonial Australians speak English, making clear that minoritarian languages are themselves multi-lingual vehicles of settler-colonial Australia.

61 Moreton-Robinson, "Whiteness Matters," 250.

62 Dylan Robinson, Kanonhsyonne Janice C. Hill, Armand Garnet Ruffo, Selena Couture, and Lisa Cooke Ravensbergen, "Rethinking the Practice and Performance of Indigenous Land Acknowledgement," *Canadian Theatre Review* 177 (Winter 2019): 20–30.

63 Ibid., 20.

Secondly, by speaking the Acknowledgement of Country in her "wild tongue," my Aunty felt she could reclaim the orthographic traditions of the Vietnamese language—her langue vulgaire. Troubling the established treatment of the Acknowledgement of Country by speaking it in Vietnamese, my aunty implicates herself into what Shim describes as the limitations of "Black-white partitioning of race relations."[64] By challenging the implicit linguistic normalisation of the Acknowledgement of Country, my Aunty did not defer the responsibility of acknowledging Australia's settler-colonial violence to yet another Anglophone procedure, but literally took responsibility into her own voice, her own tongue, and on her own terms.

Feeling guilty about how I had failed to interrogate my banal procedural treatment of these protocols, I put aside our last-minute rehearsals and sat down with my Aunty to work on a translation of the Acknowledgement of Country on the lands of the Wurundjeri and Boon Wurrung. The task of translating the Acknowledgement of Country from English to Vietnamese was more involved and complicated than I had anticipated. Thinking about the subtleties of what the plenary panel had described as "site and context specificity" required effort, especially when it involved doing this *with* my Aunty. After some negotiation, we settled on drafting our own simplified version of the Acknowledgement

64 Shim, "The Land Between Us," 8.

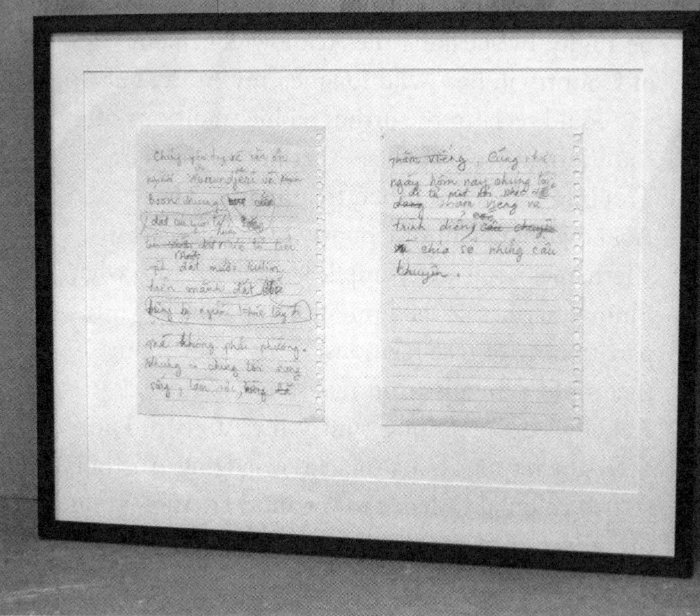

Fig. 39
Vietnamese draft Acknowledgement of Country to the Wurundjeri and Boon Wurrung by Nguyễn Thị Kim Nhung for *On the Border of Things (Part II)*, Next Wave 2018 Festival, Nguyễn Thị Kim Nhung, Nguyễn Công Aí, Hayley Forward and James Nguyen, photographed by James Nguyen, 2018.

of Country, thus reducing the probability of potential mistranslations that could overwhelm my Aunt's intent and clear articulation of the message:

We respect and thank the Wurundjeri and Boon Wurrung people
and their Ancestors, of the Kulin Nation.
On whose unceded land,
we have come from afar
to live, work, perform and share these stories today.

Chúng tôi trân thành cảm ơn người Wurundjeri và người Boon Wurrung,
và các tổ tiên của đất nước Kulin của người ấy.
Trên mảnh đất này bị người khách lấy đi, mà không phải nhừơng,
chung tôi tại đây đã đến sống, làm việc,
và hôm nay chúng tôi đến từ nơi khác, để chia sẻ những cầu chuyện này.

We found translating the term "unceded land" quite challenging, as my Aunty and I couldn't between us think of an equivalent term encapsulating the concept. We decided to spell it out in Vietnamese. Saying trên mảnh đất này bị người khách lấy đi, mà không phải nhừơng ~ *on this piece of land that was taken away by other people but was never offered up/ given away*. To my Aunty, the clarity of saying how the land bị người khách lấy đi ~ *was taken away* acknowledges the actuality of forced land theft,

making it specifically resonant for herself and other potential Vietnamese-speaking audiences whose lands and property were taken away throughout our various wars. To Dì Nhung, the memory of having land, friends, and family taken away and put into re-education camps was something that she can không bao dờ quên ~ *never forget.*[65]

In unpacking the intent behind the Acknowledgement of Country as a demonstration of respect, we began the slow process of talking about the implications of living on đất bị cướp ~ *Stolen Land.* My Aunty reminded me that our family had similarly experienced firsthand the atrocities of violent massacres and land dispossessions. This process opened up discussion about the colonising impact that my family, along with millions of other internally displaced Vietnamese refugees, had endured, and then enacted in a mass migration of our relatives and ancestors from the north to the south, crossing the Seventeenth Parallel in 1954.[66] Our family was resettled in South Vietnam under the "Highlands Resettlement Schemes which

65 Nguyen Ho, "Erasing Vietnam's Past," *Index on Censorship* 7, no. 6 (November 1978): 18-20. https://doi:10.1080/03064227808532852.

66 Jessica Elkind, "'The Virgin Mary Is Going South': Refugee Resettlement in South Vietnam, 1954-1956," *Diplomatic History* 38, no. 5 (2014): 987, https://doi:10.1093/dh/dht119.

67 Mark W. McLeod, "Indigenous Peoples and the Vietnamese Revolution, 1930-1975," *Journal of World History* 10, no. 2 (Fall 1999): 373.

removed highlander tribes and villages, often by force."[67] Mark McLeod noted that in North Vietnam, zones earmarked for "National Minorities" (to garner support from minority tribes) also paved the way for similar patterns of indigenous assimilation and removal.[68] Unfortunately, this history of displacement and resettlement of ethnic minorities continues under a unified Vietnam.[69] It is symptomatic of the historic and continuous displacement of Southeast Asian minorities and First Tribes into the present.

By recognising the complexity of personal loss, and also our complicity in the dispossessing machinery of war, my Aunty and I began to value the importance of refusal by Australia's First Nations peoples from ceding their cultural, spiritual, or material sovereignty; their land, sea, and sky. I was reminded by my Aunty that the Vietnamese term for *Country* was Đất Nước. Literally translated, Đất Nước simply means *Soil Water*. To my Aunty, our country and our nation is a composite of the physicality of our landscape. The other term for nation that I started to think about appeared in Bà Huyện Thanh Quan's poem: Quốc Gia (with multiple associated homonyms and interpretations). In my broken Vietnamese I decoded these terms as Quốc (cuốc) ~ *using a hoe to work and till the soil*, and Gia (da) ~ *your skin* ~ da *and family* ~ Gia.

68 Ibid., 372.

69 Ibid., 210.

Reflecting on the ontological combination of all these linguistic associations, I realised that in Vietnamese, Country and Nation are ultimately linked to a conceptual relationship with Soil, Water, Labour, Skin, and Kin. To have any of these elements stripped away would be a direct assault on your person—your skin and family.

By unpacking and translating the Acknowledgement of Country, my Aunty and I as recent settler-colonists have inherited the weight of being both colonised and colonising peoples. As part of the waves of migration into Australia paved by white settlement, the Acknowledgement of Country takes on a particular significance when spoken by us in Vietnamese. To us, the conventional Acknowledgement of Country that Lisa Asher, Joe Curnow, and Amil Davis describe as a form of containment "using decolonization as metaphor" and not attending to the "rematriation of Indigenous land, language, and pathways,"[70] ignites a different significance when spoken in the minoritarian language of the displaced.[71]

70 Lila Asher, Joe Curnow, and Amil Davis, "The Limits of Settlers' Territorial Acknowledgments," *Curriculum Inquiry: Essays from the 2017 Curriculum Inquiry Writers' Retreat* 48, no. 3 (2018): 316–34, https://doi:10.1080/03626784.2018.1468211.

71 Rematriation, used in Indigenous and First Nations discourse, is an alternative to "repatriation" of land, language, and culture. Here I have used the term to acknowledge the leadership and feminism of women in my family and their various linguistic endeavours.

These linguistic articulations are important for my family, as Vietnamese speakers, to open up concepts and histories that we can cleave to as dispersed and estranged people ourselves. By acknowledging Country in this way, we reconnect with our Mother tongue to the stories and truths that implicate our loss and desecrations of Đất, Nước, Quốc, Gia ~ *Soil, Water, Labour, Family, Skin, Country, and Nation.*

In Australia, there are of course many precedents to translating the Acknowledgement of Country. A notable example is Ryan Whittard, who as a First Nations Australian, gave the first Acknowledgement of Country in Mandarin at Macquarie University's Chinese Culture Festival (Appendix 1). Majoring in Law and Chinese Studies, Whittard had reached out to the Australian Mandarin-speaking community through his language of study, rather than the language of his Country. Closing his speech, Whittard notes that "my dream is to make my contribution in creating a pluralistic and harmonious Australia."[72] Another more collaborative project has been initiated by Wiradjuri man Joel Sherwood Spring, an artist and architect based in Sydney who is working with Radio Skidrow 88.9, to write and record multi-lingual messages of solidarity and

72 Claudianna Blanco, "Indigenous Student Delivers the First Acknowledgement of Country in Mandarin," *NITV News*, August 29, 2016, https://www.sbs.com.au/nitv/nitv-news/article/2016/08/29/indigenous-student-delivers-first-acknowledgement-country-mandarin.

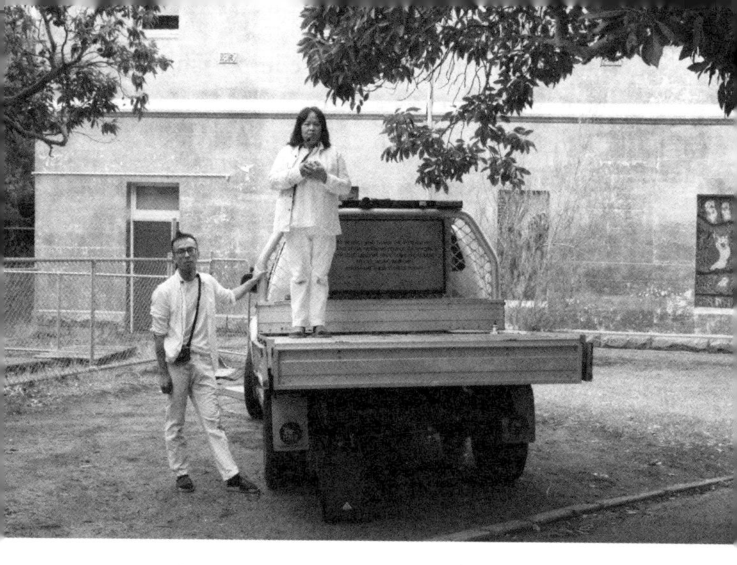

Fig. 40
Nguyễn Thị Kim Nhung performing the Acknowledgement of Country to the Wurundjeri and Boon Wurrung in Vietnamese for *On the Border of Things (Part II)*, at Next Wave Festival). Nguyễn Thị Kim Nhung, Nguyễn Công Aí, Hayley Forward and James Nguyen, performance photography by Ghosh Snehargho, 2018.

Acknowledgements of Country with Indigenous communities for bilingual broadcasters. I am taking part in this expanded collaboration of friends and local artists who come from various diasporic and linguistic backgrounds. We are building on work already done by activists from the Anticolonial Asian Alliance. Such projects, along with work made by my Mum and Aunty, have recently found resonance in connecting to communities outside of my own family. These intersectional and inter-diasporic dialogues are part of a broader movement towards acknowledging the realities of internalised racism, sexism, and estrangement to counter these with contemporary forms of self-reflection, collaboration, archival production, language-sharing, and knowledge production.

What has been most valuable to me throughout this chapter has been the time spent with my Mum and Aunty, translating between Vietnamese and English. This has allowed me to reclaim new ways of thinking and speaking. I can find new expressions to better articulate and appreciate the Vietnamese language and its feminist canon. In addition to this, these translations have helped me to gain more insight into the troubling colonial truths within my own family, and how the estrangement to language is one in a suite of troubling outcomes from resettlement, adaptation, and westernisation in Australia. Perhaps Anzaldúa was right in vehemently defending and reclaiming her "wild tongue." She notes "that if you want to really hurt me, talk badly about my

language. Ethnic identity is twin skin to linguistic identity—I am my language. Until I can take pride in my language, I cannot take pride in myself."[73] Ultimately, to perform the Acknowledgement of Country without having to rely on the default language of colonial oppression in Australia is both liberating and burdensome. By not choosing to sit with trouble and defer all colonial responsibility to English, but instead taking on the responsibility of speaking the Acknowledgement of Country in our Mother tongue, speaking becomes a contractual compact—one which honestly acknowledges our multiple histories and embodied traumas to take on the task of presencing the self as a settler-coloniser, as complicit violator.

73 Anzaldúa, *Borderlands = La Frontera*, 39.

Throughout this chapter, I have emphasised how reductive assumptions often used to simplify concepts of community, migration, and diaspora are unable to address the multi-valent dynamics of history, class, gender, and politics that percolate throughout diasporic interactions and encounters of Vietnamese people in Australia. Reductive and racialised presumptions about this community undermine the complexity of our diasporic flourishing and agency.

From the naff karaoke and cheesy pop of Vietnamese-language variety shows, to how our families have adapted to the major political and economic events of Australia's contemporary history (including the labour reforms and deregulation of manufacturing), to post-war eviction of D'harawal/Tharawal families from their lands, to the rollout of new telecommunications infrastructures—our experiences of resettlement are inevitably entangled in the Australian narrative, yet are specifically our own. Continually having to prove that we are Australian is a constant reminder of our perceived inferiority as cultural, political, moral, and linguistic minorities. Defined according to our compliance and model behaviour, 1.5th- and 2nd-generation Vietnamese experience the compounded triple domination and shame of not speaking good enough English, of being represented as faceless Asian hordes (if represented at all), and having to

perpetually demonstrate gratitude for being granted asylum as part of the narrative of being grateful.

These dominations are not merely psychological nor social but are embodied in the complex relationships we have with our voice, our accents, our Mother tongues, our wild tongues, our means of communication, and connection to our families. The impulse to adapt to the new normal of resettlement, to acquiesce to the limiting benchmarks of assimilation, and fulfilling the impossible standards of success as immigrants have blunted our ability to truly speak for ourselves. What if the normative standards of being a good or model migrant are not enough? What if we should rather reject the latent misogyny, classism, and shame that accompanies these external standards of success and failure?

This chapter returns to the central theme of connection, dialogue, mediation, and language-brokering as a way to formulate artistic and political actions that trouble the violence of being both colonised and colonising subjects, and the inclination to blindly accept the tabula rasa of resettlement, bowing in gratitude as recruits in the ongoing colonial project is profoundly troubling. Our extraordinary capacity for adaptation and resilience as migrants should not limit our capacity to think critically and act beyond a colonial mindset that tells us we are not enough. We are actually more than capable of standing up for ourselves, and speaking up against the troublesome parts of ourselves. Seen in Xu's *Letters for Black Lives*,

Nguyễn Thị Kim Dung's poem for *Portion 53*, and Nguyễn Thị Kim Nhung's refusal to speak the Acknowledgement of Country in English, these actions demonstrate that not all migrant responses are compliant, submissive, or avoidant of the trouble we inhabit.

The process of reclaiming and gaining an appreciation for my Mother tongue, spending the time to translate poetry with my Mum, and translate the Acknowledgement of Country with my Aunty has given me an insight into their feminism and women's work. As women who do not speak good English and who continue to work in piecework and low-skilled occupations, they remain perennially invisible to the broader Australian society, and shamed by the Vietnamese community. Through their insistence in writing and speaking Vietnamese, despite expectations to denounce their langue vulgaire, my Mum and Aunty are connected with Anzaldúa's refusal to tame her "wild tongue." Establishing their own feminist approach, producing their own forms of political agency, and practising a decolonising strategy with the Vietnamese language, my Mum and Aunty have engaged me and a number of my peers, my Dad, and even parts of the wider Vietnamese community to think beyond the misogynistic tendency to dismiss and undermine the capacity of migrant women. Deploying their wild tongues, my Mum and Aunty have generated artistic and critical interventions that confront our troubling settler-coloniality as people from elsewhere.

Their provocations have made me acutely aware of my own neglect of language and exposed the gendered violence reserved for the women in my family. The feminist decoloniality that Nguyễn Thị Kim Dung and Nguyễn Thị Kim Nhung are engaged in has dragged me into the epistemic disobedience that, as a family, we are only now beginning to process.

CONCLUSION

Making Chó bò: Troubling Việt-speak

The title for this thesis opens with a linguistic joke. A one-liner, a homonym for *trouble* ~ chó bò, which characterises the off-beat humour and absurdity of perpetually having to speak from elsewhere. Speaking English with a Vietnamese accent, each word uttered bears the intonations of estrangement, rupture, and loss. Marking a troubling relationship to the taming of our wild tongue, big chó bò happens when the assimilation and sedation of our Vietnamese voice is softened and absorbed into the settler-colony. Speaking good English, we become compliant subjects and industrious model citizens, yet somehow, we are never really treated as equal. Worse still, this linguistic compliance has, for me, meant a certain betrayal of my family and estrangement from my own culture. To simply speak my thoughts and be present in the lives of my parents and Vietnamese-speaking relatives is really difficult. Losing the ability to speak for myself, and with my own family, is devastating. No less so for those members of my family who continue to be dependent on me to inadequately translate, broker language, and speak *for* them. How are we then to deal with these violations? How to rehabilitate an assimilated tongue so profoundly colonised and tamed? Can we hold our tongues from repeating the violence and neoliberal inflections of the settler-colony?

The difficult task of reconnecting with language, with family, and with my family's conflicted histories is palpable. Difficult conversations are made even more difficult when our language,

memories, and family archives are so fragmented. We have little else but to throw the dog among the cows, choking on half-forgotten words and brittle accents, swallowing each and every spiky solecism. Slowly, very slowly, we learn to crawl on our bellies, spitting out and dribbling on half-remembered diphthongs. We speak. The consolation for me and my family is that we have never been strangers to such troubles. We are acquainted with the daily humiliations that trouble a broken tongue. It is, however, an extraordinary privilege for me to still have what language I do have, to reconnect and share with my family. It is deep inside these spaces that I can recover the epistemic worth to simply be present, to think, and to physically bite into the most damaging and troublesome parts of my colonised and colonising tongue.

The results of this research have, therefore, never been an individual enterprise. It has always been inextricably bound up with and facilitated by the many networks and relationships that make up the thinking, the doing, and the undoing of art. I have tried my best to foreground and provide a small sample of the wealth of practice, thinking, and important work of my artworld peers, companions, friends, and even artworld adversaries. Intrinsic to the work that I continue to do with my family, I feel that the depth of diasporic practice around me far exceeds the limited forms of perfunctory and tokenistic opportunities afforded by the contemporary artworld and academia.

Although this community of artists and practitioners has clearly asserted and maintained substantial forms of institutional self-representation and advocacy through organisations such as 4A Centre for Contemporary Art and recently Hyphenated Projects, I still feel that more needs to be done to archive and make present the important work being done here in Australia and the Indo-Asia-Pacific. The practice of Bhenji Ra, Sophia Cai, Soo-Min Shim, Lap-Xuan, Rainbow Chan, Phương Ngô, Nguyễn Thị Thanh Mai, Hoàng Trần Nguyễn, with countless and continually emerging others, continues to push our conversations into increasingly critical and conceptually rich spaces. This has invariably fed my own practice and continues to contribute to the conversations, ideas, and experiences that I share with my family. The archive for some of the work which I have integrated into this thesis is a small but important starting point. Much more needs to be done to foreground and interrogate the extraordinary depth of artistic practice in the region. The work of these artists and countless others who I am now only encountering continues to expand on what diasporic practice can be: something that far exceeds the reductive terms of identity art, minority self-representation, post-colonial practice, or even contemporary politics and activism. Continued effort is required to keep up with the knowledge coursing through these communities as vital to any serious conversation about contemporary art.

In Chapter 1, I introduced the reader to my Uncle Nguyễn Công Ái, and our collaborative work *On the Border of Things (Part II)* with my Aunty Nguyễn Thị Kim Nhung. Together, we had spent time in his market garden, reconnecting and talking about the multiple forces that had pulled us apart as we were being resettled in Australia. The everydayness of navigating services like Telstra revealed to me how I had taken for granted the vernacular language skills I had managed to develop over many years of mediating language with my family. This sounds obvious, but the automated customer services of Telstra's call centres made me realise the importance of speaking the right kind of English to be heard and access basic services. Working with my Cousins in Vietnam, I came to realise that language-brokering and mediation is just as important to the economies of business and art. Being used to doing the work of translation in Australia, I was humbled, having to rely on my Cousins to broker the Vietnamese language for me. In the end, it was the shared exchange of our imperfect communication and linguistic collusion that supported their business to generate new economic opportunities. Implementing a strategy of nuanced and shrewd linguistic deception, presenting ourselves as native English speakers based in Vietnam, we exploited the tacit arrogance and racist assumptions of international investors and global capital. From a zucchini farm in Adelaide to a biotech start-up in Vietnam, enterprising opportunities for our family

do not emerge from merely recognising the racism and bias around us. Rather, through our collective ability to engage with the absurdity and stupidity of these infrastructures, we are able to find ways that ensure we exploit these spaces. Language-brokering with my family therefore is used as an essential tool for not only navigating the traps of Globish and globalisation, but confronting parallel forms of exclusion similarly built into academia and the artworld.

My failure to make a substantive archive with my family, discussed in Chapter 2, resulted in the realisation of two almost negligible "bodies of work." Revisiting the *Nguyễn Family Photo Album* (1986–1989), I learnt how administrative mishandling of our Family Reunification Visa resulted in many years of our family separation. The second encounter involved navigating the protocols of the Human Research Ethics Committee (UNSW HREC), including the "Participant Information Statement and Consent Form" (PISC). My Dad, Nguyễn Ngọc Cư, helped me to translate the PISC to satisfy the university's ethical requirements, and by doing so, inadvertently blurred the procedural and arbitrary separation of the researcher (myself) from the research participants (my family). Interrogating both administrative folly and procedural inflexibility, I started to appreciate the distinctive coloniality and structural biases built into the immigration department and academic institutions in Australia. I saw how archives in their various manifestations

continue to violate and separate families and communities. These *archival imposts* on the family, and the procedural banality and structural indifference of the anxious settler-nation, makes permissible punitive border violence on asylum seekers offshore, whilst simultaneously doing little to resolve the incarceration and chronic deaths in custody of Aboriginal and Torres Strait Islander people on-shore.

Ironically, it is on these compounding atrocities that the immigrant myth of a new home and tabula rasa are suffused. It became clear that my family and I needed to address the situational dissonance of being forcefully displaced refugees, but finding ourselves resettled and instrumentalised deep within the colonial matrix of Australia. As people encountering the systemic violence from the multiple infrastructures around us, it was important for my family to critically review and acknowledge our own complicated relationship with colonial prejudice, racism, and misogyny. Spending time with my Mum to translate her poetry, and working with her Sister (my Aunty) to translate her Acknowledgement of Country into Vietnamese, I realised that not only were the non-English speaking women in my family engaged in important concepts of self-determined decoloniality, but through their provocations, were also exposing the latent gender violence and normative coercion of the Vietnamese community itself. The intimate proximities of making art and doing translations with my Mum and Aunty

challenged my own presumptions about the self-determination, collective responsibility, and personal accountability of confronting ubiquitous violence, misogyny, and racism as a family. Even though I was doing a PhD, it took me up to this point to realise that my assimilation into the Australian way of life entailed a profound neglect and dissociation from my own language, culture, and family for the ambition of higher education and so-called academic excellence. Without actually saying it, my Aunty told me that I knew nothing. I knew nothing of her life, nothing of my Mum's life. I knew nothing of, or had never even cared enough to ask about, their artistic and political desires, and their internal life as thinking, living people. I also knew nothing about my own linguistic inheritance and the profound feminism of the orthographic origins of the Vietnamese language itself. On a personal level, a primary outcome of this thesis has been how the women in my family have dragged me, my Dad, and others to finally recognise the embedded importance of canonical feminism, and resistance within the texts of Vietnamese women. The inter-colonial feminism of Vietnamese poetry, and its traditions, continue to have relevance in the complex situational settler-colonialism that we find ourselves engaging with as Australians today. The impulse of archival and epistemic resistance in the Vietnamese language and its orthographic feminism continues to flow from the tongues of women like my Mum and Aunty, women who in broader Australian society (myself included in this

category) one way or another, regularly dismiss as incoherent non-English speaking and invisible pieceworkers. Through our informal and imperfect family translations, we have managed to engage with each other in new decolonial feminist dialogues.

The complex and multilayered forms of resilience, prejudice, and profound coloniality embedded in ourselves as Vietnamese-Australians continues to be present in my research and in the artworks and conversations that I continue to have with my family. The conclusion to this thesis therefore feels like a beginning. As the Artistic Director of *Nirin*, Brook Andrew notes in the catalogue for the 22nd Biennale of Sydney, "colonisation is not a history but a continuum."[1] This continuum demands continued redress and reassessment. I have found that collaborating with my family has provided us with an ongoing methodology to engage in the politics and intimacies of decolonisation. This emerges not from a generalised and nebulous critique, but a contextualised and situated approach to artistic-based family collaborations. This thesis presents a series of instigations and interventions that are still in process. My family's attempts at self-presencing as we enter these fraught and unsettling conversations are still unresolved and ongoing. What is now required is to better define our roles and subject position as persistent settlers, and perhaps permanent colonisers

1 Jennifer Lavers, Hannah Catherine Jones, Paschal Daantos Berry, and Brook Andrew, "Diaspora Footprint Cycle Puzzle Oceans," 60.

and guests on Aboriginal and Torres Strait Islander Land. As other newcomers arrive onto these shores, what are our responsibilities to these more recent arrivals? And what are our responsibilities to those already present, over 60,000 years before us? Beyond unsettling the infrastructures of resettlement, we must also lay out and develop more substantive action and shared futures with our First Nations colleagues, peers, and expanded families. This is a challenge that extends far beyond the limits of this thesis.

Appendices

Appendix 1

Respectable special guests, fellow students, ladies, and gentlemen, welcome to the 2016 Chinese Culture Festival!

We acknowledge the traditional custodians of this land, the Wattmattageal clan of the Darug nation. Since the Dreamtime, their culture and customs have nurtured the land. We pay respects to Aboriginal elders past, present and future, and any other Aboriginal people present today.

My name is Ryan Whittard, I am a student at Macquarie University, studying Law and Chinese. In Year 7 of high school I began learning Chinese because my dad was learning a little bit. He encouraged me to study a foreign language. Since then, I have developed a growing interest in the Chinese culture and language. Apart from enjoying learning Chinese, I understand that this language and knowledge will have a great impact on my future. China has an important role in the world's politics, economy and other matters, and Chinese people make up the majority of new immigrants in Australia. My dream is to make my contribution in creating a pluralistic and harmonious Australia.

I am sure that continuing my Chinese learning journey will help me to reach my goals. I encourage all present and future students to stay focused, study hard, and persevere. With perseverance comes great success.

Tonight's event is a great opportunity for the talent of young students to be showcased. I hope you enjoy tonight's activities.

Thank you everyone.

尊敬的各位嘉賓、同學們、女士們、先生們，大家晚上好！歡迎來到2016年的中國文化節！

我們首先承認這塊土地的傳統托管人：Darug民族的Wattmattageal氏族。自從土著民的"夢幻時期"，他們的文化和風俗培育了這塊土地。我們在此對過去的、現在的和未來的土著長者們，以及出席今晚活動的土著民們表示我們的敬意。

我叫偉大瑞恩，是麥考利大學的學生，現在學法律和中文。從中學七年級開始我就學習漢語，因為我爸爸已經學過一點，他鼓勵我學習漢語。自那以後，我對中國的文化和語言產生了濃厚的興趣。除了喜歡學習中文以外，我認為懂得中文語言和文化知識對我的未來會有好的影響。中國在世界政治、經濟以及其它領域佔有越來越重要的地位，而華人在澳大利亞的新移民中佔了大多數。我的夢想就是為建立一個多元和諧的澳大利亞社會做出我的貢獻。

我知道，繼續我的中文學習之旅將幫我達到我的目標。我也鼓勵所有當前和未來的學生們認真、努力學習中文，不要放棄，堅持就是勝利！

今晚的活動將展現許多青少年學生的才華和才藝。希望大家欣賞今晚的節目，渡過一個愉快的晚上。

謝謝大家！

The writer, publisher, and designer acknowledge the Wurundjeri and Boon Wurrung people of the Kulin Nation as sovereign custodians of the land on which we work. Always was, always will be Aboriginal land.

Making Chó Bò
Làm *Trouble*
James Nguyen
2023

Edited by Helen Hughes and Amy May Stuart
Foreword by Brian Martin
Designed by Zenobia Ahmed
Printed and bound by Printon, Tallinn

ISBN: 978-0-9945388-9-5
Published by Discipline, Naarm/Melbourne
Edition of 400
www.discipline.net.au

The original version of this book was written as part of a practice-based PhD at the University of New South Wales, Art & Design, submitted in 2020.